CHRONICLES
OF A
CHEST

To: Maurice A. & Jacqueline Kelliher

CHRONICLES
OF A
CHEST:

Henry Sutton's
New Haven Schooners, 1875-1918

by Robert W. Feuer

The Woman's Seamen's Friend Society of Connecticut
New Haven, Connecticut

MYSTIC SEAPORT • MYSTIC • CONNECTICUT

The Woman's Seamen's Friend Society of Connecticut
291 Whitney Avenue
New Haven, CT 06511

Mystic Seaport
75 Greenmanville Avenue
Mystic, CT 06355

Cataloging in Publication data:

Feuer, Robert W.
    Chronicles of a chest : Henry Sutton's New Haven schooners, 1875-1918 / by Robert W. Feuer. —
1st ed. — Mystic, Conn. : Mystic Seaport ; New Haven : Woman's Seamen's Friend Society of
Connecticut, c2001.
    p. : ill., ports. ; cm.
    Includes bibliographical references and index.

    1. Schooners—Connecticut—New Haven—History. 2. Coastwise shipping—Connecticut—New
Haven—History. 3. Shipbuilding—Connecticut—New Haven—History. 4. Coal trade—Connecticut
—New Haven—History. 5. Shipwrecks. 6. Seafaring life. I. Title.

HE767.F37F4 2001

The publication of this book has been made possible by a generous grant
from the Woman's Seamen's Friend Society of Connecticut, Inc.

ISBN 0-913372-93-5

Book and cover design by Caroline Rowntree, New York

ACKNOWLEDGEMENTS

I am indebted to many individuals for their kind assistance in furnishing advice, information, leads, photographs and other materials in the preparation of this book. Certainly, my in-laws, Myrlon and Hortense Farnham, initiated my interest in schooners when they gave me the chest, upon which this whole investigation was based. Others are Warren E. Shindle, who restored the chest and determined its significance. Robert Egleston, former Executive Director of the New Haven Colony Historical Society, who first encouraged me to write a book about Henry Sutton's fleet and the schooner carrying trade. Dr. Everett C. Wilkie, former Editor of the Connecticut Historical Society, Hartford, Connecticut, who accepted "The Last Voyage of the Lyman M. Law" for publication in the Connecticut Historical Society Bulletin (new revised). Captain Francis E. Bowker, former Research Associate, Mystic Seaport, who was a staunch advocate of this book and who furnished technical sailing advice as well as friendly encouragement. Joseph Gribbins, Director of Publications, Mystic Seaport, who offered sage advice in reorganizing topics of the book. Captain W.J.L. Parker, USCG retired, who graciously gave information about individuals and schooners in general, as well as furnishing copies of numerous photographs displayed herein. He also provided convincing evidence that a purported picture of the Lyman M. Law was actually that of the Henry Lippett. Olivier L. Delisle, who was most helpful to me regarding French naval matters, while serving his year of military service at French Naval Archives, Chateau de Vincennes, France. Dr. Bernd Steggeman, Militaergeschichtliches Forschungsamt, Freiberg, Germany, who answered my many questions time after time and helped direct my path where I needed to go. Dr. Hans Kordik,

Office of Defense and Armed Forces Attache, Austrian Embassy, Washington, D.C., who furnished leads and information on some matters that I had no idea existed. Commander Hector A. Skare, Assistant Naval Attache, Argentine Naval Office, Washington, D.C., who authorized and followed up on the successful search in Argentina that unearthed the record of the Lucinda Sutton's loss on Lobos Bank. Henry L. De Buck, former FBI legal attache in Paris, who translated Capt. Le Merle's five-page letter, which led the way for my own translation of the remaining French, Spanish and some German materials that I picked up during the investigation for this book. Richard von Doenhoff, Naval Archivist, National Archives, who speaks French and formerly taught sailing to midshipmen at the U.S. Naval Academy, and who guided me through an understanding of French sailing idioms. Karen S. Feuer, my daughter, who was instrumental in getting me started on computers, without which this book probably never would have been written. My wife, Polly C. Feuer, who has patiently read this manuscript, furnishing pertinent observations and corrections. On many occasions, she also had dissuaded me from either an aggravated dismantling, or a deep-six, final solution of my altogether frustrating, self-minded computer. And there were countless others who helped along the way; to all those folks whom I can't name individually here, I can only repeat in print what I hope I have previously acknowledged, "Thank you one and all."

CONTENTS

CHRONICLES
OF A
CHEST

THE CHEST

After Aunt Ne Farnham died in 1974 at her old farmhouse at 93 Farnham Avenue, on the outskirts of New Haven, every family member was invited to go through the house to select an item or two as a remembrance of her. (The house is now part of the Southern Connecticut State University campus.) My father-in-law, Myrlon A. Farnham, Aunt Ne's younger brother, invited me into the basement, where I had never been before. Almost as soon as we arrived downstairs an old 15-drawer pine chest caught my eye. Every drawer had a foot-long metal name-

plate with a different individual's name painted on it. Each name was preceded by a mysterious prefix such as "Sch.," "Schr.," "Schr. Genl.," or "Genl." I asked Pop, "What is that?" "I don't know," he replied. "It belonged to my father. He built this house in 1904 when I moved in with the rest of the family. I was just six years old, and as far as I can remember it has always been here. My father used it in connection with his duties with the Governor's Horse Guard and the Governor's Foot Guard."

We tried opening a few drawers that weren't stuck and found they contained several old cans of bootblack and chalk, mementos of their prior association with military drill units of the Connecticut Governor's guards. My father-in-law's father, Arthur N. Farnham, was a farmer and businessman, and at the time of his death in 1935 was a Major in command of the Second Company of the Horse Guard. He had been its oldest living member and had been decorated for 65 years of service in that organization.[1]

For the next 40 years the chest remained in the basement of the house, where it gathered dust, insects, spider webs, and dry rot. And yes, my first choice was the chest. An attempt to move it with my nephew's assistance prompted second thoughts. First we removed the drawers that could be loosened, and with the load thus lightened we lifted the chest. This started a sudden dispersal of long thin multiped bugs. The top then separated from the rest of the piece and sections of the right rear corner simply fell away. However, this proved helpful for it allowed the remaining drawers to be taken out. After we did this we realized that the original order of placement of the drawers was lost forever. The bottom was next to go its own way, and after that the remainder of one of the lower boards in the back. This led to the frame taking on an alarming degree of flexibility. Everything was loose, and the chest seemed ready to self-destruct. All retrievable parts were gathered together and loaded into a rented truck.

Loading didn't help the chest's integrity, nor did the trip to Virginia, nor the unloading. My son helped unload the whole

piece (if one may use this terminology), and questioned my sanity. The chest began to be described as "fifteen drawers and boards"—but not for long.

A friend put me in touch with Warren E. Shindle, a restorer of antique furniture, but Mr. Shindle only did restoration work in his spare time. He worked full time at another line of work, and that job took precedence. Commitments to the Boy Scouts, canoeing, and other interests took further precedence. He said he would do the work–but it might take six to nine months.

Six months later Mr. Shindle returned the chest. He had transformed its parts into a single piece once again. It was beautiful and behaving as a proper chest should. Among other repairs, he added a front to the top; restored the sides; replaced rear bottom boards and another in the lower back, as well as the right rear support; combined the sides with the front and top; and cleaned the piece. Replacement wood was obtained from old lumber discarded from the Freeman House, which was built in 1861 and had recently been restored in Vienna, Virginia. The Freeman House was a combination dwelling and store that changed hands several times between Union and Confederate forces during the Civil War. Both sides used it as a hospital.[2]

The chest is 5' long by 4' 6" high by 1' 6" deep. Mr. Shindle determined the following: it was built circa 1880; mortise and tenon joints were used throughout its construction; it is very light in weight in proportion to its strength—similar to a Windsor chair; and each drawer has its own lock and drawer handle, patented in 1870 and 1872, respectively. Mr. Shindle was excited about the chest. He said it was one of the two most interesting pieces he had ever worked on. Mr. Shindle found some keys to the drawers with labels attached inside the chest. The labels disclosed something of its history before it came to the Farnhams. "Henry Sutton, Ship Chandler, New Haven, Conn." is printed on them, and handwriting provides data on schooners. It names four schooners, three masters, (captains), two launching dates, and a date when one vessel was lost at sea. Nothing else was found in the chest pertaining to ships.[3]

Mr. Shindle telephoned the New Haven Colony Historical Society and learned that Henry Sutton was the builder and managing owner of 16 or more vessels comprising what was thought in its time to be the largest privately owned fleet of sailing ships on the East Coast. He also learned that most of the vessels were named after New Haven businessmen. In addition, he reviewed *Lloyd's Register of Shipping* and the *List of Merchant Vessels of the United States*, from which he obtained data for all but one of the schooners that were named on the drawers. From evidence provided by the chest, Mr. Shindle correctly deduced that Henry Sutton was its original owner. Sutton probably used it to keep the construction, maintenance, and business records for his schooners.[4]

He also must have kept one other record in it. In November of 1992 my mother-in-law, Mrs. Hortense G. Farnham, asked me to look through some old notebooks that had been removed from the house where Aunt Ne died. One of these was a business ledger with entries from 1880-82. More than half the pages were missing, and more than a third of the remaining pages of ledger entries were pasted over with newspaper clippings and other articles dating from 1902 to 1915. Presumably this was done by Aunt Ne and her older sister Aunt Letty when they were much younger. The business entries, however, were Henry Sutton's ship-chandlery records for provisioning vessels and other business. Two such items were listed for the schooner *Henry Sutton* in 1881. Most entries had "Settled" or "Paid" next to them along with different initials, some of which were "HS." This ledger had to have been acquired at the same time as the chest and most likely was in one of the drawers. The family speculates that Arthur Farnham acquired the chest at an estate auction.

My curiosity about Sutton and his schooners began to grow. I wanted to know more about the people for whom the vessels were named (the eponyms). I wanted to know more about each schooner. I wanted to know what happened to them. Thus began the research for this book.

END NOTES:

1. *New Haven Journal,* 11 November, 1935, 2 (hereafter cited as *Journal*). Charles W. Burpee, *The Story of Connecticut*, 4 vols. (New York: American Historical Co., 1939) 4:1250.
2. Letter to author from Warren E. Shindle dated 16 February, 1976. *History of Freeman House*, pamphlet distributed by Historic Vienna (Virginia) Inc.
3. Telephone interview with Warren E. Shindle, 15 January, 1976, and letter from Mr. Shindle, 16 February, 1976.
4. Ibid.

SCHOONERS

Before we begin to know more about Henry Sutton's schooners, let's understand something about schooners. A schooner is a fore-and-aft-rigged sailing vessel. In its most basic form it has a gaff-headed foresail, a similar larger mainsail, and a headsail (any sail set forward of the foremast, as a jib or forestaysail). Sometime after 1630 the Dutch built small vessels that incorporated the above except for the headsail. About the end of the seventeenth century, two schooner-rigged vessels flying English colors were painted by a Dutch artist, indicating they may have been fairly common at the time. But what name they had in Dutch or English isn't known. There is an old tale, largely discounted, that is of interest in this context. In 1713 Captain Andrew Robinson built one of these vessels at Gloucester, Massachusetts. Upon its launching, a spectator allegedly cried out "Oh, how she scoons!" Robinson concurred, "A scooner let her be." Hence the name, from scoon: to skip or skim. New England records appear to have originally spelled the word as "scooner."[1]

At the start, schooners were two-masters. By 1860 the schooner rig had become all but universal in the coasting trade, and three-masted schooners appeared in New England shipyards in the 1860s. A shipbuilding industry report prepared by the U.S. Census Office after the 1880 census declared it probable that more schooner-rigged vessels were built in the U.S. each year than all other rigs combined. The first four-masters came into existence with the conversion of one schooner in 1879 and the construction of another in Maine in 1880. This inaugurated the age of the great schooners, the cheapest carriers per cargo ton of any sailing ship.

A FIVE-MASTED SCHOONER, THE *MAGNUS MANSON,* SHARES A PIER WITH THE SUTTON FLEET'S *GENERAL E.S. GREELEY.*

The demand for them after 1880 created a U.S. revival in the building of wooden ships, and they continued to grow in size and number of masts. In 1888 Maine produced the first five-master. Later, between 1900 and 1910, huge six-masted Maine-built schooners were launched. As a group, they were the largest wooden sailing ships ever constructed. One seven-master with a steel hull was built in Massachusetts in 1902; but the cost of steel for the hull and a short life span made this famous vessel, the *Thomas W. Lawson,* most unprofitable.[2]

Schooners were especially suited for transporting bulk cargos, the need for which had greatly expanded in the last half of the nineteenth century in America. Freight such as coal, lumber, phosphates, ores, etc., was often stored for long periods at both loading and unloading terminals, so speed wasn't a necessity. Capacity and economy were considerations that made schooners the coastal carriers of choice. Many schooners had drafts of comparatively little depth that enabled them to reach shallow-water docks to load or unload ice, lumber and other cargos. Some of these vessels were fitted with large centerboards (raisable keels) for this purpose. Other schooners were deep-draft vessels intended for foreign trade.[3]

The schooner rig had certain advantages over the more complex sail and spar arrangements of square-rigged vessels. While maneuvering, the schooner's sails were more easily managed, and this enabled them to get around better than square-rigged vessels in narrow coastal estuaries and rivers. Their rig was aerodynamically more efficient than arrangements of square sails, and they could beat to windward (sail into the wind) with more speed and less complication than the fastest square-rigged ships. At least one report claims that the big schooners were on a par with square-riggers in beam winds and in steady trade winds.[4]

A considerable number of men were required to handle sails and lines on square-rigged vessels. Much of this work was done aloft, where it was difficult and dangerous. On the later schooners the large lower sails could be quickly and efficiently raised or lowered by a steam winch (or later by a gasoline winch in vessels up to about 1,000 tons). Schooner hands rarely had to go aloft except to set or furl the light gaff topsails. Five- and six-masted schooners often carried two sets of steam winches. Overall manpower needs on great schooners were from 25 to 55 percent less than on comparably sized square-rigged carriers. This alone made them much more economical.[5] Great schooners had heavily constructed hulls combined with lightweight rigs. They normally sailed without ballast, thereby saving time and expense in port. In addition, they used wire standing rigging, far less running rigging, and many fewer spars than square-rigged vessels, which reduced maintenance costs.[6]

But schooners also had weaknesses. Most of the great schooners were demanding to steer with strong winds abaft the beam. In this circumstance, they often required two men to steer unless they had steam steering engines. When sailing before the wind, where high seas or long rolling swells and light breezes were encountered, the schooner might "slat herself to pieces" (tear or wear out sails and gear). If strong fair winds were blowing, square-rigged vessels were much faster. In storms, the square-riggers could reef down to topsails and not be cut off from the wind in the troughs of large seas. But the schooners' topsails were for light weather and had to be clewed up in storms. Reefing down the lower sails further reduced the effective operating area of a schooner's sails in the trough of a wave. The sails were blanketed from the wind. When the schooner crested on the following wave, the previously slack sails billowed out with explosive force and a loud report. This exacted a heavy toll on sails and gear. Schooners were generally not suitable for most deepwater commerce —around Cape Horn, for example, where it was important to be able to run in heavy weather. A schooner voyage around the Horn could be a tortured, dangerous passage, if not a disaster. The consensus on the waterfront was that the "straight fore-and-aft-rigged" schooner was a coastwise vessel and not a deepwater carrier.[7]

With respect to the great schooners, they required reinforced keels since their long hulls were subject to great strains. One of the limitations of wooden shipbuilding was wood's lack of stiffness compared with metal. The bow of a big wooden schooner held the massive anchors, a quantity of anchor chain, the windlass and headgear, while the stern had to support an overhang. As the big schooners aged, they became hogged (arched in the middle). To compensate, their keels were constructed with a deliberate sag in the center. Even so, with aging the hogging stress caused them to leak, which required frequent recaulking.[8]

After 1905 competition from steam freighters and barges reduced the demand for schooners in most of their coastal trades.

By 1914 declining freight rates pushed many coastal schooners into foreign trade. It should be mentioned that, for coastal schooners, the West Indies was not considered foreign trade. Coasters had always sailed there—albeit with stiff competition from deepwater vessels that traded with Europe and South America. A brief resurgence in building wooden schooners came with World War I, and existing schooners had all the trade they could handle during the war. Large profits were gained by great schooners trading overseas to the Mediterranean and elsewhere in Europe, to Africa, and to South America. By the teens of the twentieth century, much of the new schooner construction took place on the West Coast of the U.S., where there was ample timber. Many of the vessels built there were great four- and five-masted schooners and barkentines. The latter were schooner rigs with square-rigged foresails. For conditions encountered in the Pacific, this rig improved sailing performance and reliability and lessened wear and tear. These great schooners were used especially in the lumber trade. The end of World War I saw the virtual end of building wooden sailing vessels in the U.S., and many of the existing sailing carriers, lacking business, were abandoned, broken up, or burned to retrieve their metal. Nevertheless, a few schooners survived in both coastal and offshore routes until World War II.[9] Some of the great schooners worked foreign trade routes for many years. Indeed, a four-master reportedly made the first schooner voyage to China from an eastern port as early as 1884. These ships were particularly efficient in the tradewind belts of the Atlantic and Pacific, but the vast majority of great schooners made only coastal passages. Overall, they had little presence in American deepwater commerce.[10]

During their heyday, the big schooners were unrivaled and omnipresent along the coast from Maine to Texas and from Washington to California. In coastwise service the great American schooner was said to be "the most weatherly and economical sailing vessel in the world."[11]

END NOTES

1. W.J. Lewis Parker, *The Great Coal Schooners of New England 1870-1909* (Mystic: The Marine Historical Association, 1948), 28 (hereafter cited as Parker, *Great Coal Schooners*). *Webster's New International Dictionary*, 2d ed., (1945 unabridged), s.v. "schooner." Letter from Captain Francis E. Bowker, research associate, Mystic Seaport, dated 11 April, 1991.

2. U.S. Department of Interior, Census Office (10th Census, 1880), 8 vols., *Report on the Ship-Building Industry of the United States*, 8 (1884): 93-94 (hereafter cited as *Ship-Building Report*). Parker, *Great Coal Schooners*, 33. William Armstrong Fairburn, *Merchant Sail*, 6 vols. (Center Lovell, Maine: Fairburn Marine Educational Foundation, Inc., 1915-55), 4:2608, 2619 (hereafter cited as Fairburn, *Merchant Sail*). John G.B. Hutchins, *The American Maritime Industries and Public Policy, 1789-1914* (Cambridge: Harvard University Press, 1941), 545, 551-53, 556, 558, 565 (hereafter cited as Hutchins, *Maritime*).

3. Hutchins, *Maritime*, 545-49, 555-56.

4. Ibid., 551. Fairburn, *Merchant Sail*, 4:2618.

5. Hutchins, *Maritime*, 549-51, 554. Fairburn, *Merchant Sail*, 4:2618-2619. Letter from Captain Bowker dated 11 April, 1991.

6. Hutchins, *Maritime*, 549, 554-55. Fairburn, *Merchant Sail*, 4:2618.

7. Hutchins, *Maritime*, 383, 556. Fairburn, *Merchant Sail*, 4:2608, 2618-21. Parker, *Great Coal Schooners*, 45, 61. Francis E. Bowker, *Atlantic Four-Master* (Mystic: Mystic Seaport, 1986), 57, 58 (hereafter cited as Bowker, *Atlantic Four-Master*).

8. Parker, *Great Coal Schooners*, 41.

9. Hutchins, *Maritime*, 383, 555-57, 561-65. Fairburn, *Merchant Sail*, 4:2621. *Shipbuilding Report*, 8:94.

10. Hutchins, *Maritime*, 556, 564.

11. Ibid., 545, 547, 549, 555. Fairburn, *Merchant Sail*, 4:2618. *Shipbuilding Report*, 8:96.

CHAPTER 3

HENRY SUTTON, SHIPOWNER

In 1872, at age 29, Henry Sutton added a ship chandlery to his grocery business in New Haven. He soon saw the potential in owning vessels as well as outfitting and provisioning them. Soon enough he became an owner/manager of vessels that were the 18-wheel trucks of a growing nation during the final decades of the nineteenth century, especially for carrying bulk cargos. But no information has been located that Henry Sutton ever formed a company as such to build his schooners. He simply rounded up partners to finance construction and then built the ships. This was pretty much the custom of the day; companies weren't necessary, and in a sense each vessel was its own company.

   Sutton's career as a builder, owner, and manager of coasting schooners began at East Haven in W.O. Nettleton's shipyard, where his first two schooners, *Edward M. Reed* and *James Boyce,* were constructed in 1875 and 1877. A move to H.H. Hanscomb's Fair Haven shipyard produced the *Henry Sutton* in 1879. All of his subsequent shipbuilding was done at Gesner and Mar's yard in West Haven, where he had 13 more schooners built between 1880 and 1894, beginning with the *Orville Horwitz.* One additional schooner, the *R. & T. Hargraves,* built in Camden, Maine, in 1891, became part of the Sutton fleet in 1894 as the result of a lawsuit.[1]

Henry Sutton's Schooners With Measurements		
Edward M. Reed (1875)	421.34 gross tons	134' length overall
James Boyce (1877)	453.50 gross tons	142' length overall
Henry Sutton (1879)	602.56 gross tons	149' length overall
Orville Horwitz (1880)	515.90 gross tons	150' length overall
Harry A. Barry (1881)	469.31 gross tons	137' length overall

HENRY SUTTON, SHIP CHANDLER AND SHIPOWNER.

James D. Dewell (1882)	603.01 gross tons	151' length overall
Nathan Easterbrook, Jr. (1883)	712.58 gross tons	156' length overall
James Ives (1883)	505.76 gross tons	147' length overall
General S. E. Merwin (1884)	789.12 gross tons	170' length overall
Charles F. Tuttle (1886)	776.39 gross tons	177' length overall
Henry H. Olds (1887)	872.66 gross tons	180' length overall
W. Wallace Ward (1888)	1245.13 gross tons	206' length overall
George M. Grant (1889)	1254.27 gross tons	212' length overall
Lyman M. Law (1890)	1300.03 gross tons	211' length overall
Lucinda Sutton (1891)	1486.63 gross tons	225' length overall
R & T Hargraves (1891)	783.26 gross tons	173" length overall
General E. S. Greeley (1894)	1306.02 gross tons	219' length overall

Henry Sutton was more than just a client in the shipbuilding process. He seemed to take over the yards where his ships were built. Just prior to the launching of the *Henry Sutton*, the *New Haven Journal* reported that the schooner was built "under the personal supervision of Henry Sutton, who has the entire direction of the yard and has pushed the completion of the work along with surprising rapidity." Sutton wrote a letter to the editor, published two days after the above report, stating that giving him credit for superintending work on the vessel in the shipyard was in error. He gave credit to the ship-builders and to the vessel's future captain: "W.O. Nettleton, of Fair Haven, modeled and drafted said schooner. George W. Baldwin was the master carpenter, W.F. Noyes boss joiner, and H.H. Hanscomb furnisher of iron works, spars and blocks, and the whole has been under the able supervision of Captain Gilbert Manson, who is to command her. By inserting the above you will give credit to whom credit is due." The essence of the original newspaper article was correct, however: Sutton was the promoter and prime mover in the construction of his vessels.[2]

Gesner and Mar were listed as the master carpenters for the first two schooners constructed for Sutton at West Haven. No master carpenters were identified for the next four vessels built for him there; but Sutton was certified, at least for the record, as the master carpenter for the final seven schooners built for him at Gesner and Mar's yard.[3] His shipbuilding activities at Gesner and Mar's caused considerable confusion as to who actually owned the yard. At the launching of three of his last four vessels, the *New Haven Register* referred to "Henry Sutton's shipyard" and Henry Sutton's "shipbuilders." The *New Haven Journal* followed suit and upped the ante to make it four out of his last five vessels. Both newspapers got it right when the *Lyman M. Law* was launched and they called it Gesner and Mar's shipyard. Bringing further confu-

JOHN E. MAR, WEST HAVEN SHIPBUILDER.

sion to the issue was a profile of "Henry Sutton, Ship Builder and Ship Chandler" in *Leading Businessmen of New Haven County*, published in 1887. It stated that Sutton was the proprietor of the West Haven shipyard where he built and managed a large number of vessels that were the largest ships ever built in Connecticut. It also stated that his shipyard was the leading enterprise of its kind in the state.[4]

A modern maritime history of New Haven pointed out that Gesner and Mar had launched 13 three- and four-masted schooners between 1880 and 1893 (sic), naming the *Gen. E.S. Greeley* for the latter date, which should have been 1894. Henry Sutton's 13 vessels seem to have been all of the schooners constructed at Gesner and Mar's shipyard during this period. The confusion over the yard's ownership seems understandable.[5]

The design and construction details of Henry Sutton's schooners were typical of their time and their intended trades. Eight of the schooners were centerboard vessels —*Reed, Boyce, H. Sutton, Horwitz, Barry, Ives, Tuttle,* and *Olds.*[6] Here are some details of their rigs, accommodations, and structures, a miscellany gathered from reports on the Sutton schooners that appeared in Connecticut newspapers.

The lower masts of the *Henry Sutton* were 90', 91' and 92' in length by 27" in diameter. Extending from them were 52' topmasts. White oak was used for the *Sutton's* frame and planking. She had a large double cabin finished in black walnut and ash. A bathroom [head] and other conveniences were provided. The vessel was painted black overall with red and white striping, and her name appeared in gilt on nameboards at bow and quarters. For a figurehead she carried a wingspread eagle.[7]

The *Harry A. Barry* had a large parlor down below and two staterooms in addition to quarters for the officers. She spread 3,000 square yards of sail. An officer's gig on davits supplemented her yawlboat. At each bow was an anchor, one weighing 2,700 pounds and the other 2,300 pounds. Another 800-pound kedge completed her ground tackle.[8]

The *Nathan Easterbrook, Jr.* was metalled [copper sheathed] soon after being built. This was to protect her bottom from worms, a precaution necessary for vessels that would make passages in southern waters, such as the Gulf of Mexico. The *Easterbrook* would make a number of voyages to Galveston with railroad iron, coming back with lumber.[9]

The *James Ives* was described as "elegantly fitted up," and her accommodations were described as either "handsome" or "ornate and cozy."[10]

The salon and staterooms of the *Gen. S.E. Merwin* were "elegantly built." This vessel was well-lighted, comfortable, and supplied with a stationary bathtub and marble-top washstand. The *Merwin* had a steam engine to power winches that took the work out of handling sails and spars. Her deck was yellow pine.[11]

The *Charles F. Tuttle* had a handsome main cabin made with black walnut and sycamore, along with the best of hardware and furnishings. It was said of her that she justified the exclamation of an old sea captain that "New Haven beats the world in building schooners."[12]

The *Henry H. Olds* had a centerboard that was 26' long with a drop of 15 feet. An 11-horsepower steam engine was used for hoisting sails and cargo—a first for New Haven schooners. And a steam whistle came with the engine. Five staterooms, a pantry, and a bathroom were located off the main cabin. The *Olds* also had a figurehead.[13]

The four-masted *W. Wallace Ward* carried eight light upper sails and nine lower ones that included five jibs. Located in a cabin under the poop was a steam engine that hoisted sails and anchors and worked the pumps. Getting underway with the help of the steam engine took just 40 minutes, whereas with human muscle alone it took three to four times as long. Steam heat was furnished throughout the vessel. Heavy Brussels carpet covered the main-cabin sole.[14]

The *George M. Grant* was built substantially along the same lines as the *Ward*. The Bath [Maine] Iron Works made her 18-horsepower steam engine. Suction pumps generating a 6' stream of water were improvements over those aboard the *Ward*. Atop each mast were balls of glass that served better than lightning rods ashore. They did not conduct electricity. The chair and sofa in the Captain's cabin were described in a newspaper report as "elegantly upholstered in plush." A figurehead was carried at the ship's stem.[15]

Some particulars of Henry Sutton's largest schooner, the *Lucinda Sutton*, are length, breadth, depth, and length of keel: 225.0', 40.9', 18.6', and 203'. She was built with 470,000 feet of hard pine and 272,000 feet of hardwood in frames and keel. Lower masts fore to aft were 96', 97', 98', and 99'; topmasts were 55'. The spanker boom [her largest] was 70' long. She carried a cloud of sail–5,000 square yards.[16] The *Lucinda Sutton*'s net tonnage was 1,412.3 and her carrying capacity was 2,500 tons. She drew 9 1/2' light, and 21' fully laden. There were eight staterooms, a pantry and bathroom down below. A fine crayon portrait of Lucinda Sutton hung in the after cabin. The *Sutton* carried two immense anchors of 4,577 and 3,800 pounds, with 180 fathoms of 2" chain that alone weighed 15 tons. A steam engine was used to hoist sails, spars and anchors; to load and discharge cargo; and to work the pumps. The ship had an extra wrecking pump of 6' discharge, plus hand pumps. Her crew complement was 11 men, and she was said to have been operated as cheaply as a 1,200-ton vessel.[17]

The *Gen. E.S. Greeley* had the handsomest main cabin in the fleet, finished in gum wood and white pine with some gilt. There were six staterooms down below, a large salon, and toilet rooms. New nickel-plated garnet glass balls were mounted on the mastheads. When the sun was reflected from them, it looked like four balls of fire atop the masts.[18]

Ownership shares in these vessels were divided into 64ths or divisions thereof, and each of the schooners had anywhere from 15 to 48 owners when constructed. A great majority of the owners were from Connecticut and most of them were businessmen in the New Haven area.[19]

Henry Sutton generally held an ever-increasing ownership share in the vessels, ranging in value from a 2/64ths interest in his namesake schooner to an 18/64ths share in the *Lucinda Sutton*. He was the principal owner of the last nine schooners built, including the *Hargraves*, which he acquired through a court auction. He never held any financial interest in the *Boyce* once she was built, but he invested in all of his other vessels. He sold his shares in the *Horwitz* after about three years of ownership.[20]

The eponyms also invested financially in these vessels, except for Edward M. Reed, who had no stake in the *Reed*. Likewise, Harry A. Barry had no initial share in the schooner named after him. Later, he picked up a 1/64th interest that he maintained until the vessel was lost in 1887. When the *Horwitz* was built in 1880, six of her 31 owners were from Baltimore. Their total investment was 12/64ths of the ownership. It was unusual for this fleet to have so many owners of one ship located in a single city outside of Connecticut. However, seven of the other schooners had one or more owners from Baltimore when first built. Some eponyms also invested in vessels other than those named for them. Lyman M. Law, for example, invested in all 17 of the Sutton schooners as well as others in the Benedict-Manson fleet of New Haven.[21] The original captains invested in their vessels, again excepting the *Reed*, whose master held no financial interest in the ship. The captains often held onto their shares after leaving the ship's command.[22]

Where professions could be determined, many other part-owners of Sutton schooners were found to own ship-related businesses that supplied and/or serviced his vessels. When the *Law* was built, she had 48 owners. Of these, five were identified as masters of Sutton schooners, five as eponyms plus another eponym's wife, and six as contractors involved in the construction of the Sutton schooners. Perhaps Henry Sutton used the same financial procedure that was then current in Maine shipbuilding —i.e., to pay contractors with shares in the vessel.[23]

As with building and owning schooners, Henry Sutton formed no known company per se for managing vessels, but manage them he did, except for the first three that were constructed for him. Being new to shipbuilding at that time, it is likely that ship management was not one of his major concerns. Magnus Manson was a ship captain and one of the original owners of Sutton's first ship, the *Reed*. Later, Manson became managing owner of this schooner. He was also involved with the *Boyce*, Sutton's second vessel. When the *Boyce* was launched, Manson was her first master as well as her principal owner, holding 12/64th shares. Henry W. Benedict, who owned 6/64th shares of the *Boyce*, was the original managing owner. Benedict was in the coal business and involved to some extent with coasting vessels, but he was killed in a railway accident on 25 November, 1877, eight months after the *Boyce* was launched. His son, Frank W. Benedict, who owned 3/64th shares of the schooner, took over his father's business. Later, Frank W. became associated with J. Willis Downs and they incorporated as Benedict & Downs, with Benedict as president. It was a successful wholesale coal company with extensive shipping interests. Frank W. Benedict died in 1905. In February of 1906 a new firm, the Benedict-Manson Marine Co., was organized with Magnus Manson as president. Manson died on 24 October, 1909, following which eponym Lyman M. Law was elected president—at age 84. The Benedict-Manson Marine Co. managed the *Boyce* until she was wrecked in 1909. This firm also managed 26 other schooners in the coal trade between 1906 and 1916.[24]

Henry Sutton's namesake schooner, his third, was launched from Howard H. Hanscom's Fair Haven shipyard. Hanscom was a major shareholder with 6/32nds shares in the *Henry Sutton*. Her captain and managing owner, Gilbert Manson, [brother of Magnus], held the most shares with 9/32nds. This schooner would always be independently owned and managed. Captain James C. Clifford of Newport, Rhode Island, became managing owner sometime in the mid-1890s, apparently by buying out most of Gilbert Manson's shares. Clifford was the last managing owner when the ship was lost in 1906.[25]

In addition to receiving dividends commensurate with their ownership shares, managing owners generally received a commission of two and one-half or five percent on all charters of the vessel. Henry Sutton first became a managing owner with his 3/32nds interest in his fourth vessel, the *Orville Horwitz*. Late in 1883 Sutton relinquished his managerial interest in this ship, selling his shares to Henry W. Crawford of New Haven. When the *Horwitz* sank in 1887 the vessel was managed by the above-mentioned Frank W. Benedict of Benedict & Downs. Henry Sutton managed the remaining 13 schooners that were built for or acquired by him. At the time of his death in 1896, five of the schooners, the *Horwitz, Barry, Olds, Easterbrook,* and *Ives* had already gone down.[26]

James D. Dewell was an eponym and part-owner of 11 of Henry Sutton's ships. After Sutton's death, Dewell became the managing owner of the fleet, to which he added at least two schooners. One, the 174-ton, three-masted *Julia Frances,* joined the fleet in 1899-1900 and was sold two years later. The other, the *Jennie R. Dubois,* was a five-masted, 2,227-ton three-decker that was built at West Mystic, Connecticut. She was thought to be the largest sailing vessel ever built in Connecticut. The *Dubois* was launched on 12 February, 1902, but had such a deep draft that she stuck in the mud in Mystic. After several attempts to haul her loose, she finally was floated free at high tide nearly a month later. Her draft of more than 20' actually prevented this schooner from entering her home port of New Haven. The *Dubois* wasn't destined for a long life. On 5 September, 1903, she was maintaining her course in a dense fog about seven miles southeast of Block Island when she was knifed into by the German tramp steamer *Schoenfels.* The *Dubois* sank in five minutes. Her crew was picked up by the steamer. A few days later, the *Dubois'* masts, extending well out of the sea, had to be destroyed as a hazard to navigation. The steamer had sustained serious injury to her bow but sailed on to New York. A $128,000 lawsuit was filed by the owners of the *Dubois* against the *Schoenfels.* The value of the schooner was assessed at $110,000, cargo and freight costs at $15,000, and personal effects lost by the captain and crew at $3,000. James D. Dewell's son, James D. Dewell, Jr., was one of the attorneys representing the *Dubois* in the proceedings. The U.S. Marshal took custody of the *Schoenfels* in New York. On 14 September the *Schoenfels* cleared New York for Savannah after making only temporary repairs, permanent repairs being impossible owing to labor trouble. That the steamer was allowed to leave New York would indicate her owners had posted bond, pending the outcome of the legal dispute.[27]

James D. Dewell, Sr. not only took over the Sutton fleet in 1896, he was elected Lieutenant Governor of Connecticut, to serve from 1897-99. When the individual schooners required certificates of enrollment or registry at New Haven during his term of elective office, James D. Dewell was the one who subscribed under oath on the certificates in six out of seven possible occasions. One might say that the Lieutenant Governor did not let his official duties stand in the way of his fleet-management interests; however, there was no apparent conflict of interest since the legislature met only sporadically in Hartford for a few days each month during his first six months in office and it didn't meet again until the next legislature was elected. In addition to his state duties, Dewell was Vice President of the Security Insurance Co. at some period during this stage of his life. By the time he died in 1906 three more of Sutton's vessels, the *Merwin*, *Ward*, and *Hargraves*, had gone to the bottom.[28]

The Benedict-Manson Marine Co. picked up managing ownership of the remaining vessels of Henry Sutton's fleet in 1906 except for the *Lucinda Sutton*. This schooner was independently managed for a year or two in the early 1900s by Harry D. Sutton, Henry's son. Then Captain Herbert A. O'Brien, who was married to Lucinda Sutton's sister, became the principal and managing owner. He had been master of the ship for many prior years and he continued to function in this capacity. On 31 March, 1909, O'Brien transferred the *Lucinda Sutton*'s listed home port from New Haven to Boston. Then in 1915 O'Brien was succeeded as managing owner of the schooner by Ralph C. Emery of Newton, Massachusetts.[29]

A few months after the Benedict-Manson Marine Co. acquired them, the *Dewell* and *Tuttle* were lost at sea. By 1916 the destruction of ships worldwide, heavy demand for them, and their value, had all increased due to the strenuous prosecution of the war at sea. The Benedict-Manson Marine Co. took advantage of the escalated values of that year. Its three remaining Sutton schooners, the *Greeley*, *Grant*, and *Law*, were sold to out-of-state interests for $50,000, $35,000, and $45,000 respectively. And the *Lucinda Sutton* was sold in 1916 to the South American Shipping Co.[30]

Putting Henry Sutton's operation in the perspective of his time, it must be said that he wasn't the only managing owner to have individual vessels built locally for him. Long before he became involved in constructing and managing ships, others had shown the way. The *New Haven Journal and Courier* published an article relative to this on 7 September, 1883, one day after the launching of the *Easterbrook*. Beginning in 1862 it listed 67 two-and three-masted vessels built and registered in the District of New Haven, which encompassed both Guilford and Madison, Connecticut. Of the ships listed, 43 were identified as built for six specific parties (all managers), each of whom acquired several vessels. Sutton had seven schooners listed for him; Henry W. Benedict, four schooners; Captain Albert Thomas, nine; the Armstrongs, four schooners and five brigs (two of the latter built in Madison); the Trowbridges, three barks and three brigs (all six built in Madison); and Captain James H. Woodhouse, eight schooners. Woodhouse was a builder himself in Fair Haven, as well as a manager, merchant and shipmaster. Of the number of vessels noted above, Henry Sutton's *Easterbrook*, *Dewell* and *Henry Sutton* were the first, third and fourth largest in the whole group.[31]

Looking at the long-term merchant-shipping activities of the Trowbridges and the Armstrongs gives a sense of the maritime history of the area. The Trowbridge name in New Haven shipping dated back to 1668 when Thomas Trowbridge and William Rosewall were granted permission by the town of New Haven to cut timber to build a ship. The two men were engaged in some West Indies trading enterprises, probably involving spices, sugar, molasses and rum, and West Indies trade became a family tradition. Late in the eighteenth century, individual members of the extended Trowbridge family commanded sloops and brigs in the West Indies trade. Thomas Trowbridge & Sons, a shipping company, was founded in the next century and continued the emphasis on commerce with the islands. Henry Trowbridge's Sons followed as the successor firm. In 1892 the company was dissolved by mutual consent of its owners.[32]

Lorenzo, William and Philando Armstrong formed the shipping firm of L.W. & P. Armstrong about 1830. Like the Trowbridges, they imported sugar and molasses from the West Indies and exported food and general merchandise, including carriages made in New Haven. Long Wharf in New Haven housed the offices of both the Armstrongs and the Trowbridges. The business changed during the 1880s. Newly built sugar refineries in New York made the importation and local distribution of brown sugar and molasses unprofitable. The businesses at Long Wharf were given up; the Trowbridges sold their vessels to the Armstrongs; the Armstrongs moved their operation to New York; and imported sugar was sold directly to refiners.[33]

Except for Henry Sutton and Frank W. Benedict, Henry Benedict's son, the other builder-managers discussed above stopped acquiring new vessels after 1878. Frank Benedict had three schooners built at Madison between 1883 and 1891, one of which was the 204', four-masted, 1,114-ton *John H. Platt*. There were two other builder-managers of note in the New Haven area during the 1880s–Howard H. Hanscom and E. Harris Weaver. Hanscom owned the Fair Haven shipyard where the *Henry Sutton* was constructed. He was credited as the builder of at least 13 other schooners between 1880 and 1890, according to classified ship directories; but he managed only the last six ships he built, the final three being four-masters.[34]

One other builder-manager was E. Harris Weaver, who is being included in this group since he once was reported as being the "manager of every coasting schooner of note owned here" [New Haven]. The majority of Weaver's vessels were not built in the New Haven District, so he falls somewhat outside the scope of this survey. He was listed as an owner-manager in a classified ship directory for more than 30 years beginning in 1885. However, the maximum number of vessels attributed to his managerial stable in any one year was ten. Of course, this figure does not include ships that weren't classified, but he may not have had any of these. Twelve vessels were built for him in the decade from 1882 to 1892, of which one was constructed in Madison and two were built by Howard Hanscom in Fair Haven. Weaver acquired another schooner, the *Harold C. Beecher*, when he saw an opportunity. Abandoned in the Gulf of Mexico during a gale, the vessel was subsequently picked up and towed into Charleston. Several of her owners believed the schooner's damage was so extensive that she was not worth the salvage and repair costs. Weaver bought the interests of these stockholders, had the ship repaired, and entered her profitably in the lumber trade for a number of years.[35]

The largest vessel built by any of Henry Sutton's competitors was the *John H. Platt*. However, all five of Sutton's four-masters were larger than the *Platt*.[36]

Henry Sutton's schooners were principally engaged in the coal trade in the 1880s and 1890s, and it was a huge trade. Coal has been eclipsed in our time by electricity and petroleum products; we have no sense today of its importance in the nineteenth century or what transportation systems were in place to move it from the mines to cities and industries. Two days of coal-schooner activity in the spring of 1887 give a glimpse of how much coal was carried during all seasons of the year.

On 24 March, 1887, storms and adverse winds delayed a sizeable number of three-masted schooners in Long Island Sound, where they anchored overnight. Most carried coal from Norfolk. They were bound east for New Haven and shore points in New England. Early on the morning of the 25th a fresh westerly gale caught the ships bunched together and sent them scudding to New Haven and beyond. Fifteen of the vessels, including the *Reed* and

Boyce, brought from 12,000 to 20,000 tons of coal to New Haven—depending upon the newspaper one read. Even at the lowest figure, it was reported as the largest arrival of coal by ship on any one day at that port for 15 to 20 years. (Evidently barges were not considered in this evaluation.) At least 8,000 tons of this coal were consigned to the New York, New Haven and Hartford Railroad, known as the Consolidated Road. All of the schooners couldn't dock on the 25th—there wasn't room for them.[37]

If New Haven and other ports receiving coal were over-crowded, the coal shipping ports were worse. After 1880 the latter were often clogged with colliers awaiting their turn to load. By the late 1890s, if weather conditions prevented vessels from leaving the coal ports, fleets as large as 75 ships and barges might start out together when the weather cleared. One old captain reported that by going aloft one could see the coal fleet's sails scattered all around the horizon.[38]

Coal made the country run in those days. In the Northeast, the appetite for coal was nearly insatiable, and adding to massive domestic and industrial consumption was the Consolidated Road. Coal and the railroad were fundamental reasons for Henry Sutton to build a fleet of ships. Looking at the names of his first five vessels gives a sense of coal's primacy in Sutton's enterprises. His first schooner, the *Edward M. Reed,* named for the general superintendent of the Consolidated Road, was to be used to move coal from Baltimore to New Haven for the railroad. It may be supposed that Supt. Reed's position with the Consolidated Road was reason enough for Sutton to overlook any requirement to have Reed invest in his namesake schooner. The *James Boyce* was named for a Baltimore coal magnate; the next was named after himself; the *Orville Horwitz* was named for a Baltimore attorney who wasn't known for any coal connections but was a significant investor in Sutton's ships; and the *Harry A. Barry* carried the name of a Baltimore coal dealer. Three fourths of the Sutton schooners' known destinations on maiden voyages were to

Baltimore. Originally, Sutton used Baltimore as his principal port for loading coal, but later Norfolk became dominant. Most often the coal was destined for New England. Pointing up Norfolk's growing capacity for shipping coal was the arrival of the above-mentioned 15 schooners in New Haven in the spring of 1887. Almost all of them came up from Norfolk, although the *Reed* sailed out of Baltimore.[39]

The demand for coal and its transportation eventually produced another carrier, and thus competition for the schooners. In the early 1870s the first towed coal barges appeared on Long Island Sound. The barge traffic was documented by the 1880 U.S. Census Office Shipbuilding Report. It observed that New Haven's first two barges were built in 1876 and that the town could scarcely be said to have any other shipbuilding than coal barges four years later. It described two New Haven fleets of barges that could carry as much as 27,000 tons of coal from New York to New Haven in one trip. The barges were essentially square and were lashed together in fleets of 10 to 20. To lessen resistance, the bow and stern were raked. These scows often were wrecked or sunk and sometimes capsized. They couldn't venture into waters where they might meet a heavy ocean swell. However, if one was lost on occasion it only cost $300 to replace. The shipbuilding report stated that the two barge fleets noted above had driven a fleet of schooners out of the coal trade on Long Island Sound. They had reduced coal-carrying costs to the point that coasting schooners and colliers couldn't compete. This judgement was premature, yet it foretold events to come.[40]

The 1890s brought a new ship-shaped barge that was towed in trains of as many as five. Some old ships were cut down and refitted as part of the train. It seems that old schooners never die; they just turn into barges. These barges had some sailing capability, with short masts, baldheaded schooner rigs, and no bowsprit or head sails. Their manpower needs were minimal. In short, they were stump ships with rump crews. Sails were set when the wind was right, and they were seaworthy enough for coastal waters. By the turn of the century these barges were transporting coal to points as far removed as Bangor and New Orleans.[41]

Barges had the following advantages over schooners: less cost for maintenance and repairs; less manpower necessary; full loading possible at wharves in shallow water (schooners might have to finish loading in deeper water); ability to be employed continuously; and regularly scheduled service (schooners were more irregular, with downtime for maintenance and with unpredictable wind propulsion). Inexpensive new shallow-draft steel barges came into use before 1914, and these drove freight rates down even farther. Schooners were virtually out of coastal competition for bulk cargoes. The end of the huge schooner fleets of the final decades of the nineteenth century was at hand.[42]

END NOTES

1. *New Haven Evening Register*, 27 November, 1875, 4 (hereafter cited as *Register*); 19 March, 1877, 4; 30 November, 1883, 1; 5 June, 1886, 1; 15 August, 1887, 1; 7 September, 1889, 1; 18 July, 1891, 1; 2 June, 1894, 1; 20 February, 1903, 1. *Journal*, 26 July, 1879, 2; 7 September, 1883, 2; 19 November, 1884, 2; 17 September, 1888, 2; 29 August, 1890, 4.
2. *Journal*, 19, 21 July, 1879, 2; 7 September, 1883, 2; 29 August, 1890, 4. *Register*, 15, 20 August, 1887, 1.
3. Certificates of Enrollment: *Orville Horwitz*, 20 November, 1880; *Harry A. Barry*, 3 December, 1881; *James D. Dewell*, 3 October, 1882; *Nathan Easterbrook, Jr.*, 12 September, 1883; *James Ives*, 30 November, 1883; *Gen. S.E. Merwin*, 3 December, 1884; *Charles F. Tuttle*, 15 June, 1886; *Henry H. Olds*, 26 August, 1887; *W. Wallace Ward*, 22 September, 1888; *George M. Grant*, 13 September, 1889; *Lyman M. Law*, 29 August, 1890; *Lucinda Sutton*, 29 July, 1891; *Gen. E.S. Greeley*, 7 June, 1894, Records of the Bureau of Marine Inspection and Navigation, Record Group 41, National Archives, Washington, D.C.
4. *Register*, 7 September, 1889, 1; 18, 21 July, 1; 28 August, 1890, 1; 2 June, 1894, 1. *Journal*, 17 September, 1888, 2; 5 September, 1889, 2; 29 August, 1890, 4; 22 July, 1891, 4; 2, 4 June, 1894, 2. *Leading Businessmen of New*

Haven County, (Boston: Mercantile Publishing Co., 1887), 197.

5. *Shallops, Sloops and Sharpies*, (Derby, Connecticut: Bacon Printing, 1976), 55. The *Greeley* was launched in 1894. *Register*, 5 June, 1894, 1.

6. American Shipmasters' Association, *Record of American and Foreign Shipping*, (New York: American Bureau of Shipping, 1878-88), (1878):296; (1880):436; (1881):811; (1883):498, 559; (1885):564; (1887):251; (1888):448.

7. *Journal*, 19, 26 July, 1879, 2. Certificate of Enrollment, *Henry Sutton*, 7 August, 1879.

8. *Journal*, 28 November, 1881, 2.

9. Ibid., 7 September, 1883, 2. *Register*, 21 February, 1893, 2.

10. *Journal*, 29 November, 1883, 2. *Register*, 28, 30 November, 1883, 1.

11. *Journal*, 19 November, 1884, 1.

12. *Register*, 5 June, 1886, 1.

13. Ibid., 15, 20 August, 1887, 1. Certificate of Enrollment, *Henry H. Olds*, 26 August, 1887.

14. *Journal*, 17 September, 1888, 2. *Register*, 18 September, 1888, 1.

15. *Journal*, 5 September, 1889, 2. *Register*, 7 September, 1889, 1. Certificate of Enrollment, *George M. Grant,* 13 September, 1889.

16. *Register*, 18 July, 1891, 1. Certificate of Enrollment, *Lucinda Sutton*, 29 July, 1891.

17. *Register*, 18 July, 1891, 1.

18. Ibid., 2 June, 1894, 1. *Journal*, 4 June, 1894, 2.

19. Certificates of Enrollment: *Edward M. Reed,* 4 December, 1875; *Henry Sutton*, 7 August, 1879; *Lyman M. Law*, 29 August, 1890.

20. Certificates of Enrollment: *Henry Sutton; Lyman M. Law; Lucinda Sutton*, 29 July, 1891; *Gen. S.E. Merwin*, 3 December, 1884; *Charles F. Tuttle*, 15 June, 1886; *Henry H. Olds*, 26 August, 1887; *W. Wallace Ward*, 22 September, 1888; *George M. Grant,* 13 September, 1889; *R.& T. Hargraves*, 4 August, 1894; *Gen. E.S. Greeley*, 7 June, 1894; *James Boyce*, 21 March, 1877; *Orville Horwitz*, 20 November, 1880; 3 October, 1883.

21. Certificates of Enrollment: *Reed; Harry A. Barry,* 3 December, 1881; *Boyce; Henry Sutton; Horwitz; Tuttle; Olds; Ward; Law.*

22. Certificate of Enrollment: *Reed.*

23. *Journal*, 21 July, 1879, 2; 28 November, 1881, 2; 29 November, 1883, 2. *Register*, 7 September, 1889, 1; 18 July, 1891, 1. Certificate of Registry: *Henry Sutton,* 10 March, 1890, RG 41, NA. Certificates of Enrollment: *Reed; Barry; Law.*

24. *Register*, 21 October, 1898, 1; 11 October, 1909, 1; 17 March, 1887, 1. Certificates of Enrollment: *Edward M. Reed,* 4 December, 1875; *James Boyce,* 21 March, 1877; 19 March, 1878; 1 November, 1906; U.S. Customs

Service Wreck Report, *Edward M. Reed,* 1 October, 1898; U.S. Life-Saving
Service Wreck Report, *James Boyce,* 10 October, 1909. New Haven Colony
Historical Society Dana Collection; Scrapbook Collection: Micro 138, Box 17,
Folder D, vol. 72, 43; Micro 122, Box 11, Folder A, B 27. H. Sherman
Holcomb, *Magnus Manson and the Benedict-Manson Marine Company*
(Salem, Massachusetts: H. Sherman Holcomb, 1950), 6, 11, 19. New Haven
Colony Historical Society, *Shallops, Sloops and Sharpies* (New Haven: New
Haven Colony Historical Society, 1976), 39.

25. Certificates of Enrollment, *Henry Sutton,* 7 August, 1879; 23 February, 1892; 7
December, 1896; Certificate of Registry, *Henry Sutton,* 18 October, 1906.
Shallops, Sloops and Sharpies, 55. *Providence Journal,* 8 January, 1907, 16.
The Federal Reporter (First Series), 300 vols. (St. Paul: West Publishing Co.,
1880-1924), 26 (1886), 923.

26. Parker, *Great Coal Schooners,* 76. Certificates of Enrollment: *Orville Horwitz,* 20
November, 1880; 19 December, 1882; 3 October, 1883. *Register,* 17 March,
1907, 1; 9 November, 1896, 2. U. S. Life-Saving Service Annual Reports,
Harry A. Horwitz (1887); *Henry H. Olds* (1888). U.S. Life-Saving Service Wreck
Report, *Nathan Easterbrook, Jr.,* 20 February, 1893. U.S. Coast Guard, The
Lighthouse Board, wreck of *James Ives,* 27 January, 1895, RG 26, NA.

27. Certificates of Enrollment: *Dewell,* 3 October, 1882; *Easterbrook,* 12 September,
1883; *Merwin,* 21 June, 1900; *Tuttle,* 15 June, 1886; *Olds,* 26 August, 1887;
Ward, 22 September, 1888; *Grant,* 13 September, 1889; *Law,* 29 August,
1890; *L. Sutton,* 29 July, 1891; *Hargraves,* 5 November, 1902; *Greeley,* 7
June, 1894. *Commemorative Biographical Record of New Haven County,
Connecticut* (Chicago: J.H. Beers & Co., 1902), 30 (hereafter cited as *New
Haven Record*). *Lloyd's Register of Shipping* (London: *Lloyd's Register of
Shipping,* 1899, 1901, 1902, 1903), Appendices (List of Ship Owners and
Managers) 47. *Register,* 15 February, 1902, 1; 8 September, 1903, 3; 9
September 1903, 1. *NYMR,* 19 February 1902, 10; 9 September 1903, 10;
16 September, 1903, 10. William N. Peterson, *Mystic Built* (Mystic Seaport
Publications, 1989), 73, 74, 206, 207.

28. *New Haven Record,* 30. *Connecticut State Register and Manual* (Hartford: State
of Connecticut, 1989), 70. Dewell's oath subscriptions were on Certificates of
Enrollment for the *Hargraves,* 29 January, 1897; 25 June, 1897; 20 July,
1898; 12 December, 1898; *Tuttle,* 15 December, 1897; Certificate of Registry:
L. Sutton, 26 August, 1897. Captain George L. Kelsey signed a Certificate of
Enrollment for the *Ward* on 19 April, 1898, instead of *Dewell*. Interview with
Cheryl Schutt, Law Librarian, Law Department, Connecticut State Library,
Hartford, on 26 July, 1990, regarding meetings of the state legislature.
Register, 19 April, 1906, 1; 5 January, 1900, 1; 4 March, 1901, 1; 20

February, 1903, 1.

29. *Register*, 22 September, 1906, 1; 26 October, 1906, 1. Certificates of Enrollment: *L. Sutton*, 26 October, 1905; 31 March, 1909. Certificates of Registry: *L. Sutton*, 27 January, 1915; 18 August, 1915.

30. *Register*, 22 September, 1906, 1. *The New International Year Book for the Year 1916*, 1917 ed., s.v. "Shipping." Certificates of Enrollment *Greeley*, 28 January, 1916; 24 March, 1916; *Grant*, 13 July, 1916; 14 September, 1916; *Law*, 20 June, 1916. Certificates of Registry, *Law*, 27 November, 1916; *L. Sutton*, 18 August, 1915. *Journal*, 15 February, 1917, 1. U.S. Coast Guard Casualty Reports, Fiscal Year 1917 #1425, *Lucinda Sutton*, 31 March, 1917. Holcomb, *Magnus Manson and the Benedict-Manson Marine Company*, Exhibit B.

31. *Journal*, 7 September, 1883, 2. *Shallops, Sloops and Sharpies*, 54-55. American Shipmasters' Association, *Record of American and Foreign Shipping* (New York: American Shipmasters' Association, 1867-84).

32. *Shallops, Sloops and Sharpies*, 38, 50, 53. New Haven Colony Historical Society Scrapbook collection, micro 138, box 17, fol. D, v. 72, 43. *New Haven Record*, 1359.

33. New Haven Colony Historical Society Dana Collection, v. 129, 43. *History of New Haven*, 506-507.

34. *Record of American and Foreign Shipping*, (Review of ownership and builders for years 1867-94).

35. Ibid., years 1885-1915. New Haven Colony Historical Society Scrapbook collection, box 16, fol. B, 66. *Register*, 9 May, 1898, 1.

36. *Record of American and Foreign Shipping*, (1888-1895).

37. *Register*, 25 March, 1887, 1. *Journal*, 26 March, 1887, 2-3.

38. Parker, *Great Coal Schooners*, 52-54.

39. *History of the City of New Haven* (1638-1887), ed. Edward E. Atwater (New York: W.W. Munsell & Co., 1887), 371 (hereafter cited as *History of New Haven*). J. Thomas Scharf, *History of Baltimore City and County*, 2 vols. (Baltimore: Regional Publishing Co., 1971), 1: 390-91 (hereafter cited as *History of Baltimore*). *Journal*, 27 November, 1875, 2; 29 July, 1879, 2; 28 November, 1881, 2; 7 September, 1883, 2; 29 November, 1883, 2; 15 June, 1894, 2. *Register*, 4 November, 1880, 4; 27 September, 1882, 4; 6 September, 1883, 1; 19 November, 1884, 1; 18 September, 1888, 1; 7 September, 1889, 1; 28 August, 1890, 1; 21 July, 1891, 1

40. *Shipbuilding Report*, 8:114. Hutchins, *Maritime*, 564-65. Fairburn, *Merchant Sail*, 4:2624.

41. Hutchins, *Maritime*, 564. Fairburn, *Merchant Sail*, 4:2624.

42. Hutchins, *Maritime*, 564-65. Fairburn, *Merchant Sail*, 4:2624-2625.

BUILDING SUTTON'S SCHOONERS

The building time for Henry Sutton's schooners ranged between four months for the *Gen. S.E. Merwin*, on which approximately 60 men were employed, to about eleven months for the *Lucinda Sutton*. For the latter, construction was unhurried, although at one period some 50 men were engaged. The *Nathan Easterbrook, Jr.* took between six and seven months to complete and the *George M. Grant* eight months. On the *Grant*, 40 to 50 men worked continually when they could, although a long spell of wet weather slowed the work. Nevertheless, the *Grant* was finished only three weeks behind schedule. Weather affected the *James D. Dewell* in another way. While still on the ways, the schooner was

W. WALLACE WARD UNDER CONSTRUCTION AT THE GESNER AND MAR SHIPYARD, 1888.

struck by lightning, presumably attracted by her iron work. Although two holes were made in her bottom by the lightning bolt, she was launched one week later.[1] Ordinarily, when one schooner was completed, work on another was begun soon thereafter. However, the *Nathan Easterbrook, Jr.* and the *James Ives* were built concurrently, the *Easterbrook* being launched on 6 September, 1883, and the *Ives* on 29 November, 1883.[2]

The local populace couldn't help noticing activity in the shipyard. An article published in the *New Haven Journal* just before the *W. Wallace Ward* was launched in 1888 gives an account of the work and its impact: "It is truly a monster of a vessel for this section of New England and as one stands at the stern or bow and looks along the narrow length, the spectacle is one almost of grandeur. The huge hulk looms up over the surrounding houses like a giant and can be seen for miles across the harbor. People upon its decks look like pygmies and the long scaffolding leading up along its sides from the ground seems to be about three times as wide at the bottom as at the top. . . . Four monstrous masts rise from its decks and run up to a dizzy height while the spars and yards are almost as big as the masts themselves of many vessels seen about the Harbor. . . . Below the deck, in the body of the boat, are three tiers of flooring, and to look down through one of the hatchways reminds one of the elevator passage-way in some high building with its many floors one above the other."[3]

New Haven photographer F. H. Smith took a picture of the *Henry Sutton* in July of 1879. The schooner was up on the blocks before her launching with men busy on deck and in the yard. It was reported as "the first time one has been photographed in a like position, and the effect is novel and pretty."[4]

New Haven shipbuilding notwithstanding, from 1820 to the end of merchant sail, Maine was preeminent in building wooden ships in the United States. Initially the Pine Tree State had the advantage of cheap and easily accessible timber. But with the depletion of the forests it was said that some Maine-built ships had scarcely a piece of local timber in them.[5] Yet Maine continued to be supreme in American shipbuilding, primarily because of skilled but low-cost labor, not only natives but newcomers as well. In the late 1870s tradesmen from declining Canadian shipbuilding towns gravitated to Maine. And there were few labor problems. Attempts to unionize workers failed in Maine because there was too great a need for employment in an industry that was part of the culture. As many as 50 Maine towns continued to build ships whether there was a demand for them or not. Shipbuilding was the only trade they knew. Despite an increase in real cost, shipbuilding expenses were reduced largely at the cost of profits, builders' capital, and workmens' earnings in the State of Maine. Boss contractors earned only two or three dollars a day more than their men. There was distinct pressure on labor and capital to accept low returns. Apparently builders often asked for subscriptions from contractors and workmen. Subcontractors also passed down some of their shares to employees. So everyone involved in shipbuilding in Maine combined to build, own and operate vessels. Maine's shipyards determined the national price of wooden sailing ships.[6]

With a few exceptions, each succeeding Sutton-built schooner was larger and heavier than its immediate predecessor. And Sutton's schooners were larger and heavier than most other Connecticut-built sailing vessels. For the launchings of four of Sutton's last five ships, the press reported them individually to be the largest schooners ever built and registered from Connecticut. But not so his last vessel, the *Gen. Greeley,* since she was somewhat smaller than the *Lucinda Sutton,* her predecessor. The *Lucinda Sutton* was flagship and queen of the fleet. At the time of her launching in 1891 she was said to be the largest sailing ship ever built between New York and Boston. Construction costs of the fleet kept apace, if one can accept local newspaper figures as reasonably reliable. Some amounts reported: the *Barry,* $36,000; *Dewell,* $37,000; *Easterbrook,* $50,000; *Ives,* $39,000; *Gen. Merwin,* $50,000; *Charles F. Tuttle,* $45,000; *Olds,* $48,000; *Ward,* $60,000; *Grant,*

$64,000; *L. Sutton*, $72,000; and *Gen. Greeley*, $65,000. Contrast these figures with those of the *Hargraves*, built in Maine in 1891 and said to have cost $30,000. The *Hargraves* matches up well with the *Tuttle* in dimensions and tonnage. But the *Hargraves* was built five and one-half years after the *Tuttle*, had one additional mast, and yet cost one-third less to complete. This underscores the important differential between Maine and Connecticut construction costs and pricing, leading soon to the demise of shipbuilding at New Haven and elsewhere in Connecticut.[7]

Three of Sutton's ships, the *Reed*, *Boyce*, and *Ives*, had only one deck. All the others had two. Poop decks (a deck above the upper deck abaft the mizzen, sometimes forming the roof of a cabin) weren't counted. Sutton began by building terns (three-masted schooners) but changed to four-masters for his last five vessels, starting with the *Ward* in 1888. As his schooners became larger, their masts became taller, until a problem arose due to limitations imposed by the Brooklyn Bridge. This stage was reached when the *Easterbrook* was built in 1883. She couldn't clear the bridge at high water when light, nor apparently could any of Sutton's later vessels except for the *Ives*. After the *Easterbrook*, the masts increased still more in height so that sailing light–to the port of New York for a load of coal, for example–negated passage under the bridge unless topmasts were lowered. When U.S. Secretary of War John A. Rawlins approved plans for building the bridge in 1869 he specified that the center of the main span must be at least 135' above "mean high water of the spring tides." But even at this height it was recognized that some of the larger vessels would have to lower their topmasts. It should be noted that large schooners didn't sail under the Brooklyn Bridge, they were towed. Even so, many ships broke topmasts while attempting to pass under the span. Over the years the bridge also settled to its present 127' mid-span height. Lowering a large schooner's topmasts and raising them took about a day for each task. The alternative was to sail around Long Island.[8]

Masts for some of Sutton's later schooners were cut in Oregon forests. The *Tuttle's* and *Greeley's* masts, for example, came from Oregon via sailing ship around Cape Horn. For the *Tuttle*, her masts were 29" in diameter at the deck and appeared to maintain their girth all the way to the top. The *Greeley's* masts were a hundred feet tall and said to be without a knot. The *Grant's* masts came from Michigan and measured 30" in diameter at the base. Masts for the *Lucinda Sutton* were obtained when a new railroad line was opened in Pennsylvania. The logs were hauled through ten miles of snow to the railroad. Topmasts for these schooners were also sizeable. For the *Olds* they were approximately 60' long, projecting nearly 45' beyond the lower masts, which in turn were about 97' tall.[9]

Generally, the wood used in the construction of these schooners was oak, chestnut and yellow pine—oak and chestnut for frame members, and yellow pine for planking. Longleaf yellow pine from the American south was commonly used for planking in American shipbuilding during the nineteenth century. For six of Sutton's schooners, hackmatack was included. Galvanized fastenings were used, sometimes along with copper.[10] The most important American hardwood used in the nation's wooden shipbuilding was white oak. Originally it grew in forests of the Atlantic-coast states all the way down to Georgia. By the 1880s, after about a century and a half of harvesting, virtually all the readily accessible white oak was depleted throughout New England. And with large schooners each requiring as many as 200 large oaks, it was necessary to bring it in from other locations. At the end of the nineteenth century it typically came from Delaware, Maryland and Virginia, the Ohio valley, the Great Lakes states, and Ontario.[11]

White oak wasn't the only wood in short supply. Much of the timber used in ship construction was becoming rare in New England. Shipbuilders in Maine, Massachusetts, and Connecticut required an assemblage of timber and materials from widely separated areas of the country–at considerable cost. Some shipyards kept a supply of timber on hand for seasoning, but generally this wasn't done, and waiting for fresh-cut wood to season and be ready to use could lengthen the shipbuilding process by as much as a year.[12]

In Connecticut, there still was a small amount of white oak and chestnut to be found. Both had grown profusely along the Connecticut River, and chestnut was a regional tradition in home and barn construction as well as shipbuilding. Connecticut shipyards continued to make vessel frames from chestnut. This wood was prized for its light weight, ease in working, and durability.[13]

The last great stand of virgin American timber was located in the Pacific Northwest, and a new shipbuilding industry arose there in the 25 years before World War I. However, white oak was not native to the far west. The principal timber there was Douglas fir. This was originally determined to be unsuitable for shipbuilding because it was so rot-prone, but during the 1870s it was found to be durable when cut in winter, seasoned and salted. From 50 to 70 tons of salt were required for salting planking stock for a large vessel. If properly prepared, however, Douglas fir planking could be as good as new even after 20 years of service.[14]

It was Henry Sutton's custom to name his schooners after prominent owners of the vessels. In the case of the *General Greeley*, when the General first visited the schooner he not only took a share of her stock but also asked to name her. Sutton granted the privilege.[15] The eponyms returned the honor by furnishing the schooner's colors, which cost about $200 in the case of a four-masted vessel. The Union Jack was flown from the foretopmast. A 40'-long pennant bearing the ship's name was at the main topmast peak. The Sutton house flag, a blue "S" on a white background, was displayed at the mizzen topmast. A large 30' U.S. ensign went to the top of the spanker topmast and a long narrow streamer flew above this. A smaller American ensign was flown in the spanker rigging. The flags described can be seen in a photo of the launching of the *Lucinda Sutton* at West Haven on 21 July, 1891.[16]

At a given launching, a limited number of invitations

LUCINDA SUTTON ON THE LAUNCHING WAYS, 1891.

were generally extended to the eponyms, stockholders, special guests and families to inspect the ship and ride with it down the ways. But no special invitations were sent for the launching of the *Olds*. There it was advertised that all responsible people who could be comfortably provided for would be permitted on board the vessel for the launching. When the *Law* and the *Lucinda Sutton* made their plunges, the general public was allowed the same opportunities as invited guests, and people jumped at the chance. Due to the crush of visitors wanting to go aboard, their numbers had to be controlled.[17]

Henry Sutton's launching routine did not involve a great deal of ceremony, but when someone intimately connected with the vessel wanted it, Sutton didn't stand in the way. Ceremonies took place on two occasions. In 1879 the Rev. Mr. Parkington, pastor of the East Pearl Methodist Church, conducted appropriate exercises aboard the *Henry Sutton* before she went down the ways. This was done at the request of her master, Captain Gilbert Manson. And in 1887 the Rev. Mrs. Phoebe A. Hanaford, poet, author, and good friend of Henry H. Olds, came from her residence in Nantucket to speak at the launching of the *Olds*. After giving the invocation, she talked about the historic significance of New Haven as a seaport, then eulogized the schooner, its owners, its builders, and its eponym. She concluded with her own 56-line poem about the *Olds*, which also ended the exercises. By this time the crowd was restless, and not without reason. Not only was the speech long, but those on shore couldn't hear what was said.[18]

The launchings were colorful and exciting events. Where crowd estimates were made, they numbered in the thousands, with few exceptions. On the day the *Lucinda Sutton* went down the ways, *The New Haven Evening Register* reported that "The people began going to West Haven before 9 o'clock and at 9:30 every horse car on the West Haven road, west bound, was packed with people. In wheeled vehicles it was a varied procession. Hacks, coupes, barges, beach wagons, express wagons and fine private teams made up an almost continuous line of vehicles destined for West Haven an hour before the launch. Wheelmen and wheelwomen–a large number of the latter–were also in the procession. Then other hundreds came by water. . . . The people were not assembled en masse, but were scattered all over the big shipyard, and out on the dock near which the schooner was to rest when launched. Scores and scores of people stood on the Kimberly

avenue bridge, while down the avenue as far as the eye could reach was a line of carriages filled with eager witnesses. But there was no prettier sight than that toward the harbor, where a fleet of sloop yachts, sharpies, cat boats and row boats were lying, the sail craft at anchor. The smaller boats were only a few feet from shore, just far enough to escape a blow from the big schooner as it slid from the ways. . . ." The crowd was estimated at 5,000 people. A similar estimate had been made 11 months before for the launching of the *Lyman M. Law.*[19]

Many arrived early, and on occasion they were treated to some unfeatured side shows. For the *Ward*, a diversion was created when the ensign was hoisted to the top of the spankermast upside down. To the sailor this is a distress signal. Though quickly righted, some in the crowd must have wondered if it was an omen. For the *Law*, one young child observing from a boat in the harbor fell overboard, but he was scooped up without harm. The *Register* reported that shortly thereafter two ferocious-looking bulldogs tore into each other "and the female portion of the crowd scattered in all directions." For the launching of the *Henry Sutton* on a dog day of summer, a number of men and boys sat on floating logs in the harbor, balancing precariously. They amused everyone with numerous launches of their own, some voluntary and some not. When the big ship's stern hit the water, the wave it created catapulted dozens more from their perches, accompanied by howls from the crowd.[20]

Sending a ship down the ways was not an exact science. While the procedure was familiar, and routine for the shipyard hands, the time it might take to accomplish was always somewhat variable. *The New Haven Evening Register* gave a dramatic account of the operation when the *General Greeley* was ready to be launched and Mr. Gesner shouted the order to go ahead. ". . . the words were hardly out of his mouth before the click of a dozen mauls was heard along the keel. The first business was to wedge up the great burden so that a great portion of the weight would be transferred from the other supports to the launching ways, which had been liberally slushed with grease. This over, the men applied their mauls to half a hundred shores, or short timbers, which stood up against the bottom. The men, or a portion of them, continued at this task when others took their iron wedges and split out the keel blocks.

"It took time and lots of muscle to do this work, and just 40 minutes were expended before the last keel block was reached. Then just at noon the great hull was seen to move. The start was almost imperceptible, but there followed a creak of timbers that told well that the vessel was on her journey to the sea. She still moved slowly, but in 10 seconds or more had attained a good headway, as the ways smoked with the pressure that was transferred to them. Then the whistle on the steam launch *Ceres*, which had brought up a party, screeched a loud welcome, and two guns were fired from her deck. Two tugs which steamed over to take the great vessel to the wharf, joined in the glad acclaim, and the whistle from the *Greeley*'s engine house forward, acknowledged the salutes."[21] To this description add the gracefulness and speed of the schooner going down the slide, its final mighty splash, the wave created, the shouts of the crowd on ship and shore—and the picture is complete.

The honor of performing the christening was usually given to a young woman, often a member of the eponym's family, and she would take up a position on deck at the bow. Henry Sutton would direct her to wait until the ship was fully afloat before breaking the bottle over the bow. At the launch of the *Olds*, Miss Annie Stahl, daughter of William F. Stahl, threw the quart bottle at the bowsprit, and to her chagrin she missed. The bottle caught in the schooner's headgear and was rescued by the master, Captain Smeed. He returned it to Miss Stahl, who did better the second time around.[22]

For the *Lucinda Sutton*, Henry Sutton bought a bottle of Gold Seal wine decked out in red, white and blue ribbons. He proclaimed, "In deference to the McKinley bill, we propose to christen this vessel with wine of domestic manufacture." Then he tied a long marline to the neck of the bottle and the other end to the ship in order to save the bottle's neck as a souvenir of the occasion. Miss Lottie Bushnell, daughter of ex-alderman Frank C. Bushnell, expected to perform the honors but was rudely surprised. The vessel barely began to move along the ways when an unidentified man standing on the fo'c'sle ripped the bottle from her grasp and smashed it against the bow. Everyone wondered what had happened. Although nonplussed by the incident, Miss Bushnell quickly recovered and announced, "I christen thee *Lucinda Sutton*."[23]

A successful launch at West Haven generally called for the schooner to be towed to the wharf where its passengers could debark; but due to shallow basins and channels throughout the whole New Haven-West Haven area, launching large vessels often resulted in their being stuck on mud flats. An invitation to ride the ship down the ways could be a mixed blessing. There must have been some concern about how to get back to shore and how long that might take. For those who thought about it, possibly the best

plan was to disembark before the launch took place. Many followed this course.[24]

From the shipbuilder's standpoint, timing and seamanship
were critical in dealing with the mud. Correctly calculating the
time of highest tide, dropping anchor as soon as the vessel hit
water, operating brakes on the anchor chains, or using hawsers to
arrest the ship's momentum were procedures followed in trying to
keep it out of the mud. Nevertheless, six of Sutton's schooners
ended up in the mud and a seventh touched it. Ships trapped on
the mud flats usually would be towed out by tugs during the next
high tide. Sometimes it took longer.[25]

Getting people off the mired schooners didn't take quite
as long as waiting for the next high tide, although it may have
seemed so. On occasion, some physical dexterity was called for by
those wanting to get to shore. When the *Law* and *Lucinda Sutton*
went into the mud, each with three hundred or more people
aboard, it took time to get everyone off. From the *Law*, evacuees
began descending a rope ladder to the ship's yawl to be transported to the wharf. One report stated that people were lowered but
no particulars were given as to how this was accomplished. The
yawl's capacity was too limited, so the sloop *Jessie Dean* at Welch's
coal yard was pressed into service. Those aboard the *Lucinda Sutton*
fared somewhat better inasmuch as they were provided with regular ladders for descent. However, they didn't have the *Jessie Dean*
for transport; they were removed slowly in the ship's yawl. The
Lucinda Sutton only traveled about half her length after leaving the
ways before hitting the mud, and there she stayed for three days
before she could be moved.[26]

In the case of the *Ward*, it took considerable time for all
the people aboard to be transferred ashore in small boats. No information was available as to how those on the *Ives* debarked. That
vessel went into the mud on the opposite shore of the channel and
was still aground the next day. For the *Henry Sutton*, the tug *William*
pulled her out of the mud at New Haven and the schooner

dropped anchor in the channel. Persons aboard were allowed to get off onto neighboring coal barges. Observers on a nearby wharf also found themselves stranded. The tide had come in and enisled them, although the water wasn't too deep. Some were taken ashore in boats, others by horse and buggy. Some of the men and older women opted for wading, although a reporter observed that wading was disdained by the young women.[27]

Weather could also bring discomfort. When the *General Merwin* was launched in the middle of November of 1884 there was a storm of sleet and snow. A majority of the 200 invited guests failed to make an appearance. Those who did come huddled together in groups on deck and shivered as they waited. Even so, perhaps the sheer beauty of the scene wasn't lost upon them. The schooner's black hull, topped by her yellow masts, white upper works and colorful flags, accentuated by a set of International Code Signals, made a picture in the blowing sleet and snow. The launch was smooth and considered a success even though the schooner ended up firmly in the mud. The *Merwin*'s longboat was pressed into service to take everyone ashore, but by then the weather had deteriorated. A gale was raging and the sides of the ship and its 25' ladders were sheathed in ice. Captain John F. Sawyer was equal to the challenge. He had a bowline rigged for the women that was coiled around them under their arms. One by one they were hoisted up, out, and over the side, then lowered to the longboat in the water. The men were left to maneuver on their own down an icy ladder to the boat. It took seven or eight trips of the longboat before everybody was transported safely to shore.[28]

The launching of the *Greeley* had competition from the circus, which was then the primary attraction in town. A crowd estimate of the West Haven shipyard for the schooner's slide was only "several hundred." As time came for the launch, many people walked down the inclined platform and off the ship. Perhaps they might have been influenced by somebody's prior experience on the *Law* or *Lucinda Sutton*. However, the water was unusually high that day due to perigee tide and the *Greeley* just touched the muddy bottom.[29]

The launchings were attended by occasional mishaps or, as recounted above, some element of danger. The *Easterbrook*'s two empty rowboats were upset during launching when they were caught up in the ropes. A more significant accident occurred when the *Olds'* anchor was dropped prematurely as the ship started down the ways. Several carpenters were still in the cradle and two or three of them narrowly escaped being crushed as they dodged the huge bounding anchor. It knocked a heavy timber against carpenter John Cameron's head, leaving him stunned. He was carried from the cradle but soon recovered, apparently without serious injury. The carpenters were outraged over the incident and the jeopardy in which they had been placed. The *Olds* concluded her launch by smashing against a wharf and marring her fresh paint.[30]

After the launch of the *Ward*, she was tied by a long taut hawser to a stack of piles in the water. Five men in a small boat near the pilings were gathering pieces of timber that were floating in the water. Suddenly, the group of pilings gave way under the strain of the hawser and shot toward the boat as if fired from a giant slingshot. Hearing the sound, the men instinctively ducked as the piles sailed right over their heads, barely missing them.[31]

Wallace G. Munson, a 45-year-old laborer, was engaged in knocking down stanchions forming the braces at the sides of the *Grant* just prior to her launching. He felled a heavy stanchion but was unable to get out of its way in time. It knocked him to the ground and landed on his back. He suffered a paralyzed limb and what was thought to be a broken back and collarbone. Contributions were solicited on the spot and were said to be quite liberal. This was the first serious accident at a launching at Gesner and Mar's shipyard.[32]

About an hour before the *Greeley*'s launching, 12-year-old Albert Ricketts was scrambling over her deck along with scores of others. While between decks, he tripped over a board near the hatch and fell into the lower hold. Rescuers responded to his scream and carried him to his home. It was thought his shoulder was dislocated.[33]

END NOTES

1. *Journal*, 19 November, 1884, 2; 5 September, 1889, 2. *Register*, 18 July, 1891, 1; 6 September, 1883, 1; 7 September, 1889, 1; 21 September, 1882, 4.
2. *Journal*, 7 September, 1883, 2; 29 November, 1883, 2. *Register*, 6 September, 1883, 1; 28 November, 1883, 1.
3. *Journal*, 17 September, 1888, 2.
4. Ibid., 26 July, 1879, 2.
5. *Shipbuilding Report*, 8:96. Hutchins, *Maritime*, 386, 558-59. Fairburn, *Merchant Sail*, 5:3100.
6. *Shipbuilding Report*, 8:96. Hutchins, *Maritime*, 389-92, 394, 396, 560.
7. Review of ship's dimensions, ownership, and builders for years 1867-94, American Shipmasters' Association, *Record of American and Foreign Shipping* (New York: American Shipmasters' Association, 1867-1894). *Journal*, 7 September, 1883, 2; 19 November, 1884, 2; 17 September, 1886, 2; 5 September, 1889, 2; 29 August, 1890, 4; 22 July, 1891, 4; 22 February, 1887, 4; 29 November, 1883, 2; 4 June, 1894, 2. *Register*, 6 September, 1883, 1; 15   August, 1887, 1; 7 September, 1889, 1; 18, 21 July, 1891, 1; 21 February, 1887, 1; 27 September, 1882, 4; 21 February, 1893, 1; 28 November, 1883, 1; 19 November, 1884, 1; 5 June, 1886, 1; 18 September, 1888, 1; 2 June, 1894, 1; 20 February, 1903, 1. *Fall River* (Massachusetts) *Evening News*, 21 February, 1903, 1. *Shallops, Sloops and Sharpies*, 55.
8. Certificates of Enrollment, *Reed*, 4 December, 1875; *Boyce*, 21 March, 1877; *H. Sutton*, 7 August, 1879; *Horwitz*, 20 November, 1880; *Barry*, 3 December, 1881; *Dewell*, 3 October, 1882; *Easterbrook*, 12 September, 1883; *Ives*, 30 November, 1883; *Merwin*, 3 December, 1884; *Tuttle*, 15 June, 1886; *Olds*, 6 August, 1887; *Ward*, 22 September, 1888; *Grant*, 13 September, 1889; *Law*, 29 August, 1890; *L. Sutton*, 29 July, 1891; *Hargraves*, 21 December, 1891; *Greeley*, 7 June, 1894. *Journal*, 7 September, 1883, 2; 19 November, 1884, 2. Homer R. Seely, "Historical Features of Construction and Operation," included in "Technical Survey - Brooklyn Bridge After Sixty Years - A Symposium," *American Society of Civil Engineers Transactions* 112 (1947):185. Letters to the author from Captain Francis E. Bowker, former research associate, Mystic Seaport, dated 7 and 19 September, 1984, and from David J. Roach III, assis

tant manager, New York Marine Terminals, The Port Authority of New York and New Jersey, dated 3 May, 1984, wherein the latter advised that the rise and fall of the tide under the Brooklyn Bridge is approximately five feet. American Shipmasters' Association, *Record of American and Foreign Shipping*, (New York: American Bureau of Shipping, 1886-95), (1886):334, 421, 461, 477, 518, 520, 684, 720; (1888):448; (1890):313, 464, 899; (1895): 459, 615, 619, 741.

9. *Register*, 5 June, 1886, 1; 2 June, 1894, 1; 18 July, 1891, 1; 15 August, 1887, 1; 7 September, 1889, 1. *Journal*, 5 September, 1889, 2.

10. American Shipmasters' Association, *Record of American and Foreign Shipping,* (New York: American Bureau of Shipping, 1886-1895), (1886):334, 421, 461, 477, 518, 520, 684, 720; (1888):448; (1890):313, 464, 899; (1895):459, 615, 619, 741.

11. *Shipbuilding Report*, 8:102, 243-44. Hutchins, *Maritime*, 387.

12. *Shipbuilding Report*, 8:102. Hutchins, *Maritime*, 387-88, 558.

13. *Shipbuilding Report*, 8:113-114, 244.

14. Ibid., 8:102. Hutchins, *Maritime*, 561-62.

15. *Register*, 5 June, 1894, 1.

16. Ibid., 18, 21 July, 1891, 1. 2 June, 1894, 1.

17. *Register*, 7 September, 1889, 1; 28 August, 1890, 1; 21 July, 1891, 1. *Journal*, 20 August, 1887, 2; 29 August, 1890, 4.

18. *Journal*, 19, 29 July, 1879, 2. *Register*, 20 August, 1887, 1.

19. *Journal*, 29 July, 1879, 2; 7 September, 1883, 2; 22 July, 1891, 4. *Register*, 5 June, 1886, 1; 20 August, 1887, 1; 18 September, 1888, 1; 7 September, 1889, 1; 28 August, 1890 1; 21 July, 1891, 1.

20. *Register*, 18 September, 1888, 1; 28 August, 1890, 1; 30 July, 1879, 1. *Journal*, 29 July, 1879, 2.

21. *Register*, 5 June, 1894, 1.

22. *Register*, 20 August, 1887, 1.

23. Ibid., 21 July, 1891, 1.

24. *Register*, 7 September, 1889, 1; 21 July, 1891, 1.

25. Ibid., 21 July, 1891, 1; 18 September, 1888, 1.

26. Ibid., 28 August, 1890, 1. *Journal*, August, 1890, 4; 22 July, 1891, 4.

27. *Register*, 18 September, 1888, 1; 30 November, 1883, 1; 30 July, 1879, 1.

28. Ibid., 19 November, 1884, 1.

29. Ibid., 5 June, 1894, 1.

30. *Journal*, 7 September, 1883, 2. *Register*, 20 August, 1887, 1.

31. *Register*, 18 September, 1888, 1.

32. Ibid., 7 September, 1889, 1.

33. Ibid., 5 June, 1894, 1.

CHAPTER 5

THE SCHOONERS AT WORK

The round-trip speed of these big schooners was a relative item. It depended upon the wind and the weather, docking availability, time for loading and unloading cargos, as well as other happenstances of a voyage. Nevertheless, speed through the water was an important consideration. Along with carrying capacity, it was a factor in the profitability of a vessel. When the *Lucinda Sutton* was built, her fine lines, sharp bow, graceful stern, and great sail power were observed as being indicative of a fast sailer. For the *General Greeley*'s maiden voyage to Norfolk, sailing light, she covered the distance in just 60 hours. At the beginning of the trip a tugboat started out with her to obtain photos, but even with a full head of steam the tug was soon left behind.[1]

SCHOONERS *MAGNUS MANSON* AND *GENERAL E.S. GREELEY* LOADING ICE AT BOOTHBAY, MAINE.

When the *James Boyce* finally wrecked in 1909 she was described as an old boat but "one of the fastest 'hookers' in the coast trade." "Hooker" actually was a contemptuous term used by sailors for an old or clumsy craft, but in this case the description seems playful rather than disparaging. The *Boyce* was old, but still considered fast for an old-timer. Once, laden with 800 tons of coal, the *Boyce* made a run from New York to Boston in 48 hours. In July and August of 1890 the *Boyce*, *Ives*, and *Dewell* made four, four, and two round trips from New Haven to Norfolk to load coal and bring it back. Counting time in port, the round trips took between 11 and 14 days.[2]

What is considered most significant is the number of voyages completed by a ship and captain in one year. In 1893 the *Law* and *Lucinda Sutton* made 13 round trips each, almost entirely between Providence and Hampton Roads. These performances were considered to be good. Looking at the 1895 records of the *Law*, *Lucinda Sutton*, *Greeley*, *Merwin*, and *Grant*, (the record of this last schooner was only available for half a year and was rated on that basis), shows an average of slightly more than 13 voyages a year. Most of the trips again were between Providence and Hampton Roads or further. Their performances seem to have been fairly consistent.[3]

Transport of coal in one direction was worthwhile enough to permit the schooners to sail light to Baltimore or Norfolk. The many investors and reinvestors in Henry Sutton's schooners speaks for the profitability of the business. Certainly if the vessel persevered for a number of years the financial return could be substantial. That said, we have no really accurate measure of the degree of profitability of Henry Sutton's schooners. A few newspaper accounts gave a bare line to the subject and their statements correspond fairly well with each other and with figures available for the vessels. When the *Easterbrook* wrecked after more than nine years of service, she was reported to have just about paid for herself ($50,000). The *Ward* paid out $64,000 in dividends in 11-1/3 years ($4,000 over her cost). For the *Hargraves*, it was claimed she had paid for herself twice over, and this was after just over 11 years of sailing. As has been stated, construction costs for this Maine-built vessel ($30,000) were substantially lower than they were for the Connecticut schooners.[4]

Looking at the sailing life of the Sutton schooners, only the *Olds, Barry,* and *Horwitz* had shorter lifespans than the *Easterbrook*. The *Olds* had the shortest time of all. She sank after less than eight months of service. Nine of the ships sailed for more than 20 years, with the *Boyce* holding the record at more than 32 years. Henry Sutton's vessels averaged 17-2/3 years of sailing, which could have been longer had not two of his ships been destroyed in war. Nevertheless, the longevity of Sutton's schooners compares favorably with those of Maine's Palmer fleet of four- and five-masted schooners, built between 1900 and 1908, in which 14 of its 15 vessels averaged just 12 years. It was said that this 12-year figure would serve as a fair average for great schooners in the coal fleet. (One of the Palmer vessels, the *Harwood Palmer*, was destroyed by a German submarine.) It should be noted that the average lifespan of all ships, sail or steam, wood or steel, was but 20 years.[5]

It was important for these schooners to spend as little time in port as could be managed; if not, demurrage might be invoked. In maritime usage, demurrage is a charge made for the detention of a vessel beyond a time agreed upon (as in loading or unloading). A good example of demurrage is shown in a lawsuit brought by Gilbert Manson, master and managing owner of the *Henry Sutton*. This suit was brought against the New York, New Haven & Hartford Railroad Co. in the Federal District Court of Connecticut, which case was decided on 16 March, 1886. The schooner had carried 980 tons of coal from Baltimore to New Haven. The bill of lading called for her cargo to be delivered to the "Consolidated Road Docks" in New Haven.

On 31 January, 1885, in New Haven, Captain Manson

reported to Mr. Waterbury, the railroad's freight agent, seeking to discharge his cargo. The railroad owned three docks close to each other on the main channel where coal was delivered. The largest of these was Belle Dock. A fourth dock, the Shop Dock, was a small wharf connected to the main channel by a dredged channel three-quarters of a mile long. Only one vessel at a time could unload at this wharf, but it was designed for two ships to lie in its basin at the same time.

Mr. Waterbury instructed Captain Manson to go to the Shop Dock to discharge. Manson said he would take the *Sutton* in on the first tide that night. Waterbury said no, another ship, the *Crescent* was to enter first. He added that they had had problems before with two ships in the basin at the same time. On 1 February, the *Crescent* went to the Shop Dock and the *Sutton* was towed to the entrance of the artificial channel. Tides being good, she could have been towed to the basin that night. Thereafter thick ice formed. During the first week of February, both the *Sutton* and the *Crescent* tried to contract with tug companies to get in and out the channel but the tug companies refused, thinking it unsafe for their vessels.

Although the *Sutton* easily could have gone to Belle Dock anytime between 31 January and 15 February, Waterbury instructed the tug companies not to tow her there. Waterbury told Manson to bring the *Sutton* into the Shop Dock on 5 February since the *Crescent* was to be discharged that day. Manson advised that he would go in if the *Crescent* got out. But Waterbury said that when the *Sutton* was in, he would have the *Crescent* out. Manson refused to go in and Waterbury refused to break ice. The *Crescent* remained frozen in until 6 March. On 15 February, Manson was allowed to deliver his cargo at Belle Dock. He began unloading on the 16th and finished on the 23rd.

The court said the law held that where a bill of lading specified a dock for delivery, the vessel had to arrive at said dock as a prerequisite for demurrage. Then the court found that the *Sutton* had waited (in the dock area) at the request of the consignee. Being unable to obtain a tug to break the ice, and prevented by the consignee from unloading at its accessible dock, the defendant's liability for demurrage was found to be complete. The court issued a decree for the *Sutton* for $784 with interest and costs.[6]

The U.S. Government issued certificates of enrollment to American-flag merchant vessels engaged in coastal trade, whereas certificates of registry were necessary for vessels engaged in offshore, or foreign trade. Changes in a ship's name, ownership, description, home port, and type of trade, such as from fishing to freight or from coastal freight to foreign freight, necessitated the issuance of a new certificate. But owners didn't always file for new certificates, particularly with regard to partial changes of ownership. Sometimes the changes were allowed to accumulate before new certificates were requested. Any new certificate, after all, was an added expense.[7]

Sutton shipowners were no exception to these slack filing procedures, which made tracing ownership more difficult and sometimes impossible. For example, the last certificate of registry for the *Lucinda Sutton*, maintained at the National Archives, was issued on 10 August, 1915, and it listed 24 independent shipowners, primarily from New England. Yet the U.S. Coast Guard casualty report of 23 May, 1917, disclosed that her owner was the South American Shipping Co. of New York City. In another instance, the *Greeley* might have committed a misfeasance when she sailed to Cienfuegos, Cuba, on a 24 March, 1916, certificate of enrollment instead of a certificate of registry.[8] It is also possible that a later certificate of registry might have been forwarded to the National Archives, or it might have been misplaced there.

The Sutton schooners were built for the coastal trade, and for the most part that was where they worked. Their principal cargos, whether in domestic or foreign trade, were coal and lumber. But other cargos were transported when it was opportune.

When launched, at least four of these large schooners

were noted by local newspapers as being designated for, or adaptable to, foreign trade. The *Merwin* was said to be suitable for carrying sugar and other West Indies goods, and the *Ward* for general foreign trade. Flattering offers were made to use the *Law* in trade with South America. Henry Sutton said the *Lucinda Sutton* was adaptable to any trade and that she would work well in trade with Japan, where the freight rates were quite promising. However, aside from the *Merwin*, it all proved to be just talk. Soon after the *Merwin*'s launching, she made two voyages to Cuba and another of short duration (six weeks) to an unspecified foreign destination. Still later she visited France and Wales, stopping off in the Caribbean on her return. During Sutton's lifetime (until November 1896), only three of his other ships made overseas voyages, the sum total of which was six. The *Easterbrook* sailed to Cuba three times, once in conjunction with a trip to St. Thomas. The *Henry Sutton* traveled to the Canadian Maritime Provinces twice and the *Tuttle* went to Cuba once.[9]

After Sutton died, his schooners made just 50 more overseas voyages. Six of the ships, the *Reed, Horwitz, Barry, Dewell, Ives,* and *Olds* never sailed to any foreign shore at all. New Brunswick and Nova Scotia received 20 visits, mostly by the *Boyce* and *Henry Sutton*, delivering coal and usually picking up gypsum on the return voyage. The *Ward* went to Mexico four times. Seven vessels visited the West Indies and/or Bermuda on 27 occasions, in which Cuba was a destination 15 times. (On any given voyage, sometimes more than one country was visited. Two Puerto Rican visits were not included in this foreign trade count since the Sutton schooners did not go there until after the U.S. acquired the island as a result of the Spanish-American War.)[10]

The *Grant* was reported to have sailed from a Spanish port just in time to avoid capture when Spain declared war on the U.S. on 25 April, 1898. But the story wasn't true. The *Grant* had stopped at Barcelona in December of 1897 and sailed from there to Trapani, Sicily, arriving in January, 1898. Returning to the U.S.

much later, she encountered very strong headwinds and was blown far off her course. She was overdue when she arrived at Gloucester, Massachusetts, with her cargo of salt on 12 May, 1898. Her voyage ended when she sailed into Boston on the 24th. Playing with these dates, one might imagine the *Grant*'s sailors insinuating a miraculous deliverance from the Spaniards.[11]

As for intercontinental travel by the remaining schooners, the *Ward* completed a voyage to Barcelona and Trapani three months before the *Grant*. The *Merwin*'s trade with Wales and France has already been noted. The *Greeley* sailed to South America twice, once to Brazil and once to Argentina. South America also hosted the *Lucinda Sutton* three times. That ship's first trip was to Brazil, the second to Uruguay, and the third to Brazil and Argentina. Argentina proved to be the end of the line for the *Lucinda Sutton* in 1917.[12]

Intercontinental travel also proved to be the end of the line for the remaining Sutton ships. The *Grant* tried to return to Spain in 1916 but her fate was otherwise determined. The *Law* was forcibly prevented from reaching Italy in 1917. The *Greeley* was sold in 1917 to French interests in Algiers, where her name was changed to the *Montenegro*, and she didn't make it across the Mediterranean to France in 1918.

END NOTES

1. *Register*, 10 July, 1891, 1. *Journal*, 15 June, 1894, 2.
2. *Register*, 11 October, 1909, 1; 3, 5, 9, 12, 14, 15, 18, 26, 29 July, 1890, 1; 4, 11, 18, 21, 25, 28, 29, 30 August, 1890, 1. *Boston Morning Journal*, 3 January, 1903, 11.
3. Parker, *Great Coal Schooners*, 55, 57-58.
4. *Register*, 21 February, 1893, 1; 5 January, 1900, 1; 20 February, 1903, 1.
5. Ibid., 13 April, 1888, 1; 21 February, 1887, 1; 17 March, 1887, 1; 11 October, 1909, 1. Parker, *Great Coal Schooners*, 66, 67, app. 4.
6. *The Federal Reporter* (First Series) 300 vols. (St. Paul: West Publishing Co., 1880-1924), 26 (1886): 923-27.

7. Letter to author dated 15 July, 1981, from Kenneth Hall, archivist, Industrial and Social Branch, NA. Telephone interview with John Vandereedt, archivist, Judicial, Fiscal and Social Branch, NA, on 16 April, 1986.

8. Certificate of Registry, *Lucinda Sutton*, 18 August, 1915. U.S. Coast Guard Casualty Report #1425, *Lucinda Sutton*, 23 May, 1917. It is also possible that a later Certificate of Registry might not have been forwarded to NA or it might have been misplaced at NA. Certificate of Enrollment, *Gen. E.S. Greeley*, 24 March, 1916; *NYMR*, 17 May, 1916, 28.

9. *Journal*, 19 November, 1884, 2; 29 August, 1890, 4. *Register*, 18 September, 1888, 1; 18 July, 1891, 1. See Appendix.

10. See Appendix.

11. *Journal*, 15 February, 1917, 1. *Register*, 10 May, 1898, 8. See Appendix.

12. See Appendix.

THE SCHOONERS AND THEIR PEOPLE

A s might be expected, captains of the new schooners were usually selected from the group of masters who were sailing for the Sutton fleet. For example, Captain Alton H. Vesper was given command of the following vessels upon their launching: the *Easterbrook* in 1883; the *Ward* in 1888; and the *Grant* in 1889. Captain William L. Blake followed suit with the *Law* in 1890 and the *Greeley* in 1894. He also commanded the *Ward* in 1891. Previously, Captain Hobart E. Ives did the same with the *James Ives* in 1883 and the *Tuttle* in 1886. No information was developed whether Captain Ives was related to eponym James Ives. Captain Ives' tragic fate is discussed in this chapter.[1]

THE SHIP'S COOK, BERT CONNERS, STANDS BY THE WHEEL OF THE *LUCINDA SUTTON* IN HARBOR.

On necessary occasions, captains were temporarily replaced by substitutes; but many captains commanded particular vessels for a number of years. Captain Constant W. Chatfield was skipper of at least four vessels of the fleet, and gave Henry Sutton more than 20 years of service. He also exemplified the faith that Henry Sutton and his successor as managing owner, James D. Dewell, had in their captains. Chatfield commanded the *Barry* when she went down in 1887, yet later skippered the *Dewell*. He captained the *Hargraves* when she sank in 1903, but immediately thereafter the *Law* was assigned to him until he retired in 1916.[2]

Captain George L. Kelsey commanded the *Easterbrook* when she was wrecked in 1893. Henry Sutton backed Kelsey completely, even before learning the facts about the wreck from his captain. Sutton said at the time that he did not believe Captain Kelsey was responsible for the loss of the ship, and expressed great confidence in this man he described as a careful and experienced navigator and a first-class seaman. He offered his opinion that the vessel was lost due to springing a leak or having the steering gear break down or the sails blown away. He said he believed that Kelsey exercised his best judgment, and that the disaster was unavoidable. Kelsey also commanded the *Dewell*, the *Lucinda Sutton*, the *Grant*, and was skipper of the *Ward* when she went down in 1900. His uncle, Chauncey S. Kelsey, was the first captain of the *Reed* and subsequently commanded the *Horwitz* until she sank under him in 1887.[3] Captain Edward H. Smeed was in charge of the *Olds* when she was lost in 1888, and later was master of the *General Merwin*.[4] Captain Herbert A. O'Brien was commander of the selfsame *Merwin* in 1887 when she collided with another vessel and capsized. However, the *Merwin* was not at fault. O'Brien also served as master of the *Ward* and then the *Lucinda Sutton* from the time of the latter's launching in 1891 to at least 1906. But he had a special dispensation–he was Henry Sutton's brother-in-law.[5]

It is not known how often wives or family members accompanied the masters on Sutton's schooners. We know of a

CAPTAIN HERBERT A. O'BRIEN.

few instances where they were aboard or were scheduled to be aboard on specific voyages. For example, Captain John F. Sawyer planned to take his wife and daughter with him on the *General Merwin* for the vessel's maiden voyage in 1884. Captain Herbert A. O'Brien had his wife Lisle with him aboard the *Merwin* in 1887 when that schooner capsized in a collision. And in 1900 Captain John Kelsey's wife was among those rescued from the *Ward* on the ship's last voyage.[6]

Captain Hobart E. Ives left Henry Sutton's ships in 1895 to command the four-masted schooner *John H. Platt* of New Haven. August of 1898 found him and his nine-man crew aboard the *Platt*, in ballast, enroute to Brunswick, Georgia, from New York. They were to pick up a cargo of lumber and return it to New York. Accompanying Captain Ives on this voyage was his second wife, his 13-year-old son and 11-year-old daughter (children by his first wife), plus the son of the Brunswick postmaster. On 31 August and perhaps prior thereto, the *Platt* was accompanied by the schooner *Sarah D.J. Rawson*, of Camden, Maine. They were somewhere off Port Royal, Georgia, and were caught in a violent storm. It was, in fact, Hurricane #2 of the 1898 hurricane season. Horrendous winds and waves forced the *Platt* onto her side with masts dragging in the sea. A tremendous wave then crashed over her and sent the *Rawson* out of sight of the stricken ship. During the next two weeks, pieces of the *Platt* wreckage were driven ashore at several places along the Georgia coast. Her stern washed up at Tybee on 8 September, and on 12 September part of her cabin was found on the beach near Hilton's Point. There were no survivors.[7]

How did mariners react to having a captain's wife aboard ship? No commentary has been passed down to us by way of the Sutton vessels. But Captain Francis E. Bowker touched on the subject in his book about his experiences aboard coasting schooners when he was but a bos'n. He said he looked forward to having a captain's wife aboard; the crew kept cleaner, their language was better, and the women didn't interfere with the crew. He also had some long and pleasant conversations with at least one master's wife. He reported gaining insights into the lonely lives led by ship-masters' wives at home, noting that even coastwise captains could be away from their families for over a year. He supposed that many a captain might become an unwelcome intruder in his own domicile by giving orders as was his wont at sea, and peace would only return to his abode after he returned to sea.[8]

Sutton's schooners carried crews of from five to ten men

plus the captain. With the largest complement, there were two mates, an engineer, a steward and six men before the mast.[9] What was it like to work on a coastal schooner? To convey some understanding, most of the following is a synthesized summary from Lewis Parker's *The Great Coal Schooners of New England 1870-1909* and Francis Bowker's *Atlantic Four-Master: The Story of the Schooner "Herbert L. Rawding" 1919-1947.* As with other vessels, men stood watches for four hours on and four hours off, except for the two-hour dog watches between 4:00 and 8:00 p.m. The crew averaged 12 hours a day on watch. In emergencies, these hours of duty could stretch out to include an entire day—and night as well.[10]

During daylight, the watch handled steering (which was changed every two hours), washing down, repairs, and maintenance such as painting, tarring the rigging, occasional sail patching, and whatever else needed to be done. And there was always something to be done on a sailing ship. Good mates followed the old adage that a busy crew is a happy crew. Scheduled daily work would begin with the forenoon watch at 8:00 a.m., continue through the afternoon watch and finish during the first dog watch, perhaps at the first sitting for supper. Starting and finishing times depended upon the work to be performed and upon work procedures of the vessel, which varied from ship to ship. In the tropics for example, if there was enough light and good weather at 6:00 a.m., decks were washed down with salt water to prevent them from drying out. No ship's work was performed at Christmas, other than to man the wheel and handle necessary sails. Christmas and Thanksgiving also called for better meals. When serious damage occurred at sea, the coaster would invariably complete its voyage by tow and arrange for repairs later, rather than trying to make do temporarily.[11]

The crew lived in the fo'c'sle, usually in somewhat cramped quarters. They slept on plain cotton-filled mattresses in double tiered, board-slatted bunks built up against a bulkhead. In cold weather, they had heat from the engine room. Meals were carried to the fo'c'sle by the junior man in the watch. There were no radios. They read dime novels and old newspapers, chewed or smoked, and yarned. Seamen's wages in the mid-1880s ran about $16 to $18 per month in winter and $20 in summer. Wages varied seasonally because small coasters were laid up during winter's bad weather. When better weather returned, the small coasters entered into the competition for sailors. By 1902 seamen's wages had increased to about $30 per month.[12]

The cook's day began between 3:30 and 4:00 a.m. in order to prepare coffee when the watch changed. He served three big meals a day for each watch, along with a single sitting for the captain and mates. He cooked, baked, acted as steward, and kept everything clean in his own quarters and work spaces, and in the officers' cabins aft. His pay was $50 to $55 per month. If he was a good cook he might stay with a captain for years.[13]

The engineer, known as "chief," kept steam in the boiler and looked after heating equipment and machinery. His quarters were in a small cabin off the engineroom. He could be called whenever steam was needed but he stood no watches. His pay also was about $50 to $55 per month.[14]

The first mate on a coasting vessel received the same wage. He served as the executive officer and headed the port watch. He had his own cabin and ate with the captain and bos'n in the dining space of the after house. While his position called for respect, he nevertheless was expected to physically lend a hand with work when needed.[15]

On coasters, the bos'n generally acted as second mate. As such, he headed the captain's or starboard watch. He was a fine seaman and performed the deck-keeping duties of a mate, but his pay was only about $35 per month. On small ships, however, when gasoline engines came into use for hoisting and pumping, if he assumed the engineer's duties along with his own he might be paid more. Depending upon the design of the vessel, his quarters could vary from comfortable to decidedly cramped.[16]

The master's quarters were luxurious compared to the others. In addition to his own large paneled stateroom with double bed, desk and chair or chairs, he would have a bathroom, large salon, and perhaps one or two other spaces that could include a chart room. He had to buy an interest in the vessel, usually a 64th share. His compensation generally was $50 per month and five percent of the ship's gross earnings.[17]

Perhaps it should be mentioned here that bedbugs were a scourge of these vessels, and they didn't differentiate between officers and crew.[18] On a more positive note, American schooners had a reputation for feeding well. Typical stores aboard ship might be salt beef (known as salt horse), salt pork, salt mackerel, cod tongues and sounds (bladders), and smoked shoulders. Fresh vegetables would include potatoes, cabbage, carrots, turnips, and onions. Peas, beans, corn, beets, fruit and meat appeared in cans. Rice and cereal were available in quantity. Fresh meat would not keep since ice boxes were the only refrigeration.[19]

Getting under way required a series of sequential steps. Halyards were led to winches and lower sails were slowly hoisted and trimmed in flat. Meanwhile, the anchor was slowly hove in as the mud was hosed off the chain, which was stowed in a chain locker at the bow. When the anchor came away, engine speed increased as the strain slacked. Different sails were raised depending upon the direction and force of the wind, tide, current, and the ship's position. As the vessel gathered way, other sails might be set. Cluttered lines and gear on deck were coiled and/or properly stowed. If topsails were to be set, crewmen climbed aloft at the captain's order. With all sails spread to the wind, and knifing her way through the water, the schooner was a dramatic sight.[20]

A sailing ship at sea has an aura about her, a mystique that encompasses both romance and vivid reality. The vast heaven with its stars at night, the moon playing on the waves, the graceful rise and fall of the ship, coordinated with its roll, combine to create an unsurpassed sense of freedom, of being in a little world far from the cares left ashore. It is a mystique that calls men back again and again. The weather adds and subtracts from the magic of sailing a ship. Consider a breathtaking, multicolored sunset on the horizon. Then think of being becalmed in the tropics with the sun's heat beating down and making tar bubble in the rigging. And of trying unsuccessfully to catch fish in order to relieve a monotonous diet of salt horse, hash, and stew. Think also of collecting rain in barrels, buckets, and tanks, sweeping off the tops of the cabin and forward house in order to fill tanks below, and having enough extra water for a grand clothes-washing spree.[21]

Some rain did not encourage sprees. Accompanying a squall with blasts of wind and building seas that continually washed over a deeply-laden deck, rain made a four-hour watch on deck miserable. A sailor was glad to go below.[22]

Another misery was slatting. With large swells and light winds that alternately blow and then slack off, sails would slat. One sail or another would have to be lowered to replace stitching in the seams. At times, all sails would have to be taken in to prevent slatting. Sail would be made again when a breeze sprang up, but too often the wind would die out and sails would have to be lowered once again.[23]

Returning from the West Indies in March of 1941, Captain Bowker's schooner *Herbert L. Rawding* ran smack into a strong northwest gale. Although sails had been reefed down, she was driving into a head sea and shipping green water forward. In heavy weather, few great schooners could heave to comfortably. They shipped water forward, rolled tremendously, and kept falling off the wind. With sea room, the best maneuver was to up helm, fall off and run before the storm. This is what the *Rawding* did, but it soon became necessary to run with just bare poles and a jib. Gigantic seas, estimated at 40' to 50', towered over the stern as the schooner dropped into the trough of one wave and then was propelled high on the crest of the next one. The sea raced by underneath before dropping her into another cavernous hollow. Wind moaned in the rigging and shreiked through the taut wire stays. Gusts carrying clouds of spray lashed and heeled the big four-master. The schooner ran for three days and nights before the storm abated.[24]

Almost completing the above voyage, the *Rawding* arrived at Nantucket Shoals. Here she ran into another northwest gale, this one carrying blinding snow. Nantucket Shoals is one of the Atlantic's graveyards, a place where sailing vessels have disappeared without trace. The *Rawding* was forced to ride to a full scope of chain on her port anchor. Headsails and topsails were tied up and reefs were put in the lower sails in case it was necessary to pull out in a hurry. The schooner was jerking as seas rolled under her, and spray froze as it hit the deck and rigging. Reefing sail in freezing rain froze hands and mittens. It also froze ropes and canvas that became as hard as boiler plate and had to be beaten with belaying pins. All four sails were reefed, even though the men were soaked and half frozen and the deck was a mass of moving slush. Quitting was never an option–not when your life depended on it. The starboard anchor had to be set, and during the night the port anchor carried away. It was touch and go for two days until the schooner rode out the storm. All in all, it was not a place for the faint-hearted.[25]

Schooners were normally loaded so fully that in heavy weather their decks were never free of water. In zero-degree weather they would almost be unrecognizable when they arrived in port totally encased in ice. Sails were often so stiff that crews couldn't handle them. In such cases, the schooners were simply blown away with their exhausted crews. Some vessels sailing south to Philadelphia, for example, were caught up in successive gales and blown as far south as Savannah or out to Bermuda, sometimes heavily damaged.[26]

Weather constituted but one of the hazards coasters faced. Add to this the dangers of lee shores, shifting shoals, narrow channels, fog-hidden headlands, groundings, and an ever-present potential for collision, exacerbated by the sheer number of vessels moving in and out of ports. In addition, the coal schooner route between New England and Hampton Roads cut through steamer lanes from the West Indies and Europe to Boston, New York and Philadelphia, three of the busiest ports in the world. Indeed, the open ocean was much safer than the coastal route. The latter required exceptional vigilance, superior seamanship and navigational skills, and awareness of coastal conditions from Cape Ann to Cape Charles.[27]

Since Henry Sutton's schooners were primarily colliers, the transport of coal is of interest. What was it like to load coal? During the loading exercise, the schooner was in the middle of a cloud of soot. It sifted through the vessel's living quarters and into the food. Captains were wont to stay ashore under these circumstances and mates were left to oversee proper trimming and stowage of cargo. In the darkness and polluted air of the hold, gangs of black trimmers in coal ports shoveled coal from under the hatches to the vessel's sides. They earned seven or eight cents a ton plus a pittance for beer money.[28] After a ship was loaded, she would be towed from port and anchored. Coal would have spilled around the hatches and the whole ship would be covered with coal dust. Once the hatches were secured, the vessel would receive a good saltwater washing and scrubbing.[29]

To ready the schooner for discharging, hatch covers had to be removed, sail covers put on, booms hoisted, and falls rove. Black stevedores came aboard and lighters came alongside. Stevedores filled a big bucket with coal that was hoisted over the side by the boom and tackle, then dumped into the lighters. The process was repeated until the cargo was delivered. When it was over, everything on the schooner was covered with coal dust once again.[30]

Although coasters normally specialized in certain cargos, they could be chartered for various trades. It was not unusual to find a collier temporarily changed over to other trades such as lumber, gypsum, railroad iron, salt, ice or even goat droppings.[31]

New England men wanting to work aboard a collier generally signed on for a round-trip voyage to a coal port. After a month, if the vessel hadn't yet been loaded at the coal port, the men would be paid off. A new crew would not be signed on until the ship was laden and ready for sea. Thus the crew was turned loose with a month's pay in a southern coal port where they found alcohol and other diversions. At voyage's end, the whole crew would be paid off. The cook or mate would be kept on to look after the vessel. If both were good men and a charter was imminent, both might be retained. The crew, however, would disperse and a new crew would be signed on for the next voyage.[32]

END NOTES

1. Certificates of Enrollment: *Easterbrook*, 12 September, 1883; *Ward*, 22
    September, 1888; *Grant*, 13 September, 1889, *Law*, 29 August, 1890;
    Greeley, 7 June, 1894; *Ward*, 8 July, 1891 (Change of Master, 2 June, 1897);
    Ives, November, 1883; *Tuttle*, June, 1886.
2. *Register* 21 February, 1887, 1; 20 February, 1903, 1; 22 September, 1906, 2.
    Journal, 16 February, 1917, 1.
3. *Register*, 21 February, 1893, 1; 5 January, 1900, 1,2; 17 March, 1887, 1.
    Journal, 22 February, 1893, 4; 27 November, 1875, 2. U.S. Customs Service
    Wreck Report, *W. Wallace Ward*, 5 January, 1900, RG 36, NA. Certificates of
    Enrollment, *Lucinda Sutton*, 29 July, 1891; *George M. Grant*, 13 September,
    1889.
4. U.S. Life-Saving Service Annual Report 1888, *Henry H. Olds*, RG 26, NA.
    Register, 4 March, 1901, 1.
5. U.S. Customs Service Wreck Report, *Gen. S.E. Merwin*, 11 May, 1887. *Journal*,
    18 May, 1887, 2. *Register*, 21 July, 1891, 1. Certificates of Enrollment,
    W. Wallace Ward, 22 September, 1888; *Lucinda Sutton*, 26 October, 1905.
6. *Register*, 19 November, 1984, 1; 5 January, 1900, 1. *Boston Daily Globe*, 12
    May, 1887, 1.
7. *Register*, 10 September, 1898, 7; 13 September, 1898, 1. *New York Maritime
    Register*, 7, 14 September, 1898, 10 (hereafter cited as *NYMR*). *Tropical
    Cyclones of the North Atlantic Ocean* 1871-1977 (Washington, D.C: U.S.
    Government Printing Office, 1978), 60.

8. Bowker, *Atlantic Four-Master*, 55, 66, 67.

9. U.S. Life-Saving Service Wreck Report, *James Boyce*, 10 October, 1909, RG 26, NA. *The Federal Reporter* (St. Paul: West Publishing Co., 1903), 122:816.

10. Parker, *Great Coal Schooners*, 60.

11. Ibid., 61. Bowker, *Atlantic Four-Master*, 34-36, 56, 60.

12. Parker, *Great Coal Schooners*, 60-61. Bowker, *Atlantic Four-Master*, 32, 36.

13. Parker, *Great Coal Schooners*, 63. Bowker, *Atlantic Four-Master*, 32, 34.

14. Parker, *Great Coal Schooners*, 63. Bowker, *Atlantic Four-Master*, 27.

15. Parker, *Great Coal Schooners*, 63.

16. Ibid., 64. Bowker, *Atlantic Four-Master*, 30, 33.

17. Parker, *Great Coal Schooners*, 65. Bowker, *Atlantic Four-Master*, 32-33.

18. Bowker, *Atlantic Four-Master*, 33, 66.

19. Ibid., 29.

20. Ibid., 29-30.

21. Ibid., 38, 56-57, 60.

22. Ibid., 30.

23. Ibid., 57-58.

24. Ibid., 40-42.

25. Ibid., 45-48.

26. Parker, *Great Coal Schooners*, 67-60.

27. Ibid., 64, 66, 68.

28. Ibid., 53.

29. Bowker, *Atlantic Four-Master*, 27.

30. Ibid., 36, 60.

31. Ibid., 37, 61. Parker, *Great Coal Schooners*, 58.

32. Parker, *Great Coal Schooners*, 49, 61.

CHAPTER 7

THE DEMISE OF SUTTON'S SCHOONERS

The schooners had no eyes below. They struck things —sunken and derelict ships, submerged objects and rocks. They stuck in things—sandbars and mud. Seemingly they had no eyes above either. They ran into things—piers, land, and other vessels. And other vessels ran into them. Finally, of course, they leaked. Water pounding them incessantly, and other knocks pounding them occasionally, generally loosened things up. Hogging stress, if present, added to the condition. Vessels were recaulked on a maintenance schedule and on special occasions—as when leaking. Storms tested them, and sailing through a storm a vessel's weaknesses worsened. Hurricanes hurried this process—in the extreme![1]

While not an everyday emergency, groundings nevertheless occurred with far greater frequency than might be imagined. Coasting schooners were much more susceptible to grounding than deepwater carriers or whalers. Short hauls, courses close to shore, continual changes in destination, and full cargos creating deep draft, gave greater opportunity for running aground. With full loads, there also was greater stress on vessels when they struck. And strike often and forcefully they did. As the ships aged, repeated strikings played a part in weakening their structures.

The ways that Henry Sutton's schooners came free from groundings are typical of the coasting trade. If a vessel didn't float off an obstruction quickly, several procedures were available to get her off. The ship could wait until the next flood tide; be towed off by tugboats or other vessels; or remove part or all of a cargo to a lighter in order to lessen draft. Sometimes all of the above were necessary. On at least one occasion a Sutton vessel was sent to lighten another Sutton schooner. The coal-carrying *Easterbrook* grounded on James Point in Chesapeake Bay on the night of 31 August, 1891. A revenue cutter and four other vessels tried to haul her off, but to no avail. Finally, the *Merwin* was sent to lighten her. (The *Merwin* was indebted to the *Easterbrook* for her previous assistance in 1888. See *Gen. S. E. Merwin*, Dismasting.) The *Easterbrook* was floated on 8 September, after which a tug towed her to Plumb Point to reload the cargo that had been removed.[2]

Floating free was not always the end of the story. The ship often struck again soon after being freed. Then the release process had to be repeated. The coal-carrying *Ward* grounded on a sand bar off Mount Hope, Rhode Island, on New Year's Day, 1895. She stayed on the bar overnight but got off the next morning. After moving only a short distance, she bumped once more and mired in the mud off Tiverton. Two tugs were unsuccessful in moving her. She was left until the next high tide, and when she didn't float part of her cargo was transferred to a lighter. She was finally hauled off on January 9th, eight days after first striking.[3]

Usually, after being freed, vessels were able to proceed on their own; but in many cases they had to be towed. Groundings sometimes caused severe structural damage. One of the worst instances of damage to a ship's bottom involved the *Grant* in 1906. (See the *George M. Grant*, Grounding.)

Groundings often caused leaks, and these might be tolerated for a short time but not for long. As the *Dewell* left Noank, Connecticut, on 4 October, 1899, she struck on a rocky ledge in the channel and sprang a leak. When she arrived at her Norfolk destination she was taking on 2'6" of water a day in smooth water. The coal-laden *Merwin*, enroute to Providence, went ashore on the southern end of Prudence Island in Narragansett Bay on 12 January, 1891. Two tugs were hired to float her, as she was leaking badly. About 300 tons of coal had to be removed from the schooner before she was floated on the 16th. She had 6' of water below forward and 9' aft. She was to have been placed in dry dock in Providence, but the leak stopped after she was pumped out. It was decided to have her go to Newport News for dry-dock repairs. The *Merwin* sailed from Providence on the 22nd in ballast. She made it as far as Winter Quarter Shoals off Virginia before the leaky condition overtook her again. A tug took her in tow on 2 February and brought her into Newport News the next day.[4]

When leaks or inundations occurred, additional men and pumps or steam pumps could be placed aboard the vessel. The *Reed* grounded on Romer Shoals in New York harbor in January, 1896. She got off the shoals, although a leak was started. Twelve men were constantly on the pumps during the passage through Long Island Sound. (Her normal complement was six.) In spite of the pumps, she had 4' of water in her hold upon arrival at Allyn's Point, Connecticut.[5]

When the depth of water in the bilges was excessive, a tug might deliberately ground a schooner on some nearby mud flats to prevent sinking. This procedure was not exceptional. The *Grant* furnishes an example. On 14 December, 1910, she departed Newport News with coal bound for Guadeloupe. She grounded on Thimble Shoal in Chesapeake Bay on the same day. Tugs tried to float her during the night but failed. It wasn't until the 16th that two tugs successfully got her off. They towed her to Lambert's Point, where they ran her onto mud flats. She had 11' of water in her hold and later was taken to Newport News for repairs.[6]

Although groundings, leaks and collisions occurred with some frequency, the principal cause of damage to the schooners was weather. And weather could create almost every sort of destruction imaginable—or unimaginable. On the Sutton schooners damage to anchors and chains, sails and rigging, and spars and masts, were most common. Loss of one or more masts posed great difficulty and danger for a schooner. Sails and masts in schooner rigs were generally set closer to each other than in square-rigged vessels. Consequently, when a mast was damaged,

71

it most often affected the rigging and sails of adjacent masts and sometimes the adjacent masts themselves. A vivid example of this domino effect was the dismasting of the *Montenegro* (formerly the *Greeley*) as she attempted to cross the Mediterranean in heavy weather in 1918 (see *Greeley-Montenegro*, Destruction). The *Merwin* was completely dismasted in a storm while crossing the Atlantic in 1889 (see *Merwin*, Dismasting). The *Dewell* lost her main and mizzen masts in a gale enroute from Newport News to Boston in 1897. Other Sutton vessels suffered masts so badly sprung during storms that new masts were required.[7]

Bad weather caused delays in departures and arrivals as well as concern over the ship's safety. Adverse winds delayed the *Lucinda Sutton*'s departure from Charleston for three weeks during September and October in 1914. Years before, on 19 January, 1901, the schooner had sailed from Trinidad for Baltimore but ran into severe weather. She was blown off course seven times and hove to for 17 days. She arrived at Baltimore on 1 March without her mainsail and with deck damage. When the *Dewell* arrived in New York on 17 January, 1904, from Fernandina, Florida, Captain Hammond reported that the schooner had been blown across the Gulf Stream three times. Her sails were badly torn and there was 5' of water in her hold. The *Law* left Portland, Maine, on 7 November, 1908, with copper ore for Baltimore, normally a week-long voyage. Inclement weather created fear for her safety until she arrived at her destination on 7 December, three weeks over-due.[8]

Other types of damage, rarely experienced on Sutton ships, involved the *Henry Sutton* in two instances. While enroute from Savannah to Boston, on the night of 6 August, 1902, off Block Island, three staybolts of the *Sutton*'s boiler blew out. Engineer Donavan of Norfolk had both feet scalded and he was removed to the Marine Hospital in Boston. Several feet of water had accumulated in the ship's hold. Upon arrival at Boston on the 8th a tug was engaged to pump out the schooner during the night. In another misadventure on 11 December, 1904, a fire broke out in some sail canvas aboard the *Sutton*. She was lying at the Grand Street dock in Newtown Creek, Brooklyn. An overheated stovepipe in the cabin caused the blaze, which resulted in $300 worth of damage.[9]

The cost of repairs was not cheap. The *General Greeley* received extensive repairs at the Erie Basin, Brooklyn, from 30 July through 14 October, 1905. This included new timbers and planking aft, new knees, deck beams, ceiling, plus a bottom cleaning and painting. The total cost ran about $30,000, but the length of time the schooner was idled should also be considered in the cost computation, adding considerably to the overall expense.[10]

The 17 schooners built for or managed by Henry Sutton experienced damages and disasters such as these during their careers. Indeed, one catastrophe or another did each of them in. What follows are the stories of their known collisions, as well as accounts of unusual damage, and finally the end of each of them under the heading "Destruction." The casualty reports appear in the same order in which the ships were launched.

THE *EDWARD M. REED*

Collision: On the night of 8 March, 1888, the *Reed* collided with the three-masted schooner *Edwin A. Gaskill* 30 miles off Cape Henry, Virginia. The *Reed* was bound from Baltimore to New London. She lost all of her forerigging and backstays. Her jib, foresail, and spanker split, while five stanchions, the rail, the planksheer (a heavy plank forming the outer edge of the deck), and four planks below the sheer were broken. Pumps had to be worked constantly to keep her from sinking as she was taken to Hampton Roads. On the 11th she was towed back to Baltimore. It was estimated that the repairs would run about $2,000.[11]

Destruction: A hatch coaming and fragment from a deck, with a ship's official number still attached, washed ashore on 19 October, 1898. Also washed ashore was the body of an unidentified seaman. The place was Cumberland Beach, on an island off

SCHOONER *EDWARD M. REED.*

the Georgia coast, south of Brunswick. Captain Magnus Manson, the principal and managing owner of the *Reed*, verified the ship's number. This confirmed what had been suspected for some time, that the *Edward M. Reed* had been lost with all seven hands aboard. She was thought to have been one of many ships destroyed on 2 October by Hurricane #7 of the 1898 U.S. hurricane season, which ravaged the coast for a hundred miles north and south of Savannah. At 7:00 a.m. on the 2nd the hurricane was centered on the Georgia coast and it roared inland from there.[12]

The *Reed* had sailed from Brunswick on 28 September bound for New York with a cargo of 345,000 board feet of yellow pine. For two weeks before finding the fragment of deck, vessels that arrived in New Haven from southern ports reported passing quantities of floating wreckage, apparently from a lumber-laden ship.[13]

New Haven shipping merchants believed the *Reed* was not far from Brunswick when she was caught in the hurricane. Being an old ship, they theorized that she couldn't take the pounding and quickly broke up. Coincidentally, the New Haven schooner *John H. Platt* was lost with all hands off the Georgia coast less than five weeks earlier in the year, a victim of Hurricane #2.[14]

The *Reed* had formerly been a collier but in later years carried lumber almost exclusively. For many years she had not sailed during the winters but was laid up at Long Wharf in New Haven. Then, supposedly a year or two before her destruction, she was said to have been given extensive repairs and placed in first-class condition to operate during the winters. She sailed during her last three winters, and despite her reconditioning experienced serious leakage problems in each.[15]

The *Reed*'s commander was 35-year-old Willet H. Wilson of Fair Haven, Connecticut. Born in Nova Scotia, he was regarded as an experienced navigator and a careful and competent master. He had formerly sailed on the *James Boyce* as mate and commanded several other New Haven vessels. Captain Wilson's wife had anxiously been awaiting news about the vessel. She had planned to meet her husband when the ship arrived in New York.[16]

Because of age, the estimated value of the schooner had decreased to a mere $8,000. She carried no insurance. It was reported that stockholders stood to lose practically their whole investment due to the cost of the repairs reported to have been made before she began service in winter. Her freight and cargo were insured for $7,500, which was carried by the Security Insurance Co. of New Haven. Magnus Manson owned a 13/64ths interest in the schooner and James Boyce of Baltimore held an 8/64ths interest.[17]

THE *JAMES BOYCE*

Collision: On 18 December, 1906, the *Boyce* sailed westward from Bridgeport through Long Island Sound, destined for a southern port. The tugboat *Emma J. Kennedy* crossed the schooner's path off Stepping Stone Light and was struck. The *Boyce* suffered no damage but the tug's pilothouse was smashed and her smokestack was broken. She had to be taken to New York.[18]

Destruction: A light wind blew from the southeast as a dense fog enveloped the Maine coast about 11:00 p.m. on 10 October, 1909. The *Boyce*, sailing without cargo from Portsmouth, New Hampshire, was proceeding to Rockland, Maine, for repairs. In the murk, the schooner strayed off course and crashed into a steep bluff shore on the east side of Pleasant Island, Maine. The vessel carried well onto the rocks so that the jibboom extended into the trees on the island. Her skipper for the last 13 months, Captain P.W. Alley of Ellsworth, Maine, and his five crewmen climbed out on the jibboom onto shore. They surveyed the area and found a suitable campsite. Taking sails from the schooner, the crew jury-rigged a tent and spent the night. The ship's hull was badly broken and at high tide rapidly filled with water. The vessel was not discovered by the life-saving patrol during the night due to thick fog.[19]

Next morning, Captain Alley took the ship's boat to Whitehead Life-saving Station, about three and a half miles away, to report the shipwreck. During that day and the next, the ship's crew, aided by the life-saving crew, stripped the vessel of sails, rigging, anchors, chains, and an engine, recovering about $2,000 worth of gear. On the second night, the keeper offered to take the men to the life-saving station but Captain Alley opted to remain near the ship with his men in their makeshift quarters. With some provisions saved from the wreck, they seemed to be quite comfortable, according to the life-saving station keeper.[20] After recovering what items they could, the men were transported to Rockland on the second day after the wreck.[21]

The *Boyce* was valued at $6,000. Magnus Manson, her original master, owned 43/64ths shares in the vessel. From 1877 to 1906 the number of owners had been reduced from 17 to 12.

Before Captain Alley commanded her, Captain A.L. Swan of Essex, Connecticut, had been her skipper for many years.[22]

THE *HENRY SUTTON*

Collisions: The two-masted schooner *Eagle*, sailing from St. John, New Brunswick, for New York with lumber, was struck by the *Henry Sutton*, enroute to Boston from Newport News. The *Eagle* was towed into New London on 26 March, 1889, and from there was to be towed on to New York. She lost both masts, head-gear, and had all her rigging carried away. The *Sutton* lost her flying jibboom.[23]

The fishing schooner *Elmer E. Randall* of Salem collided with the *Sutton* on 20 July, 1897, off the lightship below Boston and sank. Her crew was saved. The *Sutton* was slightly damaged and she put back to Boston.[24]

On 8 June, 1898, the British steamer *Megantic*, sailing from Boston for London, collided off Deer Island Light with the *Sutton*,

SCHOONER *HENRY SUTTON*.

coming up from Philadelphia. The uninjured steamer stopped long enough to ascertain that the schooner did not require assistance, then proceeded. The schooner went to her anchorage. She had been struck a glancing blow on the port quarter that carried away part of her after deck, bulwarks, and rail. She had a gash in the side extending into the cabin and running down to within four inches of the waterline, but she wasn't leaking. She was to be repaired in East Boston. The *Megantic* was sued for $1,750 in repairs and $50 a day demurrage for two weeks repair time.[25]

Destruction: On 31 October, 1906, Captain Cole of Calais, Maine, and his six crewmen sailed from Cheverie, Nova Scotia, aboard the *Henry Sutton*. The *Sutton* was well known as a lumber carrier up and down the eastern seaboard, but on this occasion she was sailing for Baltimore with 1,000 tons of plaster. One report erroneously listed her cargo as lumber. Ordinarily, the vessel would have taken a few weeks to sail from Cheverie to Baltimore, but on this passage neither the schooner nor any of her crew were ever heard from again. Managing owner Captain James W. Clifford, of Middleboro, Massachusetts, first reported the ship missing. Then, on 7 January, 1907, he advised custom-house authorities at her home port of Newport, Rhode Island, that the schooner and all on board had been given up as lost.[26]

It was known that the *Sutton* sailed into violent weather soon after departing Cheverie. Vicious gales had raged for more than a week, covering immense areas of land and sea. These storms moved slowly northeast from New England through Canada's Maritime Provinces. On 31 October a severe northeaster was centered off the Massachusetts coast, accompanied by 45-knot winds and torrential rains that turned into sleet and snow in Maine and New Brunswick. Giant waves, created by the compound effects of the storm and the full moon, crashed upon the New England coast, causing considerable damage along the shore.[27]

On 4 November the main force of the gale hit Prince Edward Island and Nova Scotia. It was the worst storm seen in those provinces in years. On Nova Scotia's Cape Breton coast, the wind reached a velocity of 65 miles an hour and for ten straight hours reportedly did not fall below 60 miles an hour. On land, trees were uprooted, barns blown over, and buildings damaged. At sea, disaster after disaster was reported. Ships were driven ashore and wrecked, with attendant loss of life. Even with vessels stranded only 100 to 300 yards offshore, rescues were hazardous in the extreme and sometimes impossible to make for days.[28]

A graphic description of what it was like to sail through the storm was presented by the officers of the battered and damaged steamer *Halifax*, which arrived in Boston on 4 November after departing from Halifax, Nova Scotia, on 31 October. The steamer carried 62 passengers, including the crew of a Gloucester, Massachusetts, fishing schooner that had been wrecked six days before. The fishermen had suffered severe hardship before they were rescued. On 1 November the *Halifax* was in the grip of the gale, being pitched and rolled by tremendous seas. Around noon, the ship's carpenter was swept overboard but his loss was not discovered for another two hours or so. Captain Alfred Ellis hove to and set a double watch on the bridge with the men lashed to stanchions. Then for the next two hours the area of the steamer's previous course was searched. It was hoped that the carpenter might have gone overboard with a piece of wreckage torn from the deck but he was never found. The steamer once again hove to and stayed that way for 20 hours riding out the storm's fury. Huge seas swept along the main deck, continuously sending tons of water over the heads of the passengers below. The main cabin doors were smashed in; the deckhouse was battered but stayed together; a metal plate on the starboard side started to tear off but not enough to create a leak. During the night, the gale reached its maximum intensity and with each crash of the waves the ship seemed to stand on one end and then the other. Most of the passengers were terror-stricken and helpless from seasickness. Captain Ellis remained on the bridge throughout the storm. At times, heavy snow made observation almost impossible. The badly buffeted steamer and her demoralized passengers finally reached port.[29]

In the light of the experience of the steamer *Halifax*, the fate of the 27-year-old wooden schooner *Henry Sutton* seems fairly certain. Both ships departed Nova Scotia on the same day, sailing in a southwesterly direction and separated by less than 50 miles across the narrow waist of the province. The *Sutton* had to sail through the Bay of Fundy between Nova Scotia and New Brunswick before reaching the Atlantic, whereas the *Halifax* steamed directly into the ocean. However, the storm system encompassed the entire area. If her cargo had been lumber and if she hadn't broken up, the *Sutton* might have remained afloat even if she sprang a leak or otherwise took on water.[30]

Neither the names nor the residences of the *Sutton*'s crew were divulged by the report of the managing owner. This information was thought to be contained in duplicate papers maintained at Captain Cole's home in Calais and could not be released until those papers were inspected.[31]

Managing owner James W. Clifford held 10/64ths shares of the *Sutton* and investors from the New Haven area still maintained their interests, including Lyman M. Law with 4/64ths and Lucinda Sutton with 2/64ths.[32]

THE *ORVILLE HORWITZ*

Collision: Laden with 1,030 tons of coal from Baltimore, the *Orville Horwitz* lay at anchor in Flushing Bay, Long Island, New York, on the morning of 8 February, 1884. Captain Chauncey S. Kelsey of Clinton, Connecticut, had stopped there while enroute to New Haven. About 8:00 a.m. the 78-ton oyster schooner *Harvest Home,* of Ellsworth, Maine, sailing from New Haven to Virginia, ran into the anchored *Horwitz*. Bulwarks on the *Horwitz'* starboard bow were stove and damages were estimated at $300. No information was available as to the *Harvest Home*'s damages. A wreck report filed by Captain Kelsey attributed the collision to "bad judgment."[33]

At that time, Henry W. Crawford of New Haven was the managing owner of the *Horwitz*. He held a 3/64ths interest in the ship, while Captain Kelsey maintained a 4/64ths share. Baltimore owners held the following: James Boyce, 8/64ths; Orville Horwitz, 8/64ths; and Harry Barry, 4/64ths. The vessel was estimated to be worth $30,000 and her cargo $4,000. The schooner carried $1,150 in insurance but there was none on the cargo.[34]

Destruction: On 11 March, 1887, the *Horwitz*, still under the command of Captain Kelsey, was sailing north, several miles off the Virginia coast near the Maryland line. She carried coal from Baltimore, consigned to the Consolidated Railroad at New Haven. About 3:30 p.m. she sprang a leak for no known reason. It was assumed she had hit an obstruction. The schooner filled rapidly with water and was abandoned some three hours later. She sank in a depth of about 75'. Her position was estimated at five miles NNE of *Winter Quarter Lightship*. Fortunately the schooner *James B. Ogden,* sailing from Baltimore under Captain Toll, was close at hand. The *Ogden* picked up the *Horwitz'* captain and crew and landed them in New York on 16 March.[35]

Too deep to raise, the schooner was a total loss. She was valued at $25,000 but carried no insurance unless some of her owners had insured their private interests. The cargo was worth about $3,000, but whether it was insured is unknown. The schooner was 6-1/3 years old. She had been a successful vessel in the coal trade between Baltimore and New Haven and was said to have paid her owners several handsome dividends.[36]

THE *HARRY A. BARRY*

Destruction: Captain Constant W. Chatfield and his six crewmen on the *Barry* had picked up 850 tons of Cumberland coal at Baltimore for delivery at Fall River, Massachusetts. On 19 February, 1887, they passed through Hell Gate and proceeded up Long Island Sound. At 4:00 a.m. on the 20th they were off Point Judith, Rhode Island, about 25 miles from their destination. The weather was misty, with a light northwest breeze blowing and the seas running high. Suddenly the *Barry* struck ground only 400 yards from the U.S. Life-Saving Service Station at Point Judith. The station discovered her plight immediately. Within 30 minutes of the grounding, the surfmen and keeper had reached her in a lifeboat. Darkness and heavy breakers kept them from coming alongside the stricken schooner but they saw that the ship's yawl had been lowered. The keeper shouted to Captain Chatfield that it was too dangerous to try for shore through the surf during the night and all hands should remain on board until daylight. Disregarding the warning, one of the sailors jumped into the yawl and began stowing the crew's gear that was passed over the side to him. Several big seas were seen bearing down on them, and the keeper shouted a warning to seek shelter on deck. The water crashed over the schooner, nearly submerging the ship, but the warning saved those on deck. The yawl capsized and the sailor on board was pitched into the sea. Somehow he grasped a board as he was carried towards shore by the surf. The lifesavers in their boat attempted to intercept him but the sea carried them a quarter mile to the north before they could make a landing. Meanwhile, the life-saving station cook heard the man's cries, rushed into the surf and rescued him. The exhausted sailor was nearly drowned. Stimulants and warm clothing were administered, and these revived him after awhile.[37]

Finally it was decided to use a breeches buoy to land the crew. But by the time the apparatus was in position abreast the schooner, dawn had come and the sea was abating. Conditions now permitted launching the lifeboat anew. It was carefully maneuvered next to the schooner, and between waves one man was taken off at a time. Captain Chatfield was the last to leave.[38]

Once ashore, dry clothing was provided through supplies donated by the Women's National Relief Association. When the yawl capsized, much of the crew's gear disappeared in the ocean, leaving some of the crewmen almost destitute. The lifesavers and captain returned to the ship in the afternoon to retrieve valuables left aboard.[39]

The weather subsided on the afternoon of the 21st and it was expected that the vessel would be floated off at high water during the night. But it was not to be as the stormy weather returned. From the 21st to the 26th, a wrecking crew was employed in running hawsers, spars, and other gear ashore, along with saving some of the cargo. The Life-Saving Service assisted in the salvage operation and placed range lights in position at night to enable the work to keep going after dark. The stormy weather continued until the ship broke up on the 27th. The crew was cared for at the station until the 25th when the keeper obtained free railroad transportation for the men to travel to their homes. Captain Chatfield stayed at the station until 14 March, when the retrieved wreckage was sold at public auction.[40]

In discussions that followed the wreck, other shippers were mystified by the fact that the schooner ran aground where she did. The almost universal custom was to stay as far from Point Judith's rocks as possible, usually by steering towards Vineyard Haven. On 21 February, Henry Sutton's son Harry was quoted as saying "This is the first serious accident we have had happen to any of our schooners... I cannot understand how she came to go ashore at that point. Captain Chatfield is an able navigator and we don't know where the blame, if there is any, should be fixed."[41]

Henry Sutton held a 6/64ths interest in the *Barry*, while Captain Chatfield owned 5/64ths shares. The schooner's original cost was $36,000. The estimated value of her cargo was $4,275 and the estimated amount salvaged, including rigging and cargo, was $1,750.[42]

THE *JAMES D. DEWELL*

Collisions: The British steamer *Mentmore*, out of Baltimore bound for London, and the *Dewell*, from New Haven for Baltimore, collided about midnight on 1 December, 1883, off Point Lookout,

SCHOONER *JAMES D. DEWELL.*

Maryland, in Chesapeake Bay. The *Mentmore* returned to Baltimore on 2 December with her bow stove and rigging damaged. The schooner also arrived in Baltimore on 2 December not seriously damaged. On 4 December the owner of the steamer sued for $20,000 damages, claiming that a sudden change in course by the *Dewell* caused the accident. A cross libel was filed by the owners of the *Dewell*. The *Dewell* was to have been auctioned by the U.S. Marshal at the end of the month, but $10,000 was furnished in U.S. bonds by the schooner owners to free her from attachment. A settlement out of court was deemed probable.[43]

At 8:30 p.m. on 11 November, 1893, in clear weather and a moderate wind, the schooner *Samuel Dillaway* crashed into the *Dewell* ten miles south of Highland Light in the Atlantic near the top of Cape Cod. Both schooners were out of Boston in ballast, bound for Norfolk and Hampton Roads, respectively. The *Dillaway* lost her flying jibboom and headgear. The *Dewell* was struck on the starboard side at her mizzen rigging, carrying it away along with 25' of taffrail. Her spanker was badly torn, the mainsail less so, and the cabin house slightly damaged. Repair costs for the *Dewell* were estimated between $400 and $500. Both vessels returned to Boston, from which the *Dewell* was towed to East Boston for repairs.[44]

During a fog on 5 May, 1897, the *Dewell* collided with the tug *Santuit* and barge *Atlas* about 15 miles east of Fire Island, New York. The *Dewell* lost her bowsprit, jibboom and all attached. The *Santuit* and tow were uninjured. The schooner was bound from Newport News to Boston and the tug and barge from Boston to Baltimore. The *Dewell* arrived in New London on 8 May after which the *Santuit* towed her to New York, where the vessel was surveyed. She subsequently sailed from New York to Boston. On 10 June the schooner received new topside planking, along with being cleaned and painted at Burnham's railway at Boston.[45]

The tug *Underwriter* was anchored at Newport News on 5 October, 1897, when the *Dewell*, enroute from Boston to Newport News, ran into her. The tug's stem was bent and her foremast was carried away about 6' above the deck by the schooner's spanker boom. The *Dewell* was not injured.[46]

The steamship *Watson* arrived in Philadelphia on 18 March, 1903, from Port Antonio, Jamaica, with damage to the upper part of her port side. She had collided with the *Dewell*, bound from Providence to Norfolk. The collision took place on the 11th at midnight about 35 miles south of Winter Quarter Shoal, Virginia. The *Dewell* lost her foretopmast, bowsprit, headgear, and figurehead. The figurehead was left on the steamer's deck. The schooner was towed into Norfolk on the 18th.[47]

Destruction: On 11 September, 1906, the *Dewell* sailed from Charleston, South Carolina, for New York with a cargo of lumber. Captain C.S. Hammond of Long Island, who had commanded the vessel for eight years, carried a crew of six with him.[48]

Six days later, at 7:00 a.m. on the 17th, hurricane #4 of the 1906 U.S. hurricane season was centered 180 miles east of Georgetown, South Carolina. It was headed due west toward the mainland. The hurricane proved to be a scourge for any ship caught in its path off the Carolina coast.[49]

On the 24th the *Dewell* was reported to have met with disaster and had to be abandoned at sea. It was stated that the crew had all been picked up by a steamer and landed at Wilmington, North Carolina. The report was founded on news that the *Dewell's* yawlboat allegedly was picked up off the Cape Fear bar and towed into Wilmington. Unfortunately, the report of the rescue was unfounded, and it was not until 9 October that the *Dewell's* fate was known. A vessel had been reported drifting bottom up at sea off Murrell's Inlet, South Carolina. The tug *Alexander Jones* located the derelict and towed her into Southport, North Carolina. The vessel's identity wasn't determined until after she was brought in. It was the *Dewell*. No trace of her crew was found. All had perished in the hurricane.[50]

There was no chance to save the schooner at Southport. She had been partly broken up by the sea. The Benedict-Manson Marine Co. managed the *Dewell*. Her value was estimated at $6,000. Among the owners listed on her last certificate of enrollment in 1903 were James D. Dewell, 27/64ths (he had died on 19 April, 1906); Lucinda Sutton, 6/64ths; and Captain Hammond, 5/64ths.[51]

THE *NATHAN EASTERBROOK, JR.*

Collisions: After receiving extensive repairs in New York, the British steamship *Guildford*, under Captain Mouett, sailed for Glasgow on 10 December, 1884. Meanwhile the schooner *Nathan Easterbrook*, Jr., under Captain Vesper, departed Providence for Baltimore in ballast. On a clear night at 12:20 a.m. on the 11th of December, soon after the watch was changed on the *Guildford*, the *Easterbrook* ran into her some 30 miles southeast of Shinnecock, Long Island. The steamer was struck on the port bow, which was stove in almost to the water's edge. Her fo'c'sle also was stove; all of her headgear and the port light was carried away; and her

SCHOONER *NATHAN EASTERBROOK, JR.*

anchor was thrown from the top of the fo'c'sle deck to the fore-mast. The *Easterbrook* lost all of her headgear; her rail was carried away in several places; and her stem was crushed.

Upon impact, one of the schooner's crew, George Venue, scrambled on board the steamer. He admitted that the steamer's lights could be seen for a considerable distance. Captain Vesper remained in the steamship's vicinity for two hours. The *Easterbrook* burned flashlights during this time so the steamer could keep her in view. The *Guildford* was down at the head and Captain Mouett ordered about 50 tons of flour jettisoned from the forehold to raise the head.[52]

The *Guildford* returned to New York on the 11th, still down at the head by two feet. Her between-deck cargo was discharged; she was lightened aft to the 17' mark; a cofferdam was placed under her stem; and the damaged plates in her bow were cut out. She was drydocked at Brooklyn. The *Easterbrook* put into Narragansett Bay on the 11th and was towed to New Haven on the 13th for repairs.

The *Guildford* was ready to sail again about 15 January after reloading cargo. She had received a new port bow, fo'c'sle deck, some new rail, and slight repairs to her stem.[53]

On 2 April, 1887, The British steamship *Flamboro* sailed from Baltimore for St. Nazaire, France, and collided with the *Easterbrook*, also out of Baltimore. The *Flamboro's* steering gear was damaged and she had to return to Baltimore for repairs, as did the *Easterbrook*. The schooner's damages amounted to about $400, which Captain Carr of the *Flamboro* paid. The *Flamboro* sailed again on the 3rd.[54]

Destruction: Shortly after midnight on 20 February, 1893, the *Easterbrook* was sailing south along the notorious "graveyard of the Atlantic" corridor off the North Carolina coast. The night was clear and the winter wind strong, blowing from the southwest. The schooner carried a complement of nine, captained by George L. Kelsey. She also carried 1,000 tons of guano, taken aboard at Carteret, New Jersey, and bound for Savannah. Suddenly, at 12:40 a.m., she ran aground about 14 miles north of Cape Hatteras. The schooner stranded some 375 yards off the beach in a strong current and heavy surf.[55]

At approximately 1:00 a.m. the wreck was discovered by surfman L.B. Gray about 2-1/2 miles north of Little Kinnakeet Life-Saving Station, where he was assigned. He was on the midnight to 3:00 a.m. horseback patrol. Dismounting, he attempted to signal with a Coston light but the three lights he carried all failed. Quickly remounting, he rode back to the station and reported the wreck at 1:20 a.m. Station Keeper E.O. Hooper immediately alerted the remainder of the crew and telephoned the neighboring Gull Shoal and Big Kinnakeet Life-Saving Stations to send assistance. A red Coston light was lit to signal the schooner that help was on the way.

By 3:00 a.m. all was ready on the beach for the rescue attempt. A Lyle gun, propelling a lifesaving line, was aimed and fired at the ship. The first shot struck the forward stays and fell into the sea. The second shot was short. The third shot went over the vessel between the fore and main rigging, with the line falling across the fore gaff. Aboard the *Easterbrook*, the crew made the line fast, after which the rescuers sent out a hawser and then a breeches buoy. The hawser was tied to the mast and the breeches buoy readied for operation.

Second Mate Charles Clafford, born in Sweden and residing in Brooklyn, climbed into the breeches buoy. His experience in this apparatus was a disaster. The wind changed direction and velocity—now blowing from the north in gale force. The *Easterbrook* veered in the new direction of the wind. As the rescuers started hauling in the line, the breeches buoy became fouled in the head stays. Still in the apparatus, Clafford finally was pulled clear of the schooner. Unfortunately, when the hawser for the breeches buoy was tied to the mast, it was tied too low to keep the buoy out of the very cold ocean. So when Clafford was dragged to shore, for the most part he was underwater.

Once ashore, the rescuers presumed him dead but commenced resuscitation efforts anyway. He was finally brought to consciousness and said he was all right. Some stimulants were administered, and he was wrapped in blankets and taken to the station in a horse-drawn cart. There he was stripped of his wet clothing. Dry clothes donated by the Women's National Relief Association were furnished him. Then he was wrapped in blankets again, given additional stimulants and put to bed. At this point, Clafford requested that a telegram be sent to Norfolk to dispatch a wrecking vessel for the *Easterbrook*. Clafford told the Gull Shoal station keeper that he had been hurt badly in the breeches buoy before it cleared the ship. At 9:30 a.m. he hemorrhaged and died.

Meanwhile, efforts to rescue the remainder of the crew continued. At 6:00 a.m. Keeper Hooper and his lifesaving crew attempted to reach the wreck in a surfboat but were prevented by heavy surf, current and wind. Hooper returned to shore and signaled the *Easterbrook* to change the location of the breeches buoy hawser to the lee bow. This was done as Hooper was arranging for the substitution of a life car in place of the breeches buoy. A life car was a boat covered with galvanized sheet iron having a perforated hatch on top to admit air. It was carried on a hawser the same as a breeches buoy. Theoretically, it was designed to carry six or seven people safely. In actuality, it had some pronounced drawbacks, as will be seen. In this rescue, however, it proved to be a success. All seven remaining crew members and the captain were brought to shore, two at a time, inside the life car. Nevertheless, it must have been a miserable experience for all concerned, judging from Hooper's report: ". . . I should have ought to mentioned the operation of the life car. When sending her off through the inside brakers she would turn bottom side up every time and would continue so until she would come to the rise of the hawser to go aboard of the vessel. Then she would turn back again right side up–being about half free of water every time when she reached the vessel . . . And the third time that the life car come to the beach men just having time to get a holt of the life car. The whip line parted close to the life car on the in-shore end. . . ."[56]

The *Easterbrook* survivors were sheltered at the Little Kinnakeet Life-Saving Station from 3:00 p.m. on the 20th to 9:00 a.m. on the 21st. Sixteen meals were provided for them. The deceased second mate was wrapped in a U.S. Government sheet, placed in a box made for the occasion and buried. These arrangements were satisfactory to the captain and his crew. On 21 February, Captain Kelsey and his men accepted the invitation of the wrecking steamer captain to return to Norfolk with him.

Although managing owner Henry Sutton expressed confidence in Captain Kelsey as a careful and experienced navigator and attributed no fault to him, Keeper Hooper reported the supposed cause of the wreck as "misted his calculations."

The *Easterbrook* and her cargo were a total loss. At the time of her stranding, she was estimated to be worth from $30,000 to $35,000. Two estimates of the value of her cargo were widely variant. One was for $33,000 (Keeper Hooper) and the other for at least $10,000. Reports on the vessel's insurance also were divergent. One report indicated there was no known insurance; another stated there was; and a third disclosed that the vessel was partially insured but the amount was unknown.[57]

Among the ship's owners, Henry Sutton held a 4/64ths interest and Nathan Easterbrook, Jr., an 8/64ths.[58]

THE *JAMES IVES*

Collisions: Towards the evening of 28 May, 1890, the steam tug *Newport* was towing a canal boat westward from Brooklyn via New York's East River to a scow permanently anchored as a landing place near Ellis Island. The canal boat was on the tugboat's port side and extended somewhat ahead of the tug. The *James Ives* had been towed down the East River and was cast off in mid-river opposite the Battery at Manhattan's lower end. Her destination was south through New York Bay.

The *Ives* got under way in a westerly direction at about nine to ten knots in a fresh NNW wind. Her starting position relative to the *Newport* was on the tug's starboard side, some 300'-400' distant. The *Ives* moved roughly parallel with and slightly faster than the tug. They proceeded in their relative positions for nearly a statute mile, but owing to the *Ives'* greater leeway she continually drew nearer to the tug. As they grew dangerously close, the tug gave warning with several blasts on her whistle.

About a third of a mile east of Bedloe's Island, the schooner suddenly changed course, attempting to cross in front of the tug. The *Newport* stopped and backed, very nearly avoiding the collision. But the *Ives* struck and damaged the canal boat. A lawsuit was filed by the canal boat owner against both the *Ives* and the *Newport*.

The court listened to conflicting evidence but decided that the *Ives* should have passed astern of the tug at the start. By not doing so, the tug's pilot was misled as to the schooner's destination and had no reason to know she wanted to go to the south. Once within hailing distance, the *Ives* could have notified the *Newport* of her intentions but did not do so. Although the *Ives* was gaining on the tug, she never got fully ahead of her. The schooner's precipitous course change did not lift the burden of maintaining her course and shift it onto the tug to keep out of her way, as in a crossing situation. Witnesses for the *Ives* claimed she was forced to bear off towards the tug by a ship anchored directly ahead. Testimony from tug and canal boat witnesses completely refuted this allegation by denying that any such ship was so anchored. The court observed that if there was a vessel directly ahead, the tug also would have had to turn.

The court found that fault rested solely with the *Ives*. A decree was entered for the canal boat against the schooner with costs and the suit against the *Newport* was dismissed.[59]

At 1:00 a.m. on 29 March, 1894, the *Ives* was lying at anchor in Boston harbor after sailing from Philadelphia. The *Morancy*, a schooner out of Ponce, Puerto Rico, coming into Boston, failed to see the *Ives'* light until she was within a ship's length. *Morancy*'s wheel was put over hard—but too late. She struck the *Ives* in the bow. On her port side, the *Morancy* lost her fore and main rigging, cathead and port anchor stock. She also lost her main topmast head. Damage to the *Ives* reportedly was slight.[60]

Destruction: On 27 January, 1895, the *Ives* was sailing from Newport News to Providence with coal. Captain Godfrey Fairbrothers, a New Jersey resident, was master of the schooner and crew of seven. In the afternoon she struck ground about one-quarter mile east of the horizontal striped buoy at Five Fathom Shoal, some 13 miles east of the southern tip of Cape May, New Jersey. She was aground but a few minutes, then worked herself loose but immediately began to pound heavily against the bottom. She soon tore her bottom out and began taking in quantities of water. Captain Fairbrothers quickly assessed the situation as hopeless, raised the distress signal and ordered the lifeboats lowered.

He and his crew had barely pulled away to a safe distance when the schooner went down. Her hull was completely under water but her masts and jibboom extended out of it.[61]

About an hour later, a passing steamer, the *Charles F. Mayer,* commanded by Captain Seth Hand, observed the distress signal and picked up the crew of the *Ives.* The *Mayer* brought them to her destination at Portsmouth, New Hampshire.[62]

On 28 January, the pilot boat *Bayard* was seven miles ESE of *Northeast End Lightship.* There she picked up seven doors and other woodwork plus a secretary with papers, all from the *Ives.*[63]

The *Ives* was a total loss, including the personal belongings of her captain and crew. She was valued at $20,000 and was partially insured. Henry Sutton was a principal owner with a 5/64ths interest.[64]

Captain Fairbrothers entered a protest at Portsmouth, charging that the buoy was some distance out of position, thereby causing the wreck. An investigation was to be conducted. Captain Hand wrote a letter to the U.S. Coast and Geodetic Survey agreeing with Captain Fairbrothers' contention. Both captains confirmed that the schooner grounded in 16-$\frac{1}{2}$' of water and that the horizontal striped buoy was out of position. According to Captain Fairbrothers, the bottom was 12' higher than what the chart indicated for this buoy.[65]

THE *GENERAL S. E. MERWIN*

Collisions: The Swedish bark *Suez* was anchored in midchannel off Clifton, Staten Island, New York, on 17 August, 1886. She was scheduled to depart for Buenos Aires. But the *General Merwin,* outward bound for Baltimore, collided with the anchored *Suez,* carrying away the bark's jibboom and headgear. The schooner suffered minor damage to her boat davits and other deck structures.[66]

About 11:00 p.m. on 11 May, 1887, the *General Merwin* was approximately 10 miles north by a half mile west of the tip of

Cape Cod in Massachusetts Bay. She was sailing from Boston to Baltimore in ballast under Captain H.A. O'Brien of Thomaston, Maine. The weather was clear, the night was dark and the stars were out. A moderate northwest breeze blew over a smooth sea.[67]

The British iron steamer *Iowa*, under Captain Walters, enroute from her home port of Liverpool to Boston, was in the same area. She carried merchandise, 299 passengers in steerage, and a pilot. The third and chief officers were on the bridge and two seamen were forward as lookouts. Suddenly the two officers saw the outline of the *Merwin* a short distance off their starboard bow. Immediately thereafter a torchlight flared aboard the schooner, which was reported by the lookouts. The *Merwin* was now seen to be sailing with the wind on her starboard quarter and she was crossing the steamer's bow on a collision course. As the burdened vessel, the *Iowa* was obligated to change course or take whatever action was necessary to avoid a collision. The steamer's helm was spun hard to starboard but she carried too much way to change course in time. Engines were stopped, then thrown into reverse at full speed but it was too late. The steamer's great iron stem smashed into the schooner's port side midships. The *Merwin* crew were aware of their precarious position. As the two vessels came together, several of the *Merwin* crewmen jumped onto the deck of the steamer. The remainder of the crew and the captain's wife took to their boat as soon as the ships collided. Once the *Iowa* cleared from the wreckage, her number five boat was lowered to help with survivors, but before it could reach the schooner the *Merwin* capsized. The *Iowa* picked up the *Merwin*'s boat. All ten people who had been aboard the schooner were now on the steamer. The *Iowa*'s bow was badly stove. She had a gaping hole 20' long by 6' wide through which water was pouring into the forepeak. The situation was critical. All boats were made ready and swung outboard. But the crew managed, after some time, to place a sail over the bow and jam the hatch down in the peak. This shut off the inpouring sea and enabled the *Iowa* to reach her dock in East Boston the next morning.[68]

The *Merwin's* crew lost everything. Captain O'Brien lost his clothes and a considerable sum of money. His wife lost some money, the contents of her trunks and a valuable sealskin jacket. Steward Joe Anderson, who had sailed with the ship since she was launched, and who was the only New Haven man in the crew, lost a valuable gold watch.[69]

Two tugboats, *Camilla* and *Elsie*, began a search of Massachusetts Bay the next day looking for the *Merwin*. Being in ballast, it was expected that she would float, and if found, would be a valuable prize. Later that day she was located off Highland Light. The schooner lay on her side in the same position as when she capsized. Her sails were in the water and the gaping hole in her side was facing the sky. Had she been lying on the other side, or upright, or laden with cargo, she would have sunk. On 13 May the *Merwin* was towed into Provincetown harbor and grounded. The hole in her side was out of water at high tide.[70]

Officers on watch aboard the *Iowa* claimed they saw no lights on the *Merwin* until she displayed the torchlights just before the collision. However, officers and crew on the *Merwin* stated that the schooner's lights had been properly set and were burning bright that night. Henry Sutton averred that the torchlight had been lit for several minutes before the collision. This was done to alert the *Iowa* that the ships were on a collision course.[71]

Within a few days after the accident, a lawsuit was initiated against the *Iowa* in Boston. Agents for the *Iowa* posted bond in the amount of $75,000, which enabled the steamer, once repaired, to resume her schedule without detention or loss of business. It was believed the claim would be settled by arbitration. Costs would have to cover not only repairs but the salvage claim of the tugboat owners, plus six cents per ton of lost cargo weight each day the *Merwin* was idled. Since she could carry 1,400 tons, this would amount to $84 per day.[72] On the afternoon of the 18th the *Merwin* was pumped out and floated.[73]

To satisfy salvage demands, the *General Merwin* was sold at auction on 28 May. She was bought by her owner, Henry Sutton, for $13,000.[74] Although a New Haven newspaper report estimated the *Merwin*'s damages at less than $5,000, the official wreck report filed by Henry Sutton on 6 June, 1887, listed a $32,000 damage assessment. The cut in the vessel's side was about 27 planks deep and she was not insured.[75]

While the repairs were being carried out, the *Merwin*'s superstructure was altered, allowing a significant increase in the capacity of the enclosures on her upper deck.[76]

At 1:00 a.m. on 8 September, 1894, about six miles off *Northeast End Lightship* at the bottom of the New Jersey coast, the *General Merwin* and the schooner *Ann J. Trainer* collided. The Philadelphia-bound *Trainer*, coming down from Kennebec, Maine, had her forward rails, stanchions, headgear, and forerigging carried away. The *Merwin*, enroute to Providence from Norfolk, lost her jibboom.[77]

On 5 November, 1898, the steamboat *Pequot,* bound for Providence, ran into the *Merwin*, while the latter was in tow off the Battery, New York City. The *Pequot*'s upper works were badly damaged and her smokestack was carried away. She returned to her dock, discharged her cargo and went into dry dock for repairs. The *Merwin*'s stem was damaged and her bowsprit and headgear were carried away.[78]

On 20 March, 1899, the *General Merwin* sailed from Baltimore for Boston. About 3:00 p.m. on the 21st off Cove Point, she collided with the York River Line steamer *Baltimore*, bound from Norfolk to Baltimore. The steamer suffered a damaged bow. The schooner, however, was badly damaged and had to return to port. The *Baltimore*'s captain acknowledged that the fault was his and he made a settlement. The *Merwin* finally arrived in Boston on 16 April.[79]

On the night of 7 July, 1899, the *Merwin*, bound for Boston from Baltimore, collided with the *Shovelful Lightship* below Cape

Cod in Nantucket Sound. Other than chafing her mizzen rigging on the port side, the schooner sustained no damage. The lightship, however, didn't fare as well. She lost her bowsprit and the iron work around it as well as having her stem damaged from the water's edge to 5' above it. The schooner arrived at Boston on the 8th.[80]

Dismasting: The *General Merwin* left Cardiff, Wales, on 29 December, 1888, laden with coal for Havana. She ran into a storm and lost all three of her masts. Captain O'Brien rigged a jury mast with which he limped into St. Thomas in distress on 12 February, 1889. After notifying New Haven, her cargo was sold in St. Thomas.[81]

The *Nathan Easterbrook, Jr.* was selected to transport new masts, spars, sails, and rigging to the *Merwin*. The former had to wait for sailmakers Van Name and King to finish making new sails in New Haven before going on to New London to pick up the masts. On 12 March she left New London for Newport News, where she loaded coal to take to St. Thomas. On 15 April the *Easterbrook* arrived at St. Thomas, where she had long been await-ed. The masts and other gear were immediately transferred to the *Merwin*, which went into dry dock on the same day. She was still refitting in St. Thomas as of 29 April. Finally, on 15 May she sailed into Turks Island in the Bahamas and picked up a cargo for New York. All told, it took approximately three months for the *Merwin* to be reactivated.[82]

Destruction: In early February, 1901, the *General Merwin* either took on 500 tons of pyrites cinders at the Everett Chemical Works instead of ballast or she was loaded with copper ore. In any event, she left Massachusetts Bay with her seven-man comple-ment under command of J. Frank Rutledge, bound for Norfolk. Rutledge normally served as mate. The *Merwin*'s regular master, Captain Edward H. Smeed, had to stay at home in East Providence, Rhode Island, to care for his sick son.[83]

No word was received about the *Merwin* for weeks. Her

owners assumed that unfavorable winds had probably blown the vessel some hundreds of miles off the coast and that she was having a difficult time beating her way back. Actually, she had been blown far south in a northwest gale on 23 February when she also had lost her compass.[84]

On 4 March, 1901, 28 days out of Everett, the *Merwin* was sailing north in thick weather off North Carolina's Outer Banks. At 3:15 a.m. she ran aground in a strong surf approximately 500 yards offshore. She was a half mile south of the Gull Shoal Life-Saving Station, about 25 miles north of Cape Hatteras. A surfman from the station spotted her about the time she stranded. The Gull Shoal station-keeper requested assistance from the adjacent Little Kinnakeet Life-Saving Station, which dispatched two surfmen on horseback to the scene of the wreck. The keeper and the two surfmen launched a lifeboat from the beach. They arrived at the *Merwin* about 4:30 a.m. The sea remained high and the keeper decided to wait until daylight before continuing the rescue attempt. At daybreak, the surfboat made three trips to the *Merwin*. Her seven-man crew was brought ashore along with their personal gear and the schooner's lifeboat.[85]

The stranded vessel, which was fast filling with water, was turned over to a wreck master. On the afternoon of the first day, there was 6' of water in her hold. The captain was sheltered for five days at the life-saving station, where he awaited results of the wreck master's efforts. But except for the small boats, nothing more was saved from the schooner. The six crewmen were sheltered at the station for nine hours, then sent to Elizabeth City, North Carolina, for transportation home.[86]

The wreck reports attributed the grounding to missed calculations and an inability to see any lights ashore. The *Merwin* was estimated to be worth $33,000. She was uninsured and a total loss. Among her listed owners were: E.H. Smeed, 2/64ths; Henry Sutton, 8/64ths; E.[sic] M. Merwin, 8/64ths; and Jas. D. Dewell, 8/64ths.[87]

THE *CHARLES F. TUTTLE*

Collisions: The *Charles F. Tuttle* was anchored in the stream at Boston when a strong blow struck the area on 17 November, 1891. During the gale the *Tuttle* fouled the schooner *Minnie Rowan*, which was undamaged. The *Tuttle*, however, lost her spanker boom and gaff, had her spanker sail torn and a boat badly stove.[88]

On 26 November, 1895, a scow ran into the *Tuttle* off Lambert's Point, Norfolk, and tore away part of the schooner's sheathing.[89]

While docking at Portsmouth, New Hampshire, on 21 October, 1897, the steamship *Reading*, from Philadelphia, carried away her own foremast and injured the *Tuttle* in some unspecified way. Although it is uncertain whether this incident is related in any way to the following repair work, there may be a connection. On 23 December, 1897, the *Tuttle* received a new foremast and a foretopmast at a Brooklyn shipyard.[90]

On the afternoon of 25 September, 1903, the *Tuttle* was fully loaded and proceeding from Norfolk to New Bedford. The ship *Clarence S. Bement* was sailing from Newport News to San Francisco. They collided in Hampton Roads, Virginia. Some of the *Bement*'s headgear was carried away. The *Tuttle* returned to Norfolk on the 26th with her mizzen rigging badly damaged and her yawl boat lost.[91]

The steamship *Mascotte* was leaving Key West for Port Tampa at 2:00 a.m. on 2 November, 1904. In doing so, she ran into the *Tuttle*, carrying away the schooner's jibboom and causing other damage. The *Mascotte* also ran into the schooner *Clara Goodwin*, damaging the *Goodwin*'s boat davits and counter (that portion of the vessel's stern from the water line to the extreme outward swell).[92]

Destruction: On 15 September, 1906, four days after the *James D. Dewell* sailed from Charleston, South Carolina, with a cargo of lumber, the *Tuttle* did likewise. Captain George W. Heath of Boston commanded the *Tuttle* and a crew of seven.[93]

Hurricane #4 of the 1906 U.S. hurricane season was raging off the Carolina coast on the morning of the 17th. On board the *Tuttle* there was great concern when the schooner started taking in quantities of water through a gaping leak. Both the steam and hand pumps were employed but the water level in the schooner continued to rise. At midnight the *Tuttle* suddenly rolled over on her beam-ends before the crew could launch a boat. All hands were able to secure holds on the chain plates, the lowest, deck-level, portion of the rigging. Eight men clung to the chain plates for the next 58 hours, without benefit of sleep, food or water.[94]

On the morning of the 20th the Ward Line passenger steamship *Seguranca,* bound from Havana to New York, came upon the overturned schooner 140 miles east of Charleston. The hungry and exhausted men were picked up by the steamer and the schooner was abandoned. The seamen were fed and given clothing by the *Seguranca*'s captain. Passengers aboard the steamer donated $200 to them. They were landed in New York.[95]

The *Tuttle* was estimated to be worth about $16,000. She was managed by the Benedict-Manson Marine Co. Among the owners were James D. Dewell, 6/64ths; estate of Charles F. Tuttle, 3/64ths; Lucinda Sutton, 4/64ths; and Captain Heath, 2/64ths.[96]

THE *HENRY H. OLDS*

Destruction: In the early morning of 12 April, 1888, the *Henry H. Olds* was bound from Baltimore to Providence with 1,400 tons of coal. It was thought that she struck rocks or a submerged wreck in five fathoms of water off Point Judith, Rhode Island. She sprang a leak and sank at 2:00 a.m. near Whale Rock Light, about 2-1/2 miles from the Narragansett Pier Life-Saving Station. Discovered by the morning patrol soon after daylight, the *Olds* was boarded by the surfmen but found abandoned. Captain Edward H. Smeed of the *Olds* and his eight-man crew had boarded the schooner's boat and landed at Narragansett Ferry. Then they walked to the life-saving station where they were sheltered for a day and a night. The keeper procured free railroad transportation for them to their homes.[97]

The schooner was resting on soft bottom, which buoyed hopes she might be raised and towed into port. The Merritt Wrecking Company of New York was engaged for this task. On the 15th the wreckers removed the sails, spars, rigging and a small boat they had salvaged from the schooner and delivered it all to Newport.[98]

Meanwhile, plans were prepared for raising the *Olds*. On 4 June the tug *E. Luckenbach* arrived in Boston from New York with pontoons to be used to raise her. The attempt was to be made with the cargo aboard. Each time the pontoons were attached, a heavy sea would break them loose, and finally the work was abandoned. Nothing additional was salvaged from the *Olds*. On 12 December the schooner's sails, spars and rigging were sold at auction for $1,332.[99]

One might have thought this was the end of the story. But in July of 1889 a new attempt was planned to raise her. Some wreckers from the Boston Wrecking Co. went out from Newport and inspected her hull. They found it to be relatively free from worm damage. Her rudder worked and she wasn't buried too deeply in the sand. They decided to remove her coal first and then try to raise her. But no further reports on this effort were located, indicating a continued lack of success.[100]

The *Olds* was nearly new and had cost about $35,000. The estimated value of her cargo was $4,000. Some of her owners were Captain Smeed, 2/64ths; Henry H. Olds, 4/64ths; and Henry Sutton, 13/64ths.[101]

THE W. *WALLACE WARD*

Collisions: The *W. Wallace Ward* and the schooner *John G. Hayne* collided at Nantucket Shoals, Massachusetts, on 13 April, 1892. The tug *Right Away* towed the *Hayne* into New Bedford on the 14th. She had her starboard fore rigging carried away, one broken boom and a torn foresail. The *Ward* lost her foretopmast and incurred other slight damage.[102]

The primary source of information for the following is Case No. 652, Admiralty Case Files, Alfred C. Pelton, Master, v. The Schooner *R.& T. Hargraves*, U.S. District Court for the Eastern District of Virginia, Norfolk Division, RG 21, NA, Philadelphia, Pennsylvania. Footnoting of this source is not indicated since it encompasses practically the whole story.

On 12 June, 1894, the *Ward* left Lambert's Point, Norfolk, with 1,991 tons of Pocahontas coal bound for Providence. She carried one passenger and a crew of ten commanded by Captain Alfred C. Pelton. He anchored the next evening in Chesapeake Bay in 5-1/2 fathoms of water. His position was approximately four miles ESE of Thimble Shoal Light, between Willoughby Spit and Lynnhaven Roads. The *Ward* was some four miles from shore. The schooner was still anchored there about 10:00 a.m. on the 14th when the *R.& T. Hargraves*, light and under full sail, was observed approaching from the sea. She continued straight on her course and, as she bore down on the *Ward*, it was thought she wanted to speak. About 10:30 a.m. she smashed head-on into the starboard side of the *Ward*, one foot forward of the spanker rigging. She opened a gaping hole in the *Ward*'s side.[103]

The sea poured into the anchored schooner. Anything the crew could lay their hands on to plug the hole was used; pumps were started but all efforts were unsuccessful. After the impact, the *Hargraves*, which was only slightly damaged, hove to. The tugboat *Volunteer* of Baltimore came upon the scene and took the *Ward* in tow. The *Ward*'s crew was removed to the *Hargraves*. Towing proceeded as far as Hampton Roads, where the *Ward* sank in 4-1/2 fathoms in the James River channel.[104]

The *Hargraves* had four of her owners on board, including the mayor of Fall River, Massachusetts, and Captain John F. Allen, also of Fall River. Prior to the mishap, nobody on the *Ward* detected any action or alarm aboard the *Hargraves* to avoid running into them. Furthermore, the weather was perfectly clear and there was no wind or sea condition that might account for the accident. Captain Allen claimed that the *Hargraves'* steering gear was out of order and he was unable to avoid the collision.[105]

The *Ward* lay in 27' of water at high tide with most of her upper deck under water. The Merritt Wrecking Company was called in to try to raise her and demanded $20,000 for the task. The *Ward* was valued at $50,000. First they removed booms, sails, chains and anchors in order to lighten her as much as possible. Then a diver was sent down to examine the hull. Finally, the schooner was raised and towed to Newport News. On 20 July, she was towed again, this time from Newport News up the James River into fresh water because of worms.[106]

A lawsuit was filed on 18 June, in Admiralty against the *Hargraves* in U.S. District Court at Norfolk. After the accident, the *Hargraves* had proceeded to the vicinity of Lambert's Point on the Elizabeth River. She was seized by the U.S. Marshal on 30 June.[107]

A memorandum of agreement, made as a stipulation in

SCHOONER *W. WALLACE WARD.*

the above legal action, was concluded between parties connected with the *Ward* and those associated with the *Hargraves*. The *Ward* parties were the Providence-Washington Insurance Co., which owned the cargo of coal, and the owners, master, and crew of the vessel and their attorneys. The *Hargraves* group was comprised of her owners, master, and crew and their attorneys. It was conceded in the stipulation that the *Hargraves* alone was responsible for the collision. Liability of the *Hargraves* group was to be limited to the amount said schooner would bring at a sale, which was to be advertised and conducted by the U.S. Marshal. However, the *Hargraves'* owners would be at liberty to contest the amount of their liability to the plaintiffs, should they choose to do so.

The sale took place in Norfolk on 13 July, but it wasn't finalized until 3 August. The purchase price was $17,000 and the buyer was Henry Sutton.[108]

Since the suit didn't claim a specific amount in damages, the case was referred to Allan R. Hanckel as special commissioner to ascertain and report damages suffered by the plaintiffs. The special commissioner had the authority to examine witnesses and call for documentary evidence. He was to report his findings in writing to the court, accompanied by evidence submitted to him.

He found the items of damage listed by attorneys for the *Ward* owners to be reasonable, proper, and accompanied by vouchers in most instances. And since no objection was raised by the respondent, as no appearance was made before him, each item listed was allowed:

Drydock bill at Newport News, net	$ 9,154.05
Sails, net	885.40
Rigging, chandlery, net	1,382.47
Merritt Wrecking organization, net	9,000.00
Loss of time from 6/14/94-8/23/94, inclusive, at 6 cents per ton per day	8,003.02
Noting protest	25.00

Towing	30.00
Captain Pelton's service	150.00
Henry Sutton's service (9 days)	90.00
Estimate for cabin furniture	150.00
Estimate for painting	100.00
Estimate for tools	75.00
Freight on 1,991 tons of coal at 75 cents per ton	1,493.25
Total losses to vessel owners	$30,544.99

Commissioner Hanckel noted that the only loss borne in common by the schooner and the cargo was that of salvage (to Merritt Wrecking), which was fixed by agreement of all parties at 55 percent of the amount recovered. Losses to the cargo were computed as follows:

Undamaged value of cargo	$4,123.46
Less proceeds, sale of damaged cargo, deducting salvage	1,164.74
Net loss	$2,958.72

Since the bill for damages, as determined by the special commissioner, exceeded the purchase price, the judge decreed it was unnecessary for Sutton to pay the purchase money in full. He was asked instead to pay a sum of $5,666.66 to the court. The vessel was then delivered to him and he gave the marshal a receipt for $11,334, which consummated the sale.

Certain charges against the *Hargraves* took priority over the claims of the *Ward*'s owners and the Providence-Washington Insurance Co. For example, seamen serving on the *Hargraves* had prior liens for wages as established under the General Maritime Law of the State of Virginia.

First Mate James D. Catharin petitioned the court for his wages of $45 a month, earned between 16 March and 18 June,

1894. Steward J.B. Long, who earned $50 a month, and Engineer Stephen S.L. Schute, who earned $30 a month, both attested that they served continuously aboard the schooner up to 1 August, 1894. They averred that they were following orders from Captain Allen, who wanted them to assist in moving the schooner about as necessary until such time as the vessel was sold. Acting as attorney for the above-named seamen in this matter was none other than A.R. Hanckel, sometimes special commissioner, now wearing his lawyer's hat.

From court records, it is evident that these seamen received periodic payments on their wages. Final payments to them and to other priority claimants are set out:

James D. Catharin	$ 9.00
Stephen S.L. Schute	42.25
J.B. Long	73.48
Loper and Co. (Groceries)	59.55
U.S. Marshal	440.34
Attorney fee	20.00
Clerk of Court	182.05
A.R. Hanckel, Commr.	30.00
Total	$806.67

Considering the listing above, one can't overlook the possibility that the $20.00 attorney fee might be for Attorney/Special Commissioner A.R. Hanckel. Furthermore, it is noted that the column of figures was added incorrectly. The total should be $856.67. Nevertheless, the court subtracted the $806.67 from the sale price of the *Hargraves*, $17,000, arriving at a figure of $16,193.33 as the amount for distribution.

The court calculated the dividend due the owners of the *Ward* based on 48-$\frac{1}{3}$ percent of $16,193.33, minus the $11,334.00 paid to Henry Sutton, giving a value of $3,429.28. The determination of the dividend to the cargo owners was $1,430.05.

It is also interesting to note that the Providence-Washington Insurance Co. had authorized Henry Sutton to collect the amount payable to them. No reason was specified for this in the court records.

Henry Sutton had astutely invested $17,000 in the purchase of the *Hargraves*, of which he received $14,763.28 back from the court that could be charged against costs to the *Ward*. Had he stood by and let someone else purchase the vessel, he would have forfeited the opportunity to obtain the *Hargraves* at such minimal cost.

The first certificate of enrollment after the *Hargraves* became part of the Sutton fleet listed Henry Sutton as sole owner. A later certificate listed additional owners.[109]

Destruction: The *Ward* sailed from Tampa on 22 December, 1899, bound for Carteret, New Jersey, with 1,899 tons of rock phosphate. She had made this run many times before. Captain George L. Kelsey was in command and had nine crewmen. His wife was also aboard. Eight days out of Tampa the vessel ran into very heavy weather off the Carolinas and took a terrible beating. She was at the mercy of a violent storm for three days, during which time she sprang a leak. Green water came over her decks, flooded the cabins and swept away everything movable, including the lifeboat. The steam pumps were started but the cargo shifted and choked off the pumps. The crew kept working with hand pumps while knee deep in water. Mrs. Kelsey took her turn at the pumps and encouraged the men. For all their effort water slowly overtook the action of the pumps and the schooner started to settle in the heavy seas. The crew suffered from the continuous work, from exposure to the elements, and from lack of food and sleep. All aboard were in a complete state of exhaustion.[110]

Early on the morning of 2 January, 1900, a high sea was running and washing over the *Ward*'s decks. At times, waves tumbled over her after house as she wallowed in their troughs. Her hold contained more than 4' of water, and it was continuing to fill. The schooner was sinking and her crew had no way of leaving her safely. Furthermore, she had moved well off the shipping lanes. No ship of any kind had been sighted during the three days of the storm.

Then the Norwegian steamship *Themis* came upon the *Ward*. The steamer was on the way north from Haiti with a cargo of lumber. When her skipper, Captain Anderson, saw that all hands on the *Ward* were huddled together atop the after house, he hove to. Questioning the schooner, he learned that Captain Kelsey was prepared to abandon ship. Captain Anderson asked for volunteers on the *Themis* to attempt a rescue. Every man on the steamer stepped forward. Chief Officer K.J. Lund and two seamen were selected. With difficulty a lifeboat was launched clear of the *Themis'* side at 7:00 a.m. Approaching the lunging schooner was perilous but the boat was brought safely alongside. Mrs. Kelsey, who appeared more dead than alive, was the first one taken aboard the lifeboat. She was made as comfortable as possible in the stern sheets before three crewmen came on board.

Meanwhile Captain Anderson had maneuvered his ship to windward of the *Ward*. He attempted to hold this position in order to create calmer water between the two vessels. The lifeboat made it safely back to the *Themis*, where Mrs. Kelsey was brought on deck as the crew cheered. She was taken to the captain's cabin while the others in the lifeboat were helped aboard.

It took three trips to the *Ward* before all hands were taken off. Captain Kelsey was the last of the ship's complement to leave. Mate Lund had orders to set fire to the derelict to prevent the schooner from menacing navigation. As soon as the fire blazed up, he leaped overboard into the frigid sea with a line attached to him. He was dragged through the waves to safety.

The rescue of the 11 people took approximately four hours. Captain Kelsey said he wouldn't have been able to keep the

Ward afloat for 10 more hours. The survivors were landed at Chester, Pennsylvania, on the 4th of January.

The vessel was reported abandoned 80 miles southeast of Cape Lookout and 120 miles off Cape Hatteras, both in North Carolina.[111]

The *Ward* was estimated to be worth $20,000, but the value of her cargo was reported as unknown. Supposedly the vessel was partly insured. Among the owners were James D. Dewell, S.E. Merwin, Charles F. Tuttle, and George M. Grant, each with a 1/64th interest; Lyman M. Law, 2/64ths; W.W. Ward, 4/64ths; and Henry Sutton, 11/64ths.[112]

THE *GEORGE M. GRANT*

Grounding: On the afternoon of 27 February, 1906, the *Grant* encountered a heavy storm off Cape Henry, Virginia. She carried a cargo of railroad ties loaded in Brunswick, Georgia, and bound for Perth Amboy, New Jersey. The storm, with 60-mile-an-hour winds, blew the schooner ashore some 800 yards (almost half a mile) from the beach. Life-savers from the Cape Henry and Virginia Beach Life-Saving Stations tried repeatedly to shoot a line over the *Grant* but the distance was too great. And any attempt to rescue the crew by lifeboat was considered too hazardous.

But Captain Meredith Partridge of the Norfolk tugboat *Jack Twohy* was undaunted by the situation. On the morning of the 28th he nosed his tug outside the Virginia capes and headed for the stranded schooner. She was then pounding hard against the bottom. Every sea was breaking over her with terrific force. She was awash amidships, and with each successive wave she wedged more firmly into the bottom. It was thought that it was only a matter of time before the crew would be swept off the ship. Captain Partridge brought the *Twohy* to the windward side of the *Grant* and close to her. He dropped a line with a float that the current carried to the schooner. There the line was made fast and the tug passed to the *Grant*'s leeward side.

Every crashing wave hid the tug from view of the life-savers on shore. They were poised to launch their surfboats in spite of the danger should the tug's rescue effort prove futile.

Captain Partridge stationed two of his men at the peak of his bow, then slowly steamed the tug, bow on, to the *Grant*. When his bow barely touched the schooner, the two crewmen reached out and pulled one of the *Grant*'s shipwrecked men to safety. This procedure was repeated until all the crew were taken off, literally dragged from the deck of the wrecked schooner. Then the tug carried the rescued crewmen to Norfolk. At the time, it was expected that the schooner would be a total loss, but the weather abated during the following days. On 2 March, the *Grant*'s deck load was removed and loaded onto a barge for Norfolk. At high tide on the afternoon of the 4th the tug *Rescue* hauled the schooner seaward about one boat length. It was then discovered that the *Grant*'s bottom was gone—she was floating on her cargo of railroad ties! After assessing the problem, a decision was made to try to tow her as she was. On 7 March, tugs of the Merritt-Chapman Wrecking and Derrick Co. carefully took her under tow. And on the 8th the *Grant* arrived safely in Norfolk, to be placed in drydock.[113]

Collision: Sailing from New York, the *Grant* arrived at Fernandina, Florida, on 23 November, 1904. Her Captain Pelton reported that in a "hurricane" (possibly tropical storm #5 of the 1904 U.S. season) off Currituck, North Carolina, she collided with an unknown steamer, resulting in considerable damage to the schooner. A protest was lodged. The *Grant* then proceeded to a New York shipyard where the damage was repaired.[114]

Destruction: On 28 September, 1916, the *Grant* sailed from Baltimore with 1,697 tons of coal bound for Alicanti, Spain. Captain A. Norberg was in command, supported by a ten-man crew.[115]

During the previous two weeks, a number of administrative changes involving the schooner had taken place. The Benedict-Manson Marine Co. sold the ship to the American Star

Line, a New York firm that purchased 121/128ths interest in the ship. Her trade was changed from domestic to international. Within three days before she sailed, Captain Norberg, a new master for her, was given command. After a few days at sea, the *Grant* sailed into tropical storm #11 of the 1916 U.S. season. Pounded by big seas, the *Grant* began to leak. Captain Norberg kept the pumps operating but they could not contain the volume of water coming in. About 9:00 a.m. on 4 October, the schooner foundered "off the Bahamas." Her listed position was approximately 185 miles due east of Georgetown, South Carolina, a considerable distance north of the Bahama Islands.[116]

All 11 persons aboard the *Grant* were rescued 3-1/2 days later by the American steamship *Seward*. This data was reported by Captain Norberg on 14 October, in a U.S. Coast Guard Casualty Report filed at San Juan, Puerto Rico. There was no mention of what took place during the 3 1/2 days after the ship foundered. Accounts of the *Grant's* loss reported that "no particulars" had been furnished. It is easily understood why no other information about the foundering and rescue was located. World War I had entered its third year and German U-boats were very active. Large numbers of ships were being sunk, so scant coverage would have been given to individual sinkings from natural causes, except in unusual circumstances. The foundering of a 27-year-old sailing vessel was not an important event.[117]

The *Grant* was a total loss. She was estimated to be worth $40,000 and her cargo about $5,100.[118]

THE *LYMAN M. LAW*

Collisions: On 30 November, 1900, at 5:00 p.m. the *Law*, bound from Portland, Maine, for a coal port, collided with the schooner *Francis Shubert*, which was carrying lumber from Bangor to New York. The next day the *Shubert* arrived at Portland in distress. Her chain plates and part of her mizzen rigging had been carried away. She also was leaking. The *Law* put into Vineyard Haven

SCHOONER *LYMAN M. LAW.*

on 4 December, with her jibboom and headgear gone. She arrived at Philadelphia on the 8th.[119]

While sailing from Portsmouth, New Hampshire, to Philadelphia the *Law* collided with an unknown tug off *Overfalls Lightship* off the entrance to Delaware Bay on 3 May, 1907. The *Law* arrived at Philadelphia on 4 May with damage to several planks abreast the mizzenmast on the starboard side above the waterline. Damage to the tug was unknown.[120]

Abandonment: About noon on 31 January, 1903, the *Law*, under Captain John E. Blake, struck on Nauset Beach near the southern end of Cape Cod. She was carrying 1,935 tons of Pocahontas coal from Norfolk to Portland, Maine. Captain Blake had his ten-man crew lower the mizzen and spanker sails and hoist the flying jib, after which the ship floated free. He then attempted to sail her around the cape but the winds were very strong and the seas very rough. At 5:30 p.m. he brought her about and anchored with two anchors two to three miles from the beach. Soon water was discovered in the hold. The forward wrecking pump, the after steam pump, and the two hand pumps were put to work, but they couldn't reduce the water in the hold, which was more than 5' deep. The crew became alarmed and wanted to leave the ship. Captain Blake gave permission to set two red lights in the rigging and sound the ship's whistle as signals of distress.

At 8:10 p.m. the *Grecian*, a steamer commanded by Captain William E. Briggs, sailing from Boston to Philadelphia, came within 700' of the schooner and hailed her. Captain Blake asked to be taken in tow but Captain Briggs declined. The latter countered with an offer to take the 11 men off the *Law*, which was immediately accepted. Two of the *Law*'s boats were lost in the sea before her crew, with personal gear, was successfully transferred to the *Grecian*. Captain Blake asked to be set ashore at Vineyard Haven, where he hoped to obtain a tug to tow his schooner to a safe harbor. But the weather was so bad that Captain Briggs couldn't enter the harbor and the men of the *Law* were transported all the way to Philadelphia.[121]

The *Law* was seen on the 31st by men of the Pamet River Life-Saving Station, some four miles away on Cape Cod. When she was observed in the same place the next morning, Captain Cole, the station keeper, launched a surfboat with six men and arrived alongside the schooner at 8:00 a.m. They boarded the ship and found her abandoned with all boats gone. The life-savers concluded that the crew had been taken off by one of several steamers whose searchlights had been seen playing on the schooner the night before. Forward of the poop, the sea was level with the *Law*'s deck. Water was coming in near the stem. Her handpumps were choked and it was obvious she could not be sailed in this condition. The life-savers attempted to attract the attention of a southbound tug towing two barges. They set the schooner's flag in the fore rigging but it was no use. The tug ignored the signal and maintained her course. After this, the life-savers departed the schooner and returned to their station. They telephoned Provincetown for a steam tug but none was located. Finally they saw the steamer *North Star* approaching the *Law* from the south and a lifeboat putting off toward the *Law* from the adjacent Cahoons Hollow Life-Saving Station. Captain Cole considered that the *Law*'s problems were now being addressed and he gave the schooner no further attention.[122]

About daylight on the 1st, the four-masted schooner *Hope Sherwood*, carrying coal to Boston under Captain Gilbert, observed the *Law* at anchor, apparently abandoned. Captain Gilbert altered course to pass close by the *Law* and saw the Pamet River life-savers aboard. He continued on his way for a short distance when the life-savers were seen to leave the schooner. Captain Gilbert then turned and made for the abandoned ship.

Meanwhile the steamship *North Star*, sailing from New York to Portland with passengers and a full cargo, approached the *Law* about 10:00 a.m. The schooner was low in the water and gave no sign of life. Several blasts on the whistle elicited no response. A boat was prepared for lowering. Then the Cahoons Hollow life-savers were observed putting off from shore. Captain Bragg of the *North Star* decided to wait for the life-savers. When they arrived, he asked them to determine the situation aboard the schooner and see what assistance was needed.

By this time the *Hope Sherwood* had arrived at the *Law* and lowered a boat with three men. The boat capsized, dumping the men into the sea. The life-savers first rescued these men, then brought them aboard the *Law*. Two other men from the *Hope Sherwood* soon joined them from another boat. Captain Bowley of Cahoons Hollow Life-Saving Station inspected the *Law* and advised Captain Bragg that the ship was abandoned and "in a sinking condition." Captain Bragg then sent his chief engineer and his second officer to board the schooner to see if she could be towed to Provincetown.

A decision was made that the *North Star* would attempt to tow the schooner into Provincetown even though the steamer was not fitted for towing. Captain Bragg ordered the schooner's chains cut with hacksaws so as to lighten the vessel forward. The steam boiler was filled and the schooner's pumps were connected. The steamer provided two hawsers that were run to the *Law* by the life-saving crew. By 2:00 p.m. the chains were finally cut through and towing was started soon after. At this time the weather appeared threatening. The *Law* had settled so that 8" of water flowed over her deck forward of the poop. Four crewmen from the *North Star* and two from the *Hope Sherwood* stayed on board along with the life-savers. The forward pump was started and ran through the night. It was difficult to steer the schooner in her half-sunk condition. Two men were constantly required at the wheel. The *Law* started to settle at the bow soon after the towing began. She had to be stopped and have her hawse pipes plugged. Captain Bragg and his chief engineer stayed at the steamer's stern watching the schooner and giving orders to the engine room as to the speed of towing. Slowing down and stopping were often necessary. Once, one of the tow lines parted. Everyone feared that the vessel might sink at any time.

Captain Bowley had his life-savers keep their lifebelts on while they were aboard the schooner. He instructed his men to jump away from the ship if she began to sink, so as to be clear of her suction. He also requested that the schooner be stopped in order to bail out their boat so they might be ready if the ship went down.

The schooner arrived in Provincetown harbor at 10:00 p.m. on February 1st. However, in her unmanageable condition, momentum carried her into the *North Star*, smashing the steamer's lifeboat, railing, and ash ejector. The steamer couldn't move to prevent the collision because of the danger of fouling her propeller in the towing hawser. Upon arrival at Provincetown, water on the *Law*'s deck forward of the poop measured between 18" and 2'. Arrangements were made to have her towed into shoal water that night so that if she should sink she could easily be raised.

On the afternoon of the 3rd, Captain Blake returned to the *Law* from his unplanned journey to Philadelphia. He arranged for the schooner to be taken in tow from Provincetown on the 7th by the tug *Storm King*. Two days later the *Law* arrived in Portland, where she delivered her cargo.

On 7 May, 1903, the District Court of Maine made a determination as to the amount of compensation for the schooner's salvage. The value of the *Law* was assessed at $23,500 and her cargo at $12,500 for a total of $36,000. The court awarded $12,000 as salvage, with $9,500 granted to the *North Star* and crew and $2,500 to the *Hope Sherwood* and crew. No money could be awarded to the crew of the life-saving station, according to the court, since they were only performing their duty.[123]

Sale: In August, 1916, the *Law* underwent an extensive overhaul in Rockland, Maine, costing about $22,000. Her Connecticut owners then sold the schooner to out-of-state interests. The vessel's value before repairs was estimated at $75,000, but due to the war and a shortage of shipping the repairs enhanced her worth by more than their cost.[124]

Destruction: In November of 1916 the *Law* was chartered to carry a cargo from Stockton Springs, Maine, to Palermo, Sicily. The cargo consisted of 60,000 bundles of wooden staves, called "shooks," which were to be made into lemon-box crates after the ship arrived in Sicily.[125] This had been a common trade for decades—Maine wood pre-cut for boxes delivered to the Mediterranean where wood resources were few, and Mediterranean cargos of fruit or Sicilian salt brought back to New England.

For this voyage, the master of the *Law* was 39-year-old Stephen W. McDonough of Winterport, Maine. The son of a Winterport sailing master, he had been a schooner captain for 15 years. Stephen McDonough claimed he was a descendant of Commodore McDonough, the victor over the British fleet in the battle of Lake Champlain during the War of 1812. (The victor of that battle actually was Thomas Macdonough, who was promoted

CAPTAIN STEPHEN MCDONOUGH.

to Captain as a result of the action.) First mate on the *Law* was William R. Lowe of Winterport, also the son of a Winterport sailing captain. The rest of the crew were experienced seamen. All were Maine men from Penobscot Bay, except for two sailors who came from Jamaica and Northern Ireland. The latter was signed on when the *Law*'s engineer deserted three days before the schooner was to depart. McDonough selected 18-year-old Lee E. Thompson of Belfast, Northern Ireland, from the ranks of the crew as a replacement for the defecting engineer. Young Thompson had obtained his mechanical skills during previous employment at a Fore River, Massachusetts, shipyard, where he was engaged in building submarines.[126]

In an interview 42 years later, Captain McDonough recalled that on the final night of loading the *Law* at Stockton Springs, he had heard a scurrying from deep inside the hatches of the schooner. A few minutes later, dozens of rats were seen running along the mooring lines from the ship to the dock. The captain said he was not superstitious and attached no significance to the occurrence.[127]

After taking on her cargo, the *Law* lay at anchor off

117

Searsport, Maine, for several days, possibly due to the original engineer's desertion. Then, at 12:40 p.m. on 6 January, 1917, she set sail for Italy on a bitter winter day in a strong northwest wind.[128]

This was to be the first transatlantic crossing for McDonough and his crew, the seaman from Northern Ireland excepted. In spite of the fact that the ship was headed across in wartime, no difficulties were anticipated. America was continuing a policy of neutrality, and as added insurance the stars and stripes were painted in huge dimensions on both sides of the vessel. One positive note, from the viewpoint of captain and crew, was an increase in wages for this overseas voyage.[129]

On 31 January, 1917, Germany and Austria-Hungary sent virtually identical notes to the U.S., announcing that a new policy of unrestricted submarine warfare would commence the next day against neutral ships if they sailed into a proscribed war zone surrounding England, and in waters off France, Italy, or the Eastern Mediterranean.[130]

The U.S. reacted on 3 February when President Wilson advised a joint session of Congress that diplomatic relations with Germany had been severed. Even so, the president stated that it would take "overt acts" on the part of Germany to make him believe that German authorities really intended to do what they said they would. The U.S. did not break relations with Austria-Hungary.[131]

The *Law* carried no wireless and her complement was unaware of the German and Austrian notes or the break in relations with Germany. On the morning of 12 February the schooner was sailing peacefully along her course through the Mediterranean, approximately 25 miles off the southwest coast of Sardinia and about 250 miles from Palermo, Sicily, when the news caught up with her. In the same interview 42 years after the event (which seems to be the most reasonable version of the story), Captain McDonough said he had finished his breakfast and the crew was sitting on deck taking in the sun when suddenly a cannon shot was fired across the schooner's bow. "We hadn't seen the submarine till then," McDonough observed, "but there she was, surfaced, sitting a few hundred yards off our starboard." McDonough hauled down his sails and the schooner hove to. The U-boat bore no name, number, letters or flag of any kind that might disclose her identity. Engineer Thompson identified the submarine as being of a distinct German type.[132]

According to McDonough, the U-boat signaled by blinker for the schooner captain to come over. McDonough ordered the small dory lowered and a seaman rowed him to the submarine, where he said he talked to the commander aboard the U-boat. This officer stood in the conning tower and asked about the *Law*'s destination and cargo. McDonough described him as "a typical old German naval officer—they all looked alike." The commander "didn't seem very interested" and sent one of his lieutenants back to the schooner with McDonough. After looking over the ship's manifest, the lieutenant ordered all hands off the vessel within 20 minutes.[133]

The *Law*'s crew took food from the galley and clothing from the "slop chest" as submarine personnel placed bombs in the ship's hold, thereby saving a costly torpedo. McDonough said the submariners gathered up canned goods to take back to their vessel.[134]

Before leaving the schooner, the Americans were told the U-boat was Austrian. One report indicates they were advised to follow a certain route to Cagliari, Sardinia's capital. The weather and sea were moderate as they disembarked in the captain's motor launch. Within minutes, explosions were heard aboard the *Law*, and she was engulfed in flames. McDonough said he and the crew hoisted the American flag on the motor launch and gave a final salute to the schooner. On 13 February they arrived safely in Cagliari, some 75 miles away, after having spent 25 hours in the motorboat.[135]

U-35 UNDER THE AUSTRIAN FLAG.

America was notified of the event through U.S. Consul Roger C. Tredwell in Turin. The American minister in Rome had received dispatches from the British consul in Cagliari and the Italian Naval Ministry and ordered Consul Tredwell to Cagliari. The dispatches reported that the *Law* was burning, without a trace of crew; she had been destroyed by bombs from an Austrian submarine flying no flag; and her crew had landed at Cagliari.[136]

But the bursting of the bombs aboard the *Law* was minor compared with the bursting of the news about the vessel's demise. The event was of great interest in the U.S. and abroad, making headlines almost everywhere. In Rome, the Chinese minister called on the U.S. ambassador to ascertain the facts about the *Law*,

and stated that his government was interested in any action the U.S. would take regarding this case or other sinkings. Rome newspapers speculated whether the sinking of the *Law* would be the *casus belli*, the "overt act," cited by President Wilson, which would bring the U.S. into the conflict. Similar speculations were printed elsewhere. All agreed that everything depended upon the facts. The pivotal questions: Were American lives lost? Was the *Law* attacked without warning? Did the *Law* carry contraband?[137]

U.S. newspapers generally followed the line that the sinking added only slightly to international tension. It was not taken as an acute incident because it appeared that the vessel was warned and no lives were lost. The *Law*'s destruction was deemed illegal in the U.S. inasmuch as the cargo was not considered to be contraband. Although the German government, and thus by extension the Austrian government, regarded lumber as contraband, the U.S. position was that lumber might be considered contraband only if it could be employed for military use. The wooden staves were useful solely in building citrus crates; they had no military use. The sinking also was deemed illegal beause it violated an accepted rule of the sea: a warship must show its flag before taking hostile action. However, the violation of international law was viewed as far less serious than any destruction that might have resulted in the loss of life.[138]

Seeking more information, President Wilson asked Secretary of State Robert Lansing about the sinkings of both the *Lyman M. Law* and the steamship *Housatonic.* The latter had been sunk on 3 February by a German submarine without loss of life and after a warning had been issued. In that case, the submarine towed the *Housatonic*'s crew in three lifeboats for 90 minutes, taking them to the vicinity of a British patrol boat, where the lifeboats were cut adrift and a signal flare was fired to attract the attention of the patrol craft.[139]

Lansing's report to the president concerning the *Law* asserted that the submarine was first sighted five miles away flying a flag of undetermined nationality, which allegedly was lowered as soon as the American flag was hoisted to the *Law*'s masthead. Then the U-boat reportedly fired the shot across the *Law*'s bow. But this sequence would indicate that schooner personnel had discovered the submarine before the *Law* was seen. Since the *Law* was a "tall ship," she would have been visible on the horizon. Furthermore, her crew was not expecting trouble, whereas the U-boat was in a war zone with her crew looking for action. The report also disclosed that submarine personnel "took ship's papers and logbook and probably $1,400 worth of stores." It concluded by declaring that nothing was done to insure the crew's safety.[140]

The *Law* case was likened to that of the *William P. Frye,* an

American sailing ship sunk in 1915 by a German auxiliary. The *Frye* case was resolved through an interpretation of old Prussian-American treaties of 1799 and 1828. But those treaties could not be invoked if an Austrian submarine sank the *Law*, since no treaty existed between the U.S. and Austria-Hungary.[141]

Indeed, the statement that the submarine was Austrian was the most serious aspect of the matter since it was thought it probably would lead to a break in relations with that country. Unofficially, such a development was not welcome. The U.S. Government wanted to maintain some official contact with the Central Powers and a break was regarded as certain to precipitate similar breaks with Bulgaria and Turkey. This, in turn, would jeopardize the welfare of U.S. citizens all over the Near East.[142]

There were two other, more compelling reasons for hoping the U-boat was not Austrian, the first of which was highly confidential. President Wilson and Lansing were attempting to persuade the Entente governments to modify their peace terms so Austria would not consider that the dismemberment of her empire was at stake. Lansing advised the president that if this could be arranged it might lessen Austrian dependence upon Germany, and by so weakening the alliance it would be a step towards peace. He also pointed out that since the German ambassador was being sent home, Austria's representative would be freed from his influence in the U.S.[143]

The second reason involved a negotiation with Count Adam Tarnowski, Austria's ambassador-designate to the U.S. Austrian interests were being handled in Washington by a *charge d'affaires* whereas America's emissary in Vienna was an ambassador. The Austrian government found this very unsatisfactory and wanted to upgrade its representation. Tarnowski first called at the State Department on 3 February. Shortly afterward he was told he could not be accepted as ambassador when the German ambassador was being dismissed at the same time, unless Austria retreated from the position taken in its submarine note. Tarnowski, anxious to avoid a break in relations, suggested a commencement of communications in the hope that a breakthrough might be achieved. He was allowed to use U.S. State Department channels to send secret messages concerning these communications to his country.[144]

With all this attention on the Austrians, the report that the *Law* was sunk by one of their submarines undoubtedly was viewed with dismay by U.S. policy makers, for it would have seemed to affirm real Austrian support for Germany's position.

Meanwhile, American newspapers were printing every conceivable item related to the *Law* and her crew. One could learn that Captain McDonough was married and the father of three daughters, the oldest of whom was seven; his sister was the night operator in the Belfast, Maine, telephone exchange; and his wife was recovering from the shock of the news. The president of the Maritime Transportation Company of New York, agent for the *Law*, advised that he was going to file a protest with the State Department over the sinking of the vessel. He stated, "Captain McDonough is a 'down easter,' an American of three generations, a sailor out of New England ports for more than 20 years. His men . . . are of the staunch New England stock. Their ancestors fought in the Revolution. Now if they are not entitled to protection, who is?"[145]

The former master of the *Law* from 1903 to 1916, Constant W. Chatfield, a 60-year-old who had retired from the sea to become a member of the Connecticut State Legislature, said he had quit the schooner because he had a "hunch" she was "in for it" and he was glad he had followed his instincts. He also said, "It's too bad to see her end like that. Now if there had been a storm, or if one of those derelicts had gotten in its bad work, that would be different. But a submarine—that's bad. . . ."[146]

Lyman M. Law, the man who had given his name to the vessel, had retired from business. He was in feeble health at 91 and so was spared an interview.[147]

In Cagliari, Captain McDonough advised that he was uncertain whether the submarine was Austrian or German. Referring to the sinking, he said, "It was a nasty piece of privateering. . . . A big fat man, who seemed to be the boss, ordered us arrogantly, as though we were his slaves, to leave the boat immediately. I desired to argue with him, although there was some difficulty in making myself understood. It seemed to me that my attempts to argue irritated the boss, and he began to threaten us. My understanding of what he said was that he would send us all to the bottom of the sea, from where we might appeal to President Wilson. Thus, although overcome with rage, I was obliged, together with my crew, to leave the vessel, which was destroyed in a few moments by bombs, set off by the submarine crew."[148]

The *Law* survivors proceeded to Rome where, with additional time to consider the matter, McDonough became convinced that the submarine and its crew were German rather than Austrian and signed an affidavit to this effect. He based this conclusion upon conversations with U-boat personnel and their general appearance.[149]

During an interview on the Italian mainland, McDonough proclaimed, "If my ship had been armed with a five-pounder I could have destroyed the submarine as easily as buttering a piece of bread. Neither myself nor my men lowered our dignity by showing any resentment. I didn't ask them to spare the ship, and left her smilingly, while the Germans also smiled." He said the submariners took $1,700 worth of stores from the *Law* before she was destroyed by the U-boat commander, who declared her cargo contraband. McDonough expressed the opinion that the *Law* was seized and sunk in order to take over her ample supply of canned foods.[150]

In Vienna, on 19 February, U.S. Ambassador Frederic C. Penfield delivered an *aide-mémoire* to Count Ottokar Czernin, Austria-Hungary's foreign minister, requesting a clarification of that country's position regarding merchant shipping and submarine warfare. After meeting with Penfield, Czernin was given a lengthy audience by the Austrian emperor. Czernin decided to delay response to the U.S., ostensibly to submit the *aide-mémoire* to the Foreign Ministry for an exhaustive examination from the standpoint of international law. In reality, it was to marshal arguments purportedly showing that Austria's policy after the 31 January, 1917, note was no different than before it was sent. Czernin thought a breach with the U.S. was "very probable" and wanted to prevent it. Nevertheless, he was committed to the intensified submarine warfare campaign alongside Germany.[151]

A newspaper article datelined 20 February, Berlin, revealed that although the text of the *aide-mémoire* was not known, its purpose was well understood. It was confidently stated that the Dual Monarchy was united with Germany in submarine warfare and would not retreat in any way from their joint position.[152] On 27 February the Austrian Foreign Ministry advised that the *Lyman M. Law* was not sunk through any action of Austria-Hungary.[153]

The U.S. *aide-mémoire* was answered by the Austrians on 2 March. The U.S. considered this answer to be a redefined statement of a totally unacceptable policy and consequently rejected Tarnowski as Austrian ambassador. Diplomatic relations were maintained since Austria-Hungary had committed no positive act to warrant breaking relations.[154]

Before he left the U.S., Tarnowski wired Count Czernin advising that the U.S. undersecretary of state told him the German U-boat commander responsible for sinking the *Law* exhibited a "transparent intent" when he identified himself as an Austrian. Undoubtedly, this "transparent intent" was an attempt to inextricably tie Austria to Germany in all ramifications of the submarine warfare campaign.[155]

Ambassador Penfield was called home in order to equalize representation at the *charge d'affaires* level in Washington and Vienna. But with the U.S. declaration of war against Germany on 6 April, 1917, Austria-Hungary reacted by breaking relations with the U.S. on 9 April and Turkey followed suit on 20 April. The U.S. did not go to war with Austria-Hungary until 7 December, 1917.[156]

For the report on the other side, German military records disclosed that the German U-boat, the *U-35*, under command of Kapitaenleutnant Lothar von Arnauld, left her Austrian home port of Pola (now Pulj, Croatia) on 6 February. She was on Mediterranean patrol to the Spanish east coast. Early on the morning of 12 February, von Arnauld had his first success of the voyage when he blew up an Italian sailing ship with bombs. Later on the same date he stopped the American schooner *Lyman M. Law* and destroyed her in like manner. No further mention was made of the schooner, but there was a great deal more about the commander of the *U-35*.[157]

He was born Lothar von Arnauld de la Periere in 1886 in Posen, Germany, (now Poznan, Poland). During 1903 he entered the Imperial German Navy as a sea cadet, and in January of 1916 began his first submarine patrol as a kapitaenleutnant in command of the *U-35*. Less than ten months later he was awarded the *pour le mérite*, Germany's highest military decoration. Throughout the war, von Arnauld compiled an exemplary record. He was, in fact, the most successful U-boat commander in the world, the German "ace of aces," and the *U-35* was the most successful U-boat in the world. During 15 voyages in the *U-35*, von Arnauld was credited with destroying 189 merchant ships comprising 446,708 tons. He became the only U-boat commander in the world to sink more than 50,000 tons of shipping on each of four separate voyages. On a 29-day cruise during July and August of 1916 he established the absolute record when he destroyed 54 ships totaling 90,350 tons. After this voyage, the *U-35* returned to Pola with 54 pennants flying, signaling her successes—and the harbor went wild. Yet von Arnauld considered this record cruise tame and humdrum. He said the ships were stopped and the crews took to the lifeboats, where they were accosted and the ships' papers examined. Sailing instructions were given to the nearest land and the captured prizes were sunk.[158]

LOTHAR VON ARNAULD DE LA PERIERE.

But it wasn't tame and humdrum for von Arnauld all the time. He engaged in a number of surface firefights and was subjected to disguised and heavily armed Q-ship traps, ramming attempts and depth-charge attacks. Four months before destroying the *Law* he caused a major French naval disaster when he torpedoed the French troop transport *Gallia*, sending 1,852 men to their deaths. He lived through some extraordinary experiences, such as when an enemy torpedo leaped out of the water and clattered across the deck of the moving, surfaced *U-35*. It passed through the 4'-wide space between the deck gun and conning tower and bent the low deck rail on the far side as it carried back into the sea without exploding. In another submarine, the *U-139*, von Arnauld torpedoed a steamer in convoy, which sank directly on top of his U-boat. The submarine, seriously damaged, was carried down to dangerous depths before skillful ship handling and good luck allowed him to break free.[159]

When the *U-35* operated in the Mediterranean, she did so under the Austrian flag more than under her own. This came about through a technical quirk in the conflict. Italy and Austria were at war with each other as of 23 May, 1915, but war between Italy and Germany was not initiated until 28 August, 1916. During this 15-month interval, the German Admiralty established a policy of treating Italian naval and merchant vessels as enemy ships. There was a proviso, however, that any German attacks on Italian ships had to be carried out under the Austrian flag, just as if the German naval unit was part of the Austro-Hungarian fleet. The Austro-Hungarian Fleet Command accepted this policy and agreed to assume responsibility for whatever German actions were taken against Italian vessels. When individual German submarines were given permission to use the Austrian flag, the German officers and crew were added to Austrian staff lists. Beginning 1 October, 1916, all German U-boats in the Mediterranean reverted to the German flag except for the *U-35*, *U-38*, and *U-39*. These three submarines were credited with the highest totals of merchant shipping sunk during the entire war and they were ordered to carry out operations against all countries under the Austrian flag. The *U-35* remained under these orders until she returned to Germany for extensive repairs in September of 1918.[160]

But why did von Arnauld fly no flag, or lower the Austrian flag before intercepting the *Law*? We don't know the answer; we do know that the *Law* was the first American vessel he sank. Possibly he decided to be discreet when he discovered the schooner's nationality. A more likely explanation is that he and perhaps other German U-boat commanders may not have been overly concerned about flying a flag, despite the rules. Since submerged U-boats flew no flag, it would have been easy to rationalize not flying one when surfaced. Additionally, paramount practical considerations in the wartime operation of U-boats could have discouraged raising, lowering and flying the flag.[161]

And why didn't Austria accept responsibility for sinking the *Law* in view of the established agreement with Germany? No direct answer was located in Austrian State Archives. Nevertheless, the reason is plain: the Austrians broke the agreement because they didn't want the U.S. to break relations with them.

The *Law*'s owners estimated her value at $146,000, although they insured her for only $44,000; the cargo, however, was fully insured for $31,200. One year after the ship's destruction, her owners were advised to file a formal diplomatic claim against the German government for the actual losses, which were listed at $106,425.[162]

On 29 March, Captain McDonough and First Mate Lowe arrived home in Winterport, where they were welcomed by friends on their safe return. McDonough said that after he and his men had left the ship, the submarine stayed near the schooner for about three hours before the bombs were exploded. He presumed that during the interval the Teutons took food supplies from the schooner to their own craft.[163]

Captain McDonough retired in Winterport after some additional sea duty. He lived there with his family for 24 more years before he died in 1963 at age 85. A few Winterport residents remembered him as an honest man who had both a temper and a decided sense of humor. His daughters generally agreed with this assessment but downplayed his temper in favor of his loving nature. It was observed he had led an exciting life and had many hair-raising experiences to relate, which stories delighted his grandchildren. No one else could furnish additional details concerning the sinking of the *Law*.[164]

Trying to establish basic facts surrounding the schooner's destruction, one finds discrepancies in information, and these might logically be attributed to Captain McDonough in official government reports and newspaper interviews. A few examples: When first seen, the submarine was reported at various distances ranging from a few hundred yards to five miles.[165] Stores were taken from the *Law* worth $1,700, which value descended in scale to a mere presumption that some stores were removed.[166] (It also should be noted that when the *Law* was destroyed, von Arnauld was only into the first week of this patrol and presumably had no great need to replenish his larder.) After the schooner's crew debarked, the bombs were allegedly exploded from a few moments later to three hours later.[167] McDonough claimed he boarded the submarine, where he talked with an officer he assumed was the commander, and whom he described on different occasions as: "a big fat man;" someone having "all the physical characteristics of the German race;" "a typical old German naval officer–they all looked alike." He described the U-boat men as "all big blond husky fellows."[168] No physical description of von Arnauld was available for February 1917, but at that time he was only 30 years old. About a decade later he was described as a tall, slender, good-looking man with brown hair and eyes, a firm jaw, a nice smile and a good sense of humor. It would appear that if McDonough talked to anyone on the U-boat it was not von Arnauld. McDonough may well have boarded the U-boat as he stated, since von Arnauld has a documented record where, on a few occasions, he ordered merchant skippers to board his submarine when he took them prisoner. McDonough's statement that he attempted to argue with the submarine commander seems unlikely when one considers the jeopardy in which he and his crew were placed. An argument is further discredited by the captain himself. In Sardinia he was quoted in regard to the angry interchange. Later, on the mainland, he maintained that neither he nor his crew showed any resentment as they smilingly left their ship. Many more interviews were given but none was found where he repeated the story that a dispute had taken place. One newspaper article that cited sections of McDonough's affidavit didn't mention any boarding of the U-boat at all. It merely stated that the submarine approached the *Law* and an officer from the submarine examined the ship's papers and cargo. Then he ordered the captain and crew to leave before the schooner was blown up.[169]

The inconsistencies in McDonough's statements are simply too numerous to attribute to misquotes or journalistic error. Those Winterport residents and family members who were interviewed could not account for the variations in his story. However, on a second interview, Mrs. Oleta (Walter) McDonough, the captain's daughter-in-law, offered a suggestion. She said that Walter, her late husband (the captain's only son), was inclined to build on a story. He enjoyed telling tales and was apt to overstate the facts when he found a willing audience. She surmised that the captain might have had the same habit. And we are reminded that seafaring men have earned an historic reputation for storytelling, acquired through the age-long practice of swapping yarns in the fo'c'sle. One is left with the perception that an opportunity was surely missed. What a story Captain McDonough might have told had he been aware of the identity and reputation of his onetime adversary.[170]

Nevertheless, any statements Captain McDonough made do not alter the significant items in this little drama. He accomplished what he had to do–i.e., to get himself and his crew ashore safely and make what was then the important decision of identifying the submarine as German rather than Austrian. Of course, the reported basis of his decision seems superficial, resting as it does on brief conversations and the general appearance of the U-boat's crew. No mention was made whether McDonough relied upon Engineer Thompson's observation that the U-boat was of a distinct German type, which could have influenced his decision.

Thompson's evaluation might not have carried much weight, if indeed it did, had it been known that before the *Law* was destroyed the Austrian Navy was using five coastal U-boats that had been constructed at a German shipyard in 1915 on order from the Austrian government. However, these submarines were considerably smaller than the *U-35*. Finally it must be observed that, while he was in Italy, McDonough was talking with U.S. embassy personnel who undoubtedly questioned "Austrian" U-boat successes. Along this line, on 15 February, Ambassador Penfield in Vienna wired Washington that it was known the Austrian U-boats were "few in number and obsolete in type." He also reported that an Austrian military attache told him the Austrian submarines were doing nothing outside the Adriatic.[171]

The *Lyman M. Law* was blown up at a time when the U.S. Government was weighing the pros and cons of arming U.S. merchant vessels. On 26 February, President Wilson addressed the joint Houses of Congress requesting authority to arm U.S. merchant ships. The president used the sinkings of the *Housatonic* and the *Lyman M. Law* as examples in his speech. He stated that the lives of the *Housatonic*'s crew "were safeguarded with reasonable care. The case of the *Law* . . . disclosed a ruthlessness of method which deserves grave condemnation, but was accompanied by no circumstances which might not have been expected at any time in connection with the use of the submarine against merchantmen as the German Government has used it." He added, "The overt act which I have ventured to hope the German commanders would in fact avoid has not occurred." Although the president had the authority to act on his own in arming merchant vessels, he preferred to have the backing of Congress. In this he was frustrated in the Senate by a successful filibuster led by Senator La Follette of Wisconsin. Shortly thereafter Congress adjourned and the president exercised his constitutional powers by ordering the navy to furnish guns and gunners to American steamships bound for the war zones. So the sinking of the *Law* was used as a springboard to effect the arming of our merchantmen. But in the overview, her destruction was only one in a series of cumulative incidents that led to the U.S. declaration of war against Germany.[172]

Perhaps the blowing up of the *Law* also served to crystalize the thinking of some Americans. At the start of World War I, much of the American public was peace-loving, neutral, and isolationist in its outlook. However, German arrogance and a succession of aggressive acts against neutral nations and civilians in the war zones hammered down the national resistance to war. Maybe the beauty and romance of an old sailing ship and her destruction also exerted some influence. Boston's famous poet, Amy Lowell, was moved by the sinking and included it in her poem *Before War Is Declared:*

> "She was a four-masted schooner,
> Bound to Sicily from Penobscot Bay,
> With the foam bubbling at her cutwater,
> Her big sails out over the starboard gunwale
> All drawing,
> Bleached white in the sun,
> And blue at the turn below the gaff.
> They slapped down on the water like Monday washing,
> Held her for a moment with their spread,
> Then soaked up the waves,
> And still ballooning,
> Collapsed and sank.
> The 'Lyman M. Law'—
> And her set sails swing in the undulating water,
> And the name on her stern is fantastic
> With the waving of the sea . . ."

The poem is wrapped in an envelope of pacifism, but it

sounds a peroration of patriotism. For Amy Lowell's conflicting emotions, the *Law* was a turning point. And she was attuned to the times. Fifty-three days after the *Law* was destroyed, war was declared.[173]

After publication of *The Last Voyage of the Lyman M. Law* in 1987 I wanted to check further on Captain McDonough's seagoing career to determine if my analysis of his "yarn spinning" was correct. His next command after the *Law* was the five-masted Maine-built schooner *Mary W. Bowen* on another transatlantic voyage with William R. Lowe as his first mate. On 7 July, 1917, the *Bowen* was intercepted by another German submarine *UC-72*, in the Bay of Biscay on the Atlantic coast of France. The schooner was destroyed by bombs and gunfire after all hands were ordered into the ship's small boat. The following day they were picked up by the French sloop of war *Regulus*. The *Bowen* crew stayed aboard for three days. Two other French warships, *Gloire* and *Marne*, accompanied *Regulus*. When McDonough and Lowe arrived back in the U.S. the newspapers tracked them down. In one newspaper interview, McDonough claimed that while on board *Regulus*, they were in two gun battles with submarines. He said U-boats fired 100 shots at them but did little damage. In another interview, he said they came upon the scene of the sinking of a French steamer, where debris and human bodies floated on the water's surface. He added that a few minutes later a periscope was sighted and the French warships sank a submarine. German records didn't list any U-boat being sunk or having engaged in a firefight with French warships at that time or place. *Regulus'* sea report did not reflect any firefights with, or sinking of, U-boats, nor sighting of any ship debris or floating human bodies. It did disclose that on 10 July *Gloire* opened fire at what was thought to be a periscope with no results. An hour later *Gloire* and *Regulus* began firing at a U-boat that appeared to be in a shallow dive. This turned out to be the half-sunken wreck of a schooner. Next there was a false alert when a line of "gallettes de cire" was mistaken for the wake of a torpedo. The *Regulus* sea report carries a question mark after "gallettes de cire." Present-day French naval officials can't explain it any better. The translation of "cire" is wax and the nautical definition of "gallettes" is "sea biscuits" (hardtack). If sea biscuits is what they were, whether waxed or not, presumably they were thrown over the side of a passing ship. So McDonough did see some shooting–but it's doubtful that any sea biscuits shot back. For all his apparent yarning, McDonough was said to be the only U.S. merchant-vessel master who had two ships sunk by German U-boats within a five-month period.

After the sinking of the *Bowen*, McDonough's statements to the press became even more exaggerated. The captain had been described as a man with both a temper and a sense of humor, and humor may have influenced these new sea stories. His adult son, Walter, now deceased, wrote that his father had "a keen sense of humor." Perhaps annoyed at being asked the same questions over and over again by reporters, and knowing that the reporters would probably write whatever he told them, McDonough related some outrageous yarns, whether they contradicted any of his previous statements or not.[174]

One year later, on 27 July, 1918, McDonough signed up as a lieutenant to serve four years with the U.S. Naval Auxiliary Reserve, in a program that would allow the navy to exploit his affinity for attracting German U-boats and use him as a decoy. He would skipper an unarmed schooner, the USS *Helvetia*, which towed or was followed by a submerged navy submarine. Another submarine would operate independently, both hoping to surprise a German U-boat. McDonough later reported that "We towed a submarine with chains back and forth on the troop ship lane between Nantucket (and in another interview, Bermuda) and the Azores." He said they never met another U-boat. U.S. Navy records confirm that the decoy plan was instituted but that a towing cable was used, not chains. And *Helvetia*'s track with McDonough as skipper did not go beyond about 200 miles from the U.S. east coast and never within hundreds of miles from Bermuda. McDonough made only two voyages in *Helvetia* for a sum total of less than four weeks at sea.

There's still more to the *Helvetia* story. Having a sailing ship tow a submarine involved all kinds of problems for both vessels. Bad weather complicated the procedure enormously. A sub could not be towed well in poor weather conditions—if at all. Towing cables and hawsers broke frequently; but towing was impossible if there was little or no wind (to propel the sailing ship). If seas broke over the periscope's fair-water mark, the sub couldn't run at periscope depth; and heavy seas made depth control difficult for the sub. On one occasion when *Helvetia* tacked the submerged sub wound up close alongside the schooner and headed in the opposite direction. And when the sub wasn't being towed and was following behind the schooner, heavy weather could separate the vessels by miles.

Helvetia sailed from Newport News, Virginia, on 8 August, 1918. This was her first voyage for the navy; but McDonough was not yet her captain, nor was he aboard. On 17 August, U.S. submarine *E-2*, under Lt. Reifsnider, surfaced to pick up a tow line from *Helvetia*. They were about 125 miles off the Virginia Capes. The schooner had the duty to notify *E-2* if there were any ships in the area before allowing the submarine to surface but she failed to do so. *E-2* came up on the weather side of *Helvetia* to pick up the line. Looking over the horizon with his binoculars, Lt. Reifsnider noted a square sail about four and a half miles away. This was the Norwegian bark *Nordhav*, and there was another object immediately to its left that appeared to have two masts. The sub captain asked the *Helvetia* what the latter was and was told, "Can't make it out." At the time, the Norwegian bark had been stopped by the big new German submarine *U-117*, whose personnel placed explosives aboard the *Nordhav*. The *Nordhav* disappeared from view 35 minutes later, and shortly thereafter the *U-117* appeared on the horizon. Lt. Reifsnider identified it as an enemy U-boat and gave orders to open the towing hook and rig for diving. But the towing hook did not open; there was no strain on the towline. Possibly a minute was lost sending a man forward to do the job. *E-2* submerged immediately. When Reifsnider thought he was near the enemy sub, he came to periscope depth but saw nothing except *Helvetia*. For the next several hours *E-2* searched for the U-boat without success. In a conversation about this incident sometime after the armistice, Kapitaenleutnant Droescher of *U-117* reportedly remarked, "There was one little Yankee submarine that pretty nearly got me. He got so near that it wasn't any fun." But back in the U.S. the commander of U.S. Navy Submarine Division would report, "It is lamentable that the schooner which was to be the eyes of the force should have failed at this critical time to carry out her part of the program." The schooner's log disclosed that the masthead lookout had reported an object alongside the bark early on. But the officer of the deck and *Helvetia*'s captain took no further action.[175]

In the court martials that followed, the officer of the deck was acquitted but the captain was found guilty. However, the Judge Advocate General's Department disapproved the finding and restored him to duty. Acting Secretary of the Navy Franklin Roosevelt signed off on the latter action.[176]

Back to the *Helvetia* at sea: The next day *E-2* sighted a sub standing toward *Helvetia* in a choppy sea. *E-2* prepared to attack, but at 500 yards recognition marks were noted of *L-5*, the other submarine that had been operating independently with *E-2*. Rough seas and small length of exposed periscope had prevented recognition sooner. In October five U.S. submarines would be sent from the U.S. to the Azores. Undoubtedly this was the inspiration for McDonough's tall tale of sailing there in the *Helvetia*. McDonough didn't receive orders to report aboard *Helvetia* as commanding officer until 13 August, when *Helvetia* was at sea, and it wasn't until 27 August that he was able to take over command of the schooner, so he missed the *Helvetia*'s rendezvous with the German U-boat.

He also missed a great opportunity. With his schooner background and intimate acquaintance with U-boats, he might have added laurels as a sub-sinking schooner captain to his renown as a captain who had lost two vessels to German subs in short order. On the other hand, if his behavior had been anything like that of his predecessor in command of *Helvetia*, he might have added a court martial to his record.

On 1 March, 1919, McDonough was given command of the U.S. barge *Harvest Queen*, which was being towed from New London, Connecticut, to Yorktown, Virginia, by the minesweeper USS *Penguin,* commanded by Lt. Edgar T. Hammond. McDonough was in overall command of the operation, but the barge began taking in water. *Harvest Queen* was towed to the nearest anchorage at Gravesend Bay in Brooklyn. After pumping out, she remained at the anchorage and was tied astern of the minesweeper. But with every change in tide, there was a danger of collision when the two vessels of unequal draft swung at different times. Lt. Hammond reported the inadvisability of keeping the barge astern on a towline, but apparently nothing was done to correct the situation. On 16 March the barge collided broadside with the minesweeper, resulting in several holes being punched in the barge's port side and her small boat being smashed. A board of investigation determined that the collision was unavoidable. It also found that Lt. Hammond had taken all proper and reasonable precautions to guard against such damage, and that his officers and crew were on deck before the collision took place, doing everything possible to avoid damage. The Board's conclusion was that Lt. Hammond was in no way responsible for the damage to the *Harvest Queen*, and that Lt. McDonough appeared to be partially responsible for the damage "in that he caused no proper watch to be kept and showed an apparent lack of interest in the safety of his vessel after the collision occurred." McDonough's active duty in the navy ceased on 23 May, 1919. He received an honorable discharge on 29 June, 1922. For McDonough's part, with the war over for half a year, and his new command a leaking barge in tow—after some 16 adventurous years as a self-reliant schooner captain, he was probably more than ready to say goodbye to the U.S. Navy.[177] McDonough returned briefly to schooners, then served on tankers as chief mate. At age 61 he fell from the bridge of a tanker onto its steel deck, breaking his leg, which never healed properly. This ended his career at sea.[178]

THE *LUCINDA SUTTON*

Collisions: Reported collisions involving the *Lucinda Sutton* were limited to just two instances. Evidence for the first was a sighting of the schooner passing Vineyard Haven on 9 December, 1898, with her headgear and jibboom carried away. It was presumed she had been in a collision. The second instance occurred at 1:00 a.m. on 2 April, 1899, when, bound for Boston, she collided with the *Cross Rip Lightship*, badly damaging the lightship, but with her own damage limited to that about her stem.[179]

Deterioration: The *Lucinda Sutton* experienced few major difficulties until she sailed from Montevideo, Uruguay, for Tampa in 1911. She arrived at Barbados, West Indies, in distress on 28 December. Two masts were sprung and there was other unspecified damage. Temporary repairs were made before she set off for Mobile on 25 January, 1912, for more permanent repairs. During her remaining years the *Lucinda Sutton* had serious leakage problems that plagued her until the end.[180]

The schooner's next major damage occurred when she sailed from Baltimore with coal for Le Lamentin, Martinique. In heavy weather she damaged her sails and leaked heavily, which forced her to put into Bermuda on 27 December, 1912. Repairs were made but the voyage to Martinique had to be abandoned. She finally arrived at Fernandina, Florida, on 17 March, 1913. Then, late in the summer of 1914, she sprang a leak off Jupiter Island, Florida, on a passage north. She put into Charleston for repairs and didn't arrive at her Boston destination until 30 October.[181]

On 21 August, 1915, the *Lucinda Sutton* left Newport News for Rio de Janeiro. Five hundred miles east of Cape Henry, Virginia, she started leaking. Captain Van Name brought the ship about and returned to Virginia. The vessel arrived off Sewalls Point (Norfolk) on 8 September leaking badly. Van Name waited for a decision from the owners regarding repairs that eventually were made.[182]

On 22 February, 1916, the schooner left Buenos Aires for New York but ran into heavy weather at the start of the voyage. Leaking worse than ever, she put into Rio for repairs on 11 March. After spending 1,000 pounds ($4,760) on the damaged ship, a new survey determined that an additional 1,500 pounds ($7,140) would be needed. With practically no insurance coverage on the vessel, managing owner Captain H.A. O'Brien and the other owners decided the time had come to sell her. Her cargo was transshipped to the U.S., and then the schooner was put up for auction several times before the South American Shipping Co. of New York finally bought her.[183]

Destruction: Under new ownership and with a nine-man crew, the *Lucinda Sutton* was under the command of a new skipper, Captain J.A. Bergman of New York City, and sailed from Paranagua, Brazil, on 6 March, 1917, for Bahia Blanca, Argentina. She was laden with Brazilian wood and other miscellaneous cargo. Part of the cargo was carried on deck. Overall, the cargo weighed 1,600 tons and was estimated to be worth about $14,000. With this weight aboard she would have drawn 17' of water.[184]

The schooner was approaching Bahia Blanca on the evening of 31 March. Visibility was hazy, while wind, weather and sea were moderate. In the haze, a steamer was mistaken for a lightship. After discovering the error, soundings were taken. The schooner was in shoal water! An anchor was dropped immediately, and soon the tide swung her around. At 6:30 p.m. she struck bottom and stranded. Captain Bergman listed her location on Lobos Bank, with coordinates of 39° 24' S by 61° 17' W. (These coordinates, possibly the ship's last dead-reckoning position, were inaccurate and they led to a contretemps many years later.) On 23 May, 1917, Captain Bergman filled in a U.S. Coast Guard Casualty Report, wherein he described the ship as a total loss. Somebody penned in her estimated value on the form as $75,000.[185]

In 1985 and 1986 I sent the above information to the Argentine Embassy and Naval Office in Washington, D.C., and to newspapers in Buenos Aires requesting additional facts. No response was forthcoming. In February of 1987 I sent the data to Bahia Blanca's oldest newspaper, *La Nueva Provincia*. This paper asked for additional details and photographs, stating they had background information that they wished to exchange. They wanted to publish an article about the schooner on the 70th anniversay of her stranding. I furnished the requested information plus a photo of the launching of the *Lucinda Sutton*. Not knowing of any picture of her under sail, I had a photo of the *Lyman M. Law* at sea sent from The Mariners' Museum in Newport News. I explained by letter that the *Law* was a slightly smaller version of the *Lucinda Sutton* and the *Law* had been constructed by the same builders in the same shipyard just one year before the *Sutton*. An article written by Jose Guardiola Plubins was published in *La Nueva Provincia* on 31 March, 1987. Plubins wrote a second article about the *Lucinda Sutton* that was published with added embellishment in the Argentine Navy's newspaper, *Gaceta Marinera*, on 31 May, 1987. Both articles were sent to me with background material, history, geography, maps of the area, and picture postcards. The photo of the *Law* was published without identification as a background to the *Gaceta Marinera* article so that one could assume it was a picture of the *Lucinda Sutton*.[186]

The material furnished by the newspaper disclosed that the area was first "discovered" by Magellan's expedition on the ship *Victoria* in 1520. In 1832 the name "Banco de los Lobos" (Wolves' Bank) was applied to the region just south of Trinidad Island on a voyage by the British naval ship *Beagle*. Charles Darwin was the *Beagle*'s naturalist on this trip.[187]

Bahia Blanca's estuary has an established reputation for shipwrecks due to its winds, currents and shifting shoals. (In this respect, it appears somewhat akin to North Carolina's Outer Banks. Even the nomadic sand dunes on shore along their respective coasts are similar.) Names listed on Argentine charts such as Labertino (Labyrinth) Shoals and Bahia Falsa (False Bay) convey a message that these are tricky waters to navigate. These charts underscore the dangers with printed warnings that the water depth may be less than noted in certain areas and ships that draw more than 25' should not approach the coast any closer than the ten-fathom curve.[188]

Neither the archives of *La Nueva Provincia* nor the periodical library, Biblioteca Bernardino Rivadavia, had any record of the *Lucinda Sutton*'s stranding. I also was informed that in 1917 no

Argentine government agency had any responsibility to note maritime movements or events in the area.[189]

The undulating northern coast of Argentina is known as the Monte Hermoso coast. For a ship adrift within ten miles of this coast, prevailing currents would take it north to this beach. But if a vessel was adrift south of Trinidad Island (Lobos Bank, for example) or 25 miles south of the Monte Hermoso coast, then prevailing currents would move the ship in an easterly direction to where the Argentine coast bends north towards Brazil. Captain Bergman's erroneous coordinates placed the *Lucinda Sutton* some 25 miles south of the Monte Hermoso coast and more than 27 miles ESE of Lobos Bank. So if the schooner was adrift at either Lobos Bank or at captain Bergman's position more than 27 miles to the ESE, the current would have carried the ship to the east, not to the north.[190]

The Argentine Institute of Oceanography (IADO) marked the map location of an international sailing ship's remains a few miles south of Recalada Light and approximately eight meters deep. Its coordinates are 39° 04' S by 61° 14' W. Longitudinally, this matches up fairly closely with Captain Bergman's coordinate (61° 17' W) but presents a 20' difference latitudinally (39° 24' S). The derelict of another sailing ship, a North American vessel sunk at the mouth of the Sauce Grande River sometime in the early 1900s, was personally known to Jose Guardiola Plubins, author of the two *Lucinda Sutton* articles.[191]

Along with this background, some contemporary Bahia Blanca history throws further light on *Nueva Provincia*'s interest in the *Lucinda Sutton*. Recalada Light first commenced operations on 21 February, 1906. A young engineer, Esteban Dufaur, built a home for his parents and established a cattle ranch amongst the desolate sand dunes abutting Recalada Light. He called the property "El Recreo" (Recreation Place) and began to build up the area. He laid out a road, built a bridge over the Sauce Grande River and irrigated the land. Within a few years, the sandbanks were covered with foliage that resonated with the trill of parrots. The celebrated Argentine naturalist and anthropologist, Florentino Ameghino, who explored these Atlantic sand dunes while searching for Pleistocene fossils, often was a guest of the Dufaur family. Ameghino repeatedly suggested to the young rancher that he establish a summer recreation center in that strange latitude of the coast where one had the rare privilege of seeing the sun rise and set on the sea.[192]

At some unspecified time (but evidently in 1917), the beach in front of Recalada Light was covered for a distance of about five kilometers by a large scattering of valuable Brazilian timber that had washed ashore. A longshoreman contractor, Senor Juan Natali, selected ten sturdy stevedores to gather up the timber. He also rented a tugboat, the *Marrocain*, and a great barge for the operation. When the task was completed, the barge was loaded to its gunwales—just in time for a storm to sink the barge. Once again the wood was strewn on the beach.[193]

This second shipwreck of the lumber was considered by Esteban Dufaur as an invitation to act upon Ameghino's suggestion. He gathered up the timber and with it built the first hotel balneario (bathing spa) at Monte Hermosa. It opened for business on 4 January, 1918, and in time turned the area into a little seaside resort.[194]

The telling of this story of the frustrated cargo salvage and the errant timber has been repeated over and over on the shores of Bahia Blanca. It is a favorite tale, but nobody ever knew where the Brazilian wood had come from. The temptation to establish the *Lucinda Sutton* as the source of the Brazilian timber must have been overwhelming. The schooner carried Brazilian wood, some of it ostensibly on deck. She ran aground in the right year. Her captain erred as to the coordinates where she grounded. One of his listed coordinates was close enough to that of two known shipwrecks, where the cargo could easily have been dispersed onto the Monte Hermoso beach. But stranding on that coast in moderate weather presented a problem, particularly with the proximity of the light beacon. It just wasn't likely.

However, Jose Guardiola Plubins solved the dilemma. He invented a storm, a big storm. Both newspaper articles described the fictional tempest and shipwreck in lurid detail. It is a colorful tale. In it, the *Lucinda Sutton*'s struggle with a raging storm lasted for hours. Recalada Light became obscured. A giant wave destroyed the ship's rudder. Sails and rigging were damaged. Many times the hull was heeled almost to the point of no return under the brutal weight of the waves. The cargo of timber was jettisoned, but to no avail. Finally the schooner ran aground on the coastal banks. "The violence of the impact broke her old frame, and with a moan of agony and wound of death, the veteran ship disappeared from the sea's inventory." The crew's fate wasn't given, but the needed point was gained. The tale was now complete.[195]

The fictional solution could not stand. While searching for history, one doesn't want to create history. But the point became moot when I discovered a new source of information—at least it was new to me. It was the *New York Maritime Register (NYMR)*. This source had some highly relevant and previously unknown data (to me) about the stranding of the schooner. It stated that the *Lucinda Sutton* had grounded about nine miles southwest of the Bahia Blanca lightship. This would indeed have placed her on Lobos Bank. *NYMR* reported that the grounding took place on 30 March, 1917, which was an error. The correct date was the 31st, as mentioned in the U.S. Coast Guard Casualty Report. *NYMR* stated that the ship filled with water the next morning. On 1 April the mainmast worked up through the deck, thereby giving evidence that the keel was broken. The crew was removed on this date. On 3 April surveyors noted that the ship had filled with water to sea level; her decks had burst and were forced up amidships. The surveyors didn't believe it was possible to save the ship or her cargo. Nevertheless, both ship and cargo were to be offered for sale by auction on 15 April.[196]

The final entry in *NYMR* disclosed that on 16 April, 1917, the schooner was sold with her cargo of Brazilian wood at public auction for $203,000.[197]

I sent this information to author Jose Guardiola Plubins and to *La Nueva Provincia*. At a later date I also sent it to the Argentine Naval Office in Washington, D.C., with a further request for more information. That office contacted a number of government offices and other Argentine sources as well as the newspaper library of *La Prensa* in Buenos Aires. Only *La Prensa* furnished any pertinent information and this was from articles that had been published in its issues of 3 and 4 April, 1917.[198]

The article of 3 April indicated that the Chief of the Military Port sent the gunship *Republica* to gather the survivors of a ship that was stranded on Lobos Bank. The tugboat *Ona* was sent to rescue the vessel and the tugboat *Querandi* was also alerted.[199]

The 4 April article advised that Rear Admiral Lagos, Chief of the Military Port, informed the Navy Ministry that it was the *Lucinda Sutton* that was stranded in the Bahia Blanca estuary. Admiral Lagos said that Captain Gully, who was sent with the rescue ships to the scene of the accident, furnished the following information about the schooner's situation: The ship was located five miles southwest of Baliza Lobo (Wolf Buoy). It had filled with water up to sea level and was sunk four feet in the sand. It had heeled over about ten degrees in just eight feet of water at low tide. Captain Gully thought it unwise for the tugboats to try to tow the vessel and risk losing both hull and cargo. He thought it better to use more men and bigger scows, observing that all efforts would be futile with the few salvage elements available. Admiral Lagos ordered Captain Gully to return and then advised the schooner's maritime agent of the situation.[200]

I sent the *La Prensa* information to *La Nueva Provincia*. The latter newspaper responded with a letter of appreciation. But no additional data has been discovered. That anyone would purchase the schooner for $203,000 under the circumstances set forth is extremely unlikely. It must also be remembered that Captain Bergman had listed the schooner as a total loss on the U.S. Coast Guard Casualty Report dated 23 May, 1917, some five weeks after her reported sale. One can only conclude that the report of a sale was erroneous, and that the *Lucinda Sutton* ended her sailing days on Lobos Bank.

A final irony concerns the background photo of the *Lyman M. Law* that I had The Mariners' Museum in Newport News, Virginia, send to *La Neuva Provincia* in Bahia Blanca. Jose Plubins used this photo in his *Gaceta Marinera* article. After the picture was sent to Argentina, Captain W.J.L. Parker, formerly of the U.S. Coast Guard and an expert on old sailing vessels, told me that this photo was of the schooner *Henry Lippett* and not the *Law*. During a visit to Mystic Seaport I saw a book by Paul C. Morris, *Schooners and Schooner Barges*, with the same photo on the dust cover of the book, identified as the *Henry Lippitt*.

I notified Mr. R. Thomas Crew, Jr., Archivist at The Mariners' Museum, of the dual identification, and he responded to me by letter dated 28 September, 1989, advising that the museum was aware of the existing confusion. The photo's donor, Albert M. Barnes, was described by Mr. Crew as being an expert on whaling, fishing and sailing vessels of the northeast but unfortunately Barnes had died two years before. The Mariners' Museum would have to stand by their identification unless documentation could be provided to amend it. Tom Crew asked me to help verify or disprove the photo's identity. He also asked me to contact author Paul C. Morris about his information and the authenticity of this same photo, which had been provided to Morris by one James Stevens. Mr. Crew concluded with, "Maybe together we can solve this mystery."

Eventually I learned from James Stevens (previously unknown to me) that he and Captain Parker were both trustees of the Maine Maritime Museum and that Captain Parker had identified the photo to him as that of the *Henry Lippett*. In turn, Stevens told me he had identified it as the *Lippett* to Paul C. Morris. I notified the interested parties of these developments in the fall of 1990 and again in the fall of 1992. On 5 October, 1992, The Mariners' Museum queried Captain Parker by letter (copy to me). Nine days later Captain Parker wrote a three-page reply to The Mariners' Museum (copy to me) detailing many differences between the *Law* and the *Lippitt*. He also advised that the picture donor, Albert M. Barnes, was an old friend of his and that he and Barnes had each acquired a duplicate copy of the photo from the photographer, N.S. Stebbins, many years ago. But Barnes had cropped the identification from his photo (presumably to fit into one of his albums) while Captain Parker's copy still reads "12460 Henry Lippett." Not hearing from Mr. Crew, I telephoned him on 14 October, 1993. He told me then that the museum would go along with Captain Parker's assessment that it was the *Lippett* and not the *Law*. In all, it took four years to resolve the issue.[201]

So the *Gaceta Marinera* article was not only wrong about the storm, the background photo they used wasn't the *Lucinda Sutton*, nor was it even a ship of the same schooner family.

THE *R. & T. HARGRAVES*

Collision: The collision between the *Hargraves* and the *W. Wallace Ward* on 12 June, 1894, is reported under the *Ward*.

Destruction: On a bitter cold night in February of 1903, a strong northwest wind propelled the *R. & T. Hargraves* on a NNE course off the New Jersey coast. She carried 1,203 tons of bituminous coal loaded at Norfolk and destined for Providence. Soon after midnight on the 19th, the weather became squally at times, with short, sudden gusts of wind and occasional snow flurries. Then visibility improved as the moon appeared, its light reflecting on the sea. Captain Constant W. Chatfield, the vessel's master, was below in his quarters. Mate Oscar Neilson had the watch with the schooner on a port tack, some eight miles northeast of Absecon Light. She was under jib, staysail, foresail and single-

SCHOONER *R.&T. HARGRAVES.*

reefed spanker. About 1:30 a.m. her lookout sighted a red light off the port bow. Neilson and the man at the helm confirmed the sighting.[202]

Over a brief interval, the light seemed to brighten but its bearing didn't change. It was another ship—on a collision course with the *Hargraves.* Neilson ordered the helmsman to bear off and give the approaching vessel more room, which was done. Both continued on their way until the other vessel abruptly and unexpectedly changed course, opening up her green light. She was on top of the *Hargraves* almost immediately. Her bow smashed into the mizzen chain plates on the port quarter of the *R.&T. Hargraves,* cutting a wide gash in the hull. The other vessel tore away the *Hargraves'* standing rigging aft but left her own jibboom, splintered in two, on the *Hargraves'* deckhouse. With the suddenness of the collision and the moon providing the only real illumination, all that could be determined about the unknown ship was that she was a large four-masted schooner. She disappeared to the south almost as soon as she struck.[203]

Inspection of the *Hargraves* disclosed that water was rapidly pouring into the hold. The powerful wrecking pump and hand pumps were put into action but water was coming in faster than it was going out. It was gaining at the rate of about a foot an hour, which foretold the schooner's sinking within a few hours. Captain Chatfield decided to anchor her to prevent drifting farther from shore. But efforts to maneuver the vessel were greatly handicapped by the ice that covered her. In order to drop the sails before anchoring, the halyards had to be cut. Preparations were made to abandon ship. The yawl was fitted with provisions and lowered, for it was not known how long it would take before they might be rescued. Captain Chatfield and his seven-man crew waited aboard the schooner, hoping to see a passing ship.[204]

At 6:30 a.m., just before daybreak, a steamer was sighted about three miles away. Torches and newspapers were burned as signals of distress. The steamer was the Clyde liner *Goldsboro*, Captain Geohegan in command. When the *Goldsboro* neared, the men from the schooner took to their boat, a few with some personal effects. They rowed to the steamer and were picked up. A last look from the *Goldsboro* showed the upper deck of the *Hargraves* awash, and soon after the schooner sank in seven fathoms of water with only the tops of her masts visible. Captain Chatfield and his crew were landed in New York.[205]

Managing owner James D. Dewell stated that no attempt would be made to raise the *Hargraves* for she had sunk in water too deep for salvage operations. Reports conflicted as to whether she carried any insurance. Among the owners were: Captain Chatfield,

1/64th; James Dewell, 1/64th; and Lucinda Sutton, 15/64ths.[206]

On February 21 it was learned that the unknown four-master was the *Eagle Wing*, a 210', 1,079-ton schooner enroute light from Boston to Newport News. Her Captain Morgan reported a collision at 1:30 a.m. on the 19th off Atlantic City with an unknown schooner, wherein the *Eagle Wing* lost her jibboom and all attached headgear.[207]

On the 25th a lawsuit was initiated in Norfolk in Captain Chatfield's name against the owners of the *Eagle Wing*. The claim valued the *Hargraves* at $23,000, her cargo at $7,000, and the crew's personal effects at $500, for a total of $30,500. U.S. authorities placed the *Eagle Wing* in custody until a bond could be furnished. One of the attorneys representing the *Hargraves'* interests was James D. Dewell, Jr.[208]

Lawyers for the *Eagle Wing* contended their vessel was sailing on a starboard tack with spanker reefed and taken in, foresail reefed, and proceeding with her remaining lower and three head sails. Her lookout reported a vessel approaching head on, a little on the starboard bow, on a port tack with the wind free. The *Eagle Wing's* mate verified these findings. Knowing the other vessel was the burdened one and had to keep clear of him, he maintained his course. Soon after, the other ship allegedly changed course and went directly across the bows of the *Eagle Wing*, which held her course. The ships were so close to each other just before the course change that it was argued nothing could be done by the *Eagle Wing* to prevent the collision.[209]

The court had to decide the following: For the *Hargraves*, it was alleged that the ships were meeting with lights red to red and the *Eagle Wing* crossed her path. The *Eagle Wing's* position was that they were meeting green to green and the *Hargraves* crossed her bows. No collision would have occurred unless one of the ships crossed the path of the other. Under the Rules of Navigation, the *Eagle Wing*, sailing close-hauled, was the privileged vessel and was obliged to keep on course. But simply because she was favored with the presumption of having maintained course, it did not necessarily mean that she did.[210]

The court was of the opinion that only the men engaged in navigating the two vessels before the moment of impact were qualified to give an account of the collision. A single lookout was posted on both ships, and on both ships the mates were on duty and in charge of the watch. Two seamen manned the wheel of the *Eagle Wing*, while one sufficed for the *Hargraves*. The men at the *Eagle Wing*'s helm did not see the *Hargraves* until the actual collision and the *Hargraves'* helmsman was not examined. Both masters were below although, alerted to danger, they scrambled topside. Captain Chatfield arrived in time to see the collision as well as the lights and courses of both schooners before impact, but the *Eagle Wing*'s master was too late. Supposedly no other persons were on the decks.[211]

So the testimonies of the *Hargraves'* master, mate and lookout, along with those of the *Eagle Wing*'s mate and lookout, were the ones crucial to the matter. The court found that navigation of the *Hargraves* was entrusted to a competent mate, with the master present, both having had long experience in coastal navigation. An able seaman served as lookout, with another at the wheel. The ship was going at a reasonable speed and upon sighting the *Eagle Wing*, made the proper maneuver to give the privileged vessel more room.[212]

Although the mate and lookout of the *Eagle Wing* testified contrary to the above, evidence given by them in many important particulars was in conflict, and in some features it corroborated statements made by the *Hargraves'* crew. Furthermore, the court found that neither the mate nor the lookout was reliable as a navigator or witness and both were incompetent for the positions they held. The lookout was an 18-year-old boy who did not ship on as an able seaman. He had been aboard the schooner for six months, where he served on the master's watch and was described as a pet of the master. His prior experience was that of a mess boy on an ocean steamer. The court noted that for some unexplained reason he appeared to have been lookout on the mate's watch at the time of collision. But the mate testified that his lookout wasn't the boy but one of two Portuguese sailors on his watch who couldn't speak English. The mate said he couldn't understand this lookout when he reported a ship ahead. The mate had to go forward to see for himself.[213]

The *Eagle Wing*'s mate, the court noted, seemed to be a roaming individual. He had sought different types of work but most of his time was spent at sea. He had often acted as mate on smaller vessels but was not responsible for navigation. For this voyage he replaced a drunken mate. Although he had worked for the master several months before, he knew none of the crew, which was comprised of five Portuguese sailors and the boy. Of the Portuguese, only two had made more than one prior voyage on the *Eagle Wing*. After the collision, the mate stayed with the ship for several days in Newport News. Then he disappeared. Some weeks before the trial he was found. Pressed for details as to why he left the ship, he said, "I felt bad enough about this collision. It is the first collision I have ever had in all my going to sea, and I have not wanted to see anybody connected with it since it happened. I have done them injury enough, I suppose. I did not want anybody to come to me and say, 'Why did you do this?' and 'Why didn't you do that?' I have heard enough of that."[214]

The court considered that this statement could be an admission of responsibility for bringing about the collision. If not, the court said it shouldn't be difficult to establish the cause of the collision, especially when the mate, whom the judge described as unfit and inefficient, was in charge of navigation. Added to this, his lookout was either an inexperienced boy or a Portuguese whose language he couldn't understand.[215]

Another serious fault in the *Eagle Wing*'s case was that the mate was unlicensed, in violation of U.S. statutes. The court commented that it was highly probable he never would have been licensed. By not complying with the statute, a presumption was raised that this contributed to the collision unless it was overthrown by contrary evidence, which wasn't done. So the court found that the collision was caused by the *Eagle Wing*'s negligence and a decree was so entered.[216]

On appeal, the Circuit Court of Appeals reversed the decision. Then a rehearing of the reversal was granted in which the critical considerations were the credibility of the witnesses and the conflicts in their testimony. Two out of three judges reaffirmed that the *Eagle Wing* was solely at fault. Finally, the *Eagle Wing*'s owner filed a petition for certiorari (review) by the U.S. Supreme Court, which was denied on 4 January, 1909.[217]

THE *GENERAL E.S. GREELEY-MONTENEGRO*

Collision: On 14 December, 1910, the *General Greeley* was anchored about one mile northwest of *Pollock Rip Lightship* at the southeastern corner of Cape Cod. The schooner *Belle Halliday*, loaded with 480 tons of granite paving blocks for New York, drifted across the *Greeley*'s bow and struck her. The *Halliday* stove a hole in her own port bow and commenced taking on water. The *Greeley* lost all of her headgear. Before the collision, Captain Brown of the *Halliday* was hit on the head and seriously injured by a block from his spanker-boom tackle. He was taken into Boston by the steamer *H.F. Dimock*, to be treated at a hospital. The *Halliday*'s steward accompanied him. About an hour after the collision, the *Halliday* sank alongside the *Greeley*, going down directly on top of the *Greeley*'s ground tackle. The four remaining *Halliday* crewmen were taken aboard the *Greeley*. Before the *Greeley* could be towed out of the *Halliday*'s wreckage, the *Greeley* had to abandon her anchor and 30 fathoms of chain. Damages to the *Greeley* were estimated at $2,000. She arrived at Boston on the 15th for examination and repairs. On the 17th the U.S. derelict destroyer *Seneca* left New York for *Pollock Rip Lightship* to remove the wreck of the *Halliday*.[218]

SCHOONER *GENERAL E. S. GREELEY.*

Sale: The Maritime Transportation Co. of New York bought the *Greeley* in July, 1917. They sold her later that year to R. van Hemelryck & Co. of Paris, a French shipping firm. The schooner was turned over to her new owners in Algiers, Algeria. There she was rebaptized the *Montenegro*.[219]

Before beginning the strange tale of the *Montenegro*'s loss, I'd like to relate my personal experience regarding "The File of the *Montenegro*."

It was September, 1981, when I called the number of the French Naval Archives from a street phone booth in Paris. A poor telephone connection, the rapid-fire response given by a male voice in French, and a background din of traffic and other street noises were not music to my ears. I could scarcely hear, much less understand what was said and responded by shouting "Does anybody there speak English?" The man I was talking to told me to wait a moment. After a short while, another male voice asked what I wanted–in English. I gave him the background in two sentences and said I had a French Naval Archives file number for some material I wanted to review. He told me to come out to the Chateau de Vincennes–by metro if I didn't have a car.

Arriving at the Vincennes station, I was directed to the old Fort de Vincennes. There a soldier on guard duty sent me to another location a few blocks away. But it wasn't where I wanted to go. Asking questions, I learned that my original directions were correct. I went back to the soldier on guard duty and told him the Chateau de Vincennes was inside the enclosed property, just beyond the old Fort de Vincennes. He seemed surprised and somewhat incredulous but allowed me onto the premises.

Once inside the walls of the guarded area, I found French soldiers milling about everywhere. I soon arrived at an open courtyard with walls enclosing it. A sign in front of a building on one side of the courtyard identified it as part of the Chateau de Vincennes. I entered and was immediately intercepted by a man who asked what I wanted. I explained my purpose and he sent me to wait in a room upstairs.

It seemed to be a school room with several large desks and seats. As I entered, my footfalls resounded on the old wooden floor. The windows were covered by dark green shades, giving the room a gloomy atmosphere. Nobody else was there. I sat down at one of the desks.

Shortly thereafter I heard the "Marseillaise" sounding from the courtyard below. I moved quickly to the window and

Fort de Vincennes.

raised the shade. A square of inward-facing soldiers was standing at attention. Each side of the square had several lines of men, with one side being filled by a military band. They had their backs against the old brick wall of the fort. Flying high over the fort was the French "tricolore." After the music stopped, an officer came to the center of the square, made a short speech and called out a name. A soldier from the ranks stepped smartly forward and came to attention in front of the officer. The officer spoke a few words, pinned a medal on the soldier's chest and kissed him on both cheeks. Then the procedure was repeated with a few other soldiers. I couldn't believe what I was seeing. It was right out of "Beau Geste." As the "Marseillaise" struck up again, I had goose bumps. If a recruiting officer had been standing by, I would have signed up then and there for a hitch in the Foreign Legion. And I'm not even a Francophile.

The spell was broken when a young French matelot

(sailor) entered the room. This was the person who had invited me to come to Chateau de Vincennes. He was Olivier Leschallier De Lisle and he was serving his year of required military service in French Naval Archives at the Chateau. His English proficiency was good—helped by a visit to the U.S. during the previous summer. He asked again what I wanted. I explained in more detail, gave him the archives file number and said I would like to review the file. He excused himself for a time and came back about a half hour later carrying a large grey cardboard box. He opened it in front of me and brought out a stack of papers many inches thick. It was the file of the *Montenegro*.[220]

I spent two days looking it over. Then Olivier gave me a rough verbal summary of some pages where I had questions. Whatever pages I wanted to have copied were duplicated (at my expense of course). There was so much photocopying to be done that it wasn't ready when I had to leave at the end of the second day. But it was finished and mailed to my home in Virginia. I couldn't have had better cooperation, and I told Olivier this before I left. Olivier said I was lucky because it usually is necessary to obtain permission of the Office of the Navy to review files such as this, but nobody had objected.

I later called the two FBI agents stationed in Paris, whom I knew. They were serving there as legal attachés to the U.S. Embassy. Both expressed amazement that I was able to obtain access to the file on my own. The senior legal attaché, Mike Zinc, told me "We can't even get that."

The thick file of the *Montenegro* I examined was the result of an investigation by a four-man Board of Inquiry looking into the circumstances surrounding the loss of the ship and the actions of her commander. Testimony was obtained from members of the ship's crew and the gun crew. Except as noted elsewhere, the tale has been pieced together primarily from this file and no additional footnotes are listed for this source.

Destruction: In December, 1917, the schooner was awaiting a captain and crew in Algiers. She was to be towed across the Mediterranean to Marseille. Shortly after Christmas, Second Captain Charles Lemerle and Bos'n Jean Mattei reported for duty. They assisted a commission conducting the vessel's inspection, required before she could put to sea. The commission found there were no spare sails or rigging and recommended their procurement before sailing. But only a few spare coils of rope were actually obtained. The ship was loaded in Algiers with zinc ore, wine, horsehair and wool, all consigned to Georges Regis & Co. in Marseille.

Lemerle and Mattei were soon joined by a T.S.F. (wireless) telegraphist, five mariners, an apprentice and a ship's boy. But Lemerle, Mattei and one of the mariners, Aime Manya, who had formerly been a captain in the coasting trade, were the only ones with experience aboard a sailing ship. The designated captain never appeared. Lemerle was appointed permanent captain on 2 January and Manya was raised to second captain.

Answering a request from the Algiers Naval Command at this time, the navy department in Paris rescinded the order for the *Montenegro* to be towed to Marseille. Then four more men were added to the crew by the Algiers Flotilla, which provided for the mobile defense of the area. Of these, only one had ever worked on a sailing vessel and he had only been a fisherman. The civilian trade of another was that of men's hair stylist.

With the ship ready to leave on 28 January, 1918, a telegram from the navy department ordered the 4th special ordnance group, a twelve-man gun crew, to be embarked on the *Montenegro*. However, one of these men was hospitalized in Marseille, another in Algiers, and neither one ever made it aboard the schooner. Ensign Antoine Henri Niox-Chateau was in command of the gun crew. He supervised the mounting of four 75-mm rapid-fire cannons on deck and made sure they were concealed from view.

Along with the guns, a T.S.F. telegraph was to be installed.

A new apparatus was expected from France but it never arrived. At the last minute a telegraph set was requisitioned at the dock from another ship, the *Nelly II*. This telegraph used a 28-volt battery and had a very limited range, about 30 miles. It was installed on the *Montenegro* by the responsible service in Algiers. The schooner's T.S.F. Petty Officer Marcel Pleven talked to the telegraphist of the *Nelly II*, who told him that the battery had not been charged for some time. There was no time to charge it, but a test showed the set to be in good working order just before leaving Algiers.

On 5 February at 7:00 a.m. the *Montenegro* was towed out of port by two tugboats. An hour later outside the jetties she was taken in tow by the steam trawler *La Rosita*. At 5:00 p.m., some 40 miles out to sea, the trawler signaled the schooner to set her sails and at 5:40 p.m. the towing ceased.

A NNE course was steered in a light breeze and a speed of three to four knots was maintained. Captain Lemerle had received instructions from the Directorate of Shipping in Algiers specifying that the vessel should not pass within 30 miles of the (Spanish) Balearic Islands.

The wind died at 5:00 a.m. on the 7th and the vessel was nearly becalmed. Then about 6:30 a.m. cannon fire erupted from a large submarine that had surfaced 6,500 meters off the schooner's port quarter.[221] The *Montenegro* was its target. It kept up a barrage and closed rapidly on the schooner. At the first shot, Ensign Niox-Chateau called his gun crew to their combat positions where they hid themselves as best they could. Operating the range finder, Telemetrist Hamon reported distances to the submarine.

With almost no way on, the *Montenegro* was greatly encumbered and almost impossible to steer or maneuver. Stationary, she made an easy target. As a precaution, her boiler was lit in case the pumps were needed. The crew of sailors were at their posts for maneuvering duties. Because of the calm, they were available to carry ammunition up to the deck.

The submarine was firing from what was thought to be

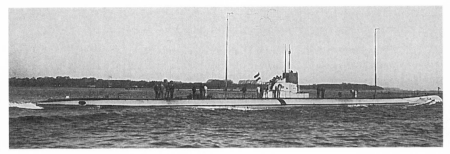

U-64 UNDERWAY IN APRIL, 1916.

two deck guns—77 and 105 mm cannons.[222] The shots, short at first, were rectified and soon bracketed the schooner. When the U-boat closed to 4,700 meters, Niox-Chateau gave the order to unmask the guns and open fire. The *Montenegro*'s shots were well adjusted. Now the submarine was bracketed. Using binoculars, the gun crew commander observed the impacts in the waters around the U-boat. He told Gunnery Petty Officer Second Class Jean Soulimant that the shooting was very good. The submarine withdrew at top speed, zigzagging as the range opened. Its sudden swerves threw the schooner's shots off. At 8,000 meters the bursts of the *Montenegro*'s shells could no longer be seen. Niox-Chateau ordered the firing stopped so as not to waste ammunition.

The submarine changed position relative to the schooner. It sailed out of the morning sun and approached to 6,000 meters. The *Montenegro* opened fire anew. Again the schooner's shots were well placed. And again the submarine withdrew, back into the sun. The routine was repeated a few times. The submarine stayed in the sun's azimuth and at the same time maintained the best possible axis for raining down destruction on the schooner. The U-boat nearly always positioned itself on the *Montenegro*'s beam. And its guns apparently had the greater range. But at long range they were unable to destroy the schooner. Hence the repeated sorties —always out of and back into the sun.

Although the *Montenegro* couldn't really maneuver during

the fight, she moved, mostly with the current. Her heading changed from north to south. This necessitated a change in tack.

The French strategy was to wait as the submarine approached. When the U-boat reached a certain range or its shells impacted closely, the schooner responded with heavy fire. This forced the U-boat to move off, disarranging its fire in turn.

About 8:00 a.m., after the submarine had been repulsed once again, the *Montenegro* ceased firing for the last time. The U-boat discharged ten more projectiles from long range and disappeared in the sun.

Telemetrist Hamon was convinced the submarine had been hit during the last exchange of shots. However, nobody aboard the schooner really knew whether it had submerged or had been sunk. A double watch was set to look for periscopes, U-boats or torpedos. All momentarily expected the arrival of a torpedo. But nighttime came and nothing had happened. This was thought by some to be proof that the submarine had been sunk.

The combat lasted from one and one-half to two hours or more, depending on who gave testimony later to the Board of Inquiry. The *Montenego* fired from 288 to 291 shells. Incoming shots from the submarine were estimated as numbering between 350 and 500. Approximately 20 of them hit the schooner's sails and rigging, putting holes in the sails and cutting several lines. Most of the rigging survived intact. But a jib downhaul and at least one shroud and one backstay were severed. Others were damaged. Six shells hit the hull and deck, all above the waterline, although one that burst in the lower hull was only a half meter above the water. A projectile passed through the foremast about eight meters above the deck. The spar deck was pierced on the starboard side forward; another blast was at the foot of the spanker mast in the rear; hatchway number two took a hit; and still another shot damaged the crew's quarters.

The shot on the spardeck exploded in bursts on deck and in the hold. On deck it wounded Seaman Pierre Crasto in the leg and lips. It knocked Second Captain Manya down and wounded him in the right leg with a flying piece of deck planking. In the hold it exploded amongst the wine casks, rupturing several of them. Another bursting shell bruised Seaman François Pappalardo and scorched his beard and hair. The ship's boy, Georges Ferrero, was bruised. One shell impacted alongside the schooner, sending up a shower of water that soaked several of the crew. Seamen François Romano and Auguste Fournier, both frightened, seized upon their wet clothing as an excuse to abandon their posts. They took refuge in the crew's quarters under pretext of changing to dry clothes. Their timing could not have been worse. They walked into a bursting shell. Romano was killed and Fournier seriously wounded in the head. All four men supplied by the Algiers Flotilla, Crasto, Pappalardo, Romano and Fournier were victims of the U-boat's gunfire. But not one of the gun crew was touched by it.

With his first awareness of the submarine, Telegrapher Pleven signaled "Hello" four times but received no response. As the action continued, he sent out "S.O.S. *Montenegro* shelled" three times before the shot landing on the spar deck blew out a corner of the T.S.F. cabin and cut the telegraph antenna. The geyser of water that soaked the crewmen also soaked the T.S.F. telegraph. Pleven made a provisional repair of the antenna and wiped off the telegraph. He continued to send S.O.S. messages at intervals during the battle but received no reply. After the combat ended, he made a permanent repair of the antenna.

Eight members of the gun crew had previously fought two battles against enemy submarines in 1917 while serving on the French steamers *Vaucluse* and *Chateau Latour*.[223] The *Montenegro*'s gun crew stood the fire fight with high spirit and morale, everyone performing his duties well. Ensign Niox-Chateau, who had never worked with this group before, said "I did not believe them capable of doing what they did."

Among the sailors, Second Captain Manya and Seamen Crasto and Pappalardo all stayed at their posts and resumed their duties soon after being wounded. Except for Romano and Fournier abandoning their posts, the remainder of the shiphandling crew conducted themselves correctly. Several had assisted in provisioning the guns.

Captain Lemerle's conduct was less commendable. At the commencement of the battle, he was quite normal. During combat, Niox-Chateau observed that the captain had become very nervous, speaking quickly and somewhat incoherently. Lemerle tried to involve himself in directing the shooting. He pulled the ensign by the arm and told him "Shoot but shoot so—smack inside. You will get them. You will get them." He was impatient to have the submarine sunk. Soon thereafter he started singing a sailor's chantey. At the first cessation in the firing, the captain gave a drink of vermouth to a few of the gunners. Niox-Chateau testified that he gave authorization—his men were very thirsty.

When the shooting started up again, the captain grew more excited. He began talking disagreeably. "The French Navy are all idiots; it is Napoleon who cheats us, Napoleon and Clemenceau." He spoke as if Napoleon were present. His manner was almost deranged. He quarreled with the wounded Pappalardo, whom he wanted to carry munitions. Second Captain Manya and Cook Joseph Gasperini intervened on behalf of the wounded sailor. Pappalardo later complained to Niox-Chateau that the captain had brutalized him. Second Captain Manya thought Lemerle had been drinking during the shooting. Ship's boy Ferrero thought he was drunk. Yet as the battle continued there was little attention paid to the captain or his behavior. After it ended his antics drew more notice. He made speeches to the air, gave seemingly unexecutable orders, sometimes speaking in English. Alone, he bound the mainsail flat, then the spanker. He took the wheel himself, putting it to port, then to starboard. He was always trying to tack in order to head north. He told Manya it was necessary to go north to stir the clod (the submarine).

One of the shells had burst in the ship's center topside to

port. Captain Lemerle went to the edge of the deck as if to inspect the damage. He climbed up on the railing, took a few steps along it and fell into the sea. He was able to reach up and grasp a line dangling overside. Hanging on with one arm, he alternated between trying to sing a sea chantey and calling out to Napoleon. He used his free arm to gesticulate.

The bos'n and one of the gun crew finally hoisted him back aboard ship. It was suggested he might want to go below to change. He went below but five minutes later was back on deck—completely naked. He called to Niox-Chateau, remarking that the ensign had expended a large amount of ammunition. Niox-Chateau replied, "You have called me to see this spectacle." The ensign turned his back and walked away.

Captain Lemerle went down to his quarters again where he put on an old shirt and pair of pants and returned to the deck. He promenaded from one end of the ship to the other with no apparent purpose in mind. He went below where he tried to prevent the wounded from obtaining dressings for their injuries. Niox-Chateau had to go below to insure access to the medicine chest.

Lemerle's attitude became increasingly belligerent towards his crew. He scolded everyone and appeared to be looking for a fight. Bos'n Mattei reported a matter to the captain that required action. Lemerle didn't seem to comprehend and gave no orders. Instead, he quarreled with the bos'n, making reference to "dirty Corsicans." Mattei told him he was unfit to command the ship. The captain knocked the bos'n's hat to the deck, then threw a punch at his head but missed. Mattei made no attempt to fight back. Ensign Niox-Chateau, who observed the fracas, called two gunners to separate the men.

It was obvious to all that Captain Lemerle was out of his senses and it was impossible to leave him in command of the ship. Manya told Niox-Chateau, "You take command or I will take it." Niox-Chateau said he would assume control but specified that this would be limited to the watch and the guns; Manya would be in charge of shiphandling. Niox-Chateau later testified that he knew the succession of command normally would fall to the second captain. But because of the special circumstances and submarine alert, he deemed it his duty to take command. He also considered that his rank was superior to that of the second captain, whose experience was only as a captain in the coastal trade.

The gun-crew commander told Captain Lemerle, "Go down to your cabin, I am taking command." Two men from the gun crew escorted Lemerle to his quarters. But with the double watch for U-boats, and the gunners at the ready, no crew could be spared to watch the captain. Soon he was back on deck promenading anew. He cried out, gesticulated, and uttered ethnic slurs against southern Frenchmen and Corsicans. Again he was taken below. And the procedure was repeated a few more times. It was impossible to keep him in his cabin. During his sojourns on deck, he attempted to seize the wheel from Apprentice Frederic Cayla; he insulted Manya, claiming the second captain could not tack in a dead calm; and he threatened Ferrero, who was at the wheel and who had to run away to avoid being hit. When he wanted to climb on the sail locker, Niox-Chateau threatened to have him locked up. He ignored the threat and continued as before. He handled the jibs and struck the boom, all the while dancing and singing "the Tipperary" and some opera airs. Niox-Chateau testified before the Board that the captain's conduct was scandalous in view of the presence of one dead and several wounded seamen. Niox-Chateau finally ordered Lemerle to be secured in the rope locker down in the hold. Supposedly he could not escape from there, although some testimony asserted that he did. Regardless, the lockup did not stop him from howling and singing. Later in the evening he was released to sleep in his own quarters.

The next day, when the captain appeared on deck, he said he had a bad headache and a shellburst in his head. At dinner he took a little drink and showed some new excitement. The following day his behavior was generally back to normal, although T.S.F. Petty Officer Pleven said he didn't talk much and was somewhat taciturn. Petty Officer Second Class Soulimant expressed his opinion that the captain had no recollection of what he had done during or after the battle.

The Board of Inquiry established that Captain Lemerle and Bos'n Mattei had spent 40 days in Algiers together just before the *Montenegro* sailed and that they had been on good terms with each other. Mattei said he never noticed anything abnormal in the captain's prior behavior.

Testifying before the Board, Lemerle said he could not remember how he fell into the sea nor why his command was removed.

The Board took notice that the captain had a drinking habit as set forth in his military record, to wit: In the autumn of 1917 he was a lieutenant in the French Navy aboard the auxiliary transport *Jules Henri* at Port Said. At that time he was disciplined with 15 days arrest for an illegal absence of three hours, repeated intoxication, acting incorrectly to his commanding officer and being deficient in his duties, specifically creating a danger to his ship. In this last instance, he disregarded orders by smoking on the deck of his ship, an oiler, thereby risking an explosion. The punishment also provided that if he did not resign from the navy within 15 days he was to be reduced in rank to petty officer. Finally he was sent back to France. His service record at that time disclosed that he was 35 years old; he had rendered service to the state for one year; and he was a veteran of seven and one-half years as an oceangoing merchant captain.

During the next few days the *Montenegro* experienced very light breezes alternating with periods of dead calm. The schooner's speed was very slow, two knots or less. Since she had remained in close proximity to the area of combat all this time without having been attacked or even having had a single alert, it was thought to be added proof that the submarine had been sunk.

On the afternoon of the day of battle, smoke from a steamer appeared on the horizon. In the next two days convoys were sighted as close as 15 miles away. Pleven's telegraphic requests for assistance went unanswered in each instance. Romano was buried at sea on the morning of the 8th. Later that afternoon, *Minorca*, in the Balearic chain, was sighted. It remained in view through the 10th. On the 9th, with the air and sea calm, the ship would not steer. A sounding of the hold determined she had taken on appreciable water. The pumps were started and engineman Jean Pasqualini found them working well. They raised a meter or so of water from the hold each day for two days.

Some repairs were effected during this period of good weather. Most of the holes in the deck and sides were covered with canvas and pieces of planking were nailed over them. The only able-bodied men in the shiphandling crew available for this duty were Bos'n Mattei, seaman Stoker Napoleon Giafferi, apprentice Cayla and ship's boy Ferrero. The gun crew also gave a hand in repairing the holes on deck.

Second Captain Manya testified that the only spars they might have used to strengthen the pierced foremast were five capstan bars that seemed to be too short. If used, they would have immobilized the foresail, whose hoops holding the sail to the mast had to slide along the length of the mast. Furthermore, the mast's supporting shrouds, stays, and base were undamaged. Niox-Chateau, Manya and Mattei agreed that strengthening the foremast seemed superfluous since the projectile hole didn't appear to compromise the mast's solidity in any dangerous way.

The broken backstay was repaired and Mattei assigned Giafferi to splice the jib downhaul. Nothing was mentioned in the proceedings about fixing the severed shroud. Lemerle, Niox-Chateau and Manya all testified that they judged the lower shrouds and rigging to be solid enough to continue sailing.

Bos'n Mattei attested that before departing Algiers he told Captain Lemerle it was necessary to take up the slack in the lower shrouds. Lemerle allegedly told Mattei it wasn't possible to do this because they were shorthanded. Nevertheless, the bos'n said he personally had tightened the lower mizzenmast shrouds. Upon questioning, Mattei admitted that nobody had gone aloft to repair the rigging after the battle. Nor did he request any assistance from the gun crew for other repairs.

Giafferi testified that sometime after the combat Mattei thought he detected movement of the mizzenmast. Giafferi was sent to assess the strength of this mast on which he reported favorably. Giafferi added that he and the bos'n checked all the lower shrouds and found them to be in good shape.

Niox-Chateau stated that the ship experienced a strong shaking aft when a shell exploded there. No determination could be made whether it caused any breach or leak. On the whole, Niox-Chateau seemed to think that the damages were not critical and the vessel was in fairly good shape. However, Captain Lemerle observed in his sea report that the *Montenegro* had suffered from the firing of its own guns. She had absorbed very strong vibrations that carried through her hull and masts.

Captain Lemerle asked Niox-Chateau on the 8th and again on the 9th to restore his command. The ensign refused these requests. However, he relented somewhat, and allowed the captain to return to service, but only as an officer of the watch and only when he, Niox-Chateau, was on duty.

Seizing the opportunity, Lemerle set a reveille call for himself at 4:00 a.m. to take up his watch. The bos'n said that after this moment the captain calmed down and abused nobody any longer. Mattei also related that two days after the battle the captain wanted to tack with the wind ahead, which was alternately blowing from one side to the other. The order was executed to please Lemerle but two hours later Niox-Chateau put the ship back on its original course.

The good weather continued until the 12th when the sea rose along with a fresh breeze. Although the wind died, the sea remained high. About 5:00 p.m. on the 13th a strong wind started blowing from the northwest and the waves grew larger. The wind increased in intensity so that by midnight the schooner was pitching and rolling heavily. The *Montenegro* was making about seven and one-half knots. Her position was approximately 50 miles from Marseille. A little before midnight the bos'n and his crew began taking in the jibs. At 12:30 a.m. on the 14th, while preparing to haul down the flying jib, the working crew heard an ominous crack overhead. The foremast broke near the projectile hole. Crew members ran aft as the mast oscillated several times before falling into the sea on the starboard side. It was held alongside by the shrouds and stays that hadn't broken. As it fell, it carried away the mainmast's topmast and stays of the jibs. It also shook the mainmast shrouds severely. The mainmast's topmast dangled along the mainmast, hanging by its backstays. It battered against the mainmast from one side to the other in the wind and rolling sea. The lower shrouds of all the masts had too much slack now if not before, particularly those of the mainmast. The masts were working in their mast steps below.

A port tack was tried but the ship steered badly without headsails, to say nothing of the foremast dragging ahead on the starboard side. Lemerle, back in service as an officer of the watch, declared it necessary to heave to, which was done.

Early in the morning, the boiler was lit to use steam power for hoisting sail in order to maneuver. At 6:00 a.m. the spanker sail was raised. With great difficulty, it was backed completely so as to bear off (pivot the ship) and run with the wind aft. If successful, this would lessen the strain on the masts and might take them to Corsica. But the maneuver did not come off very well.

An attempt was made to bring the foremast back on board in order to improve the steering. This too was unsuccessful.

A line fouled in a block aloft was creating problems. Lemerle offered to climb up and clear it. Niox-Chateau prohibited him from doing this, saying it was too dangerous. Under the prevailing conditions, nobody else could do it either.

The spanker sail was necessary to maintain the ship's heading, now into the seas, but with the weather worsening the sail was under too great a strain. At 10:00 a.m. two reefs were taken in it. About an hour later the sail tore in two.

The schooner yawed back and forth and heaved to very poorly. Oscillations increased in the mainmast, and in the other masts to a lesser degree, as slack in the shrouds and stays grew greater. The masts moved in one direction, only to be abruptly stopped by the restraining lines and then jerked back in the other direction.

Finally, about 1:00 p.m. the mainmast snapped, but without detaching itself completely. It acted like a balancing pole, secured loosely at the mizzenmast, and hammering that mast with every roll of the ship. Soon after, the mizzenmast broke, striking the spankermast when it fell. The mizzenmast's topmast landed in the midst of the spankermast rigging, and with every roll of the ship the integrity of the spankermast deteriorated. About 1:40 pm. the spankermast broke off. The *Montenegro* was now completely disabled.

The destruction on high also affected the schooner's firepower on deck. When the mainmast fell, the platform under the forward portside cannon was loosened. After several rolls, the gun plunged into the sea. The other cannons were also damaged by falling debris and movement of the ship. Foresights, elevation readings and hammers were broken; traversing handwheels were torn out. The sea took care of some loose materiel on deck such as tool boxes, lookout paraphernalia and masks that were swept away.

According to Niox-Chateau, after the mizzenmast fell, liferafts and lifeboats were launched to prevent their destruction by a falling spankermast.

The ship had suffered extensive damage. With the masts gone, she no longer steered and she shipped great quantitites of water, mostly on deck. In the hold, the several casks of wine that had burst during the fighting became unwedged. With every roll of the ship they smashed against the sides of the hull.

The toppling of the masts brought with it some personal injuries, largely among the gun crew. Telemetrist Hamon was thrown to the deck and injured his knee. Gun Layer Quelfeter was hit on the head by a falling block. Niox-Chateau was injured in the head and small of the back when the spanker mast came down, and was forced to his berth by the injuries. At this time he restored command of the *Montenegro* to Captain Lemerle, and the captain proved himself worthy. Everyone questioned by the Board of Inquiry spoke highly of his actions in the emergency. Niox-Chateau said of him, "I ought to point out this officer's splendid conduct during the time of the wreck; he did everything to redeem his prior weakness, giving everyone an example of courage, coolness and good humor. When we were disabled, he remained standing up all night, giving a hand to all, encouraging everybody, going forward to the pumps frequently despite serious danger from materiel rolling about on deck."

Captain Lemerle saw to it that all discernible holes on deck were plugged as best possible and the pumps ran continuously. This was necessary since the ship was being swept by the seas. The repairs held up, the pumps did their job, and water diminished in the hold. However, distress flares were lit at 6:00 p.m.

About 2:00 a.m. on the 15th, the pumps stopped working. The steam injector of the boiler malfunctioned and would not feed. Efforts to correct the problem weren't effective. The fire in the boiler was allowed to go out. Water mounted in the hold. The Board of Inquiry reported that the sailing ship was at the mercy of the waves and there wasn't anything to be done about it.

Looking over the deck early in the morning, Captain Lemerle found it too obstructed for safety. He ordered the men of the gun crew to jettison all materiel on deck, including the other three guns. Petty Officer Second Class Soulimant, silently disagreeing with the order, went to Niox-Chateau's quarters. The gun crew chief, still in his berth from his injuries, also believed it necessary to retain the guns as long as possible. Nevertheless, he told Soulimant that if the captain thought they were impeding passage on deck, the gun crew must begin by jettisoning the remaining forward gun but might try to keep the two rear ones. The rear cannons had suffered less damage.

Upon arriving back on deck, Soulimant found that the gun crew had already loosened the platform of one of the rear guns. At the same time, about 7:30 p.m., smoke was sighted on the horizon. Soulimant stopped all attempts to rid the deck of guns and rewedged the rear gun platform himself.

A distress flag was raised on the *Montenegro*. The signal was observed by the unknown ship, which altered her course and closed on the schooner. She was the English minesweeping vessel HMS *Petunia*. The Frenchmen referred to her as a gunboat. She had been zigzagging her way from Phillipville (now Skikda, Algeria) to Marseille.[224]

Captain Lemerle was the only one on the schooner who spoke English. Moreover, he considered it his duty to make the English commander aware of the *Montenegro*'s critical situation and to try to convince him to tow the schooner. When the gunboat drew close, Lemerle was given permission to come aboard. After a brief conversation, the British captain agreed to try towing the sinking vessel. Lemerle thought the *Montenegro*'s wounded would fare better on the gunboat. He passed the order to have them removed to the HMS *Petunia*. Lt. McClelland, the *Petunia*'s executive officer, left to pick them up from the schooner in his ship's lifeboat. At 8:30 a.m. he boarded the *Montenegro* to take off seven of her crew. Lemerle was very disagreeably surprised to see the lifeboat return to the gunboat with no wounded aboard. Instead, there were five healthy members of his own crew: T.S.F. Petty Officer Pleven, Engineman Pasqualini, Seamen Luciani and

Giaferri, and Apprentice Cayla. The gun crew carpenter, Alexandre, and one other gun crewman rounded out the passenger list.[225]

Captain Lemerle then proposed to return to the *Montenegro* with the healthy men in his crew, but the five had no intention of going back to the doomed schooner. They hid themselves on the *Petunia*. Lemerle tried to find them with the assistance of Alexandre and an English second class petty officer but without success. He now found himself in a most awkward position. The engineman could be very helpful to the towing operation. What to do? Lemerle finally decided to ask the English captain for an engineman. He said he made this request "with great dignity." The English captain obliged, but time was passing and the English were anxious to get on with the towing. Lemerle was taken back to the schooner so the operation could start. With him came a towline, an English officer and an English engineroom artificer. Niox-Chateau attested that his two gun crewmen were left aboard the *Petunia* due to Captain Lemerle's abrupt departure. He also testified that Engineman Pasqualini's absence was particularly resented.[226]

The English artificer wasn't able to reactivate the boiler, so it wasn't possible to make the pumps work, but thanks to the presence of the gun crew and the few healthy schooner crewmen still on board, towing could begin. A towing hawser was tied to the *Montenegro*'s cable, and wreckage along her sides was cut away. By 10:00 a.m. towing commenced. Of course, zigzagging couldn't be carried out in this condition.[227]

The weather was already bad, and in the afternoon it changed for the worse. Strong northwest winds began to blow again and the sea rose. Waves swept continuously over the schooner's decks, and the *Montenegro* was taking in more water. Water in the after part of the hold was nearly three meters deep and up forward it was more than two and one-half meters. The English commander signaled that if the waves became any larger he would have to stop towing. He also cautioned that it would be imprudent to remain on board during the night.

Captain Lemerle said he sought the advice of the gun crew chief, the second captain, the bos'n, and men of the schooner's shiphandling and gun crews. They were unanimous in their agreement to leave the ship. This decision was signaled to the *Petunia*, which let go the towline shortly after 4:00 p.m. The British vessel came to windward of the schooner and stood by to take off the crew.[228]

Captain Lemerle then asked permission of the English captain and Niox-Chateau to remain on board alone overnight. Niox-Chateau insisted strongly that this would be a useless sacrifice seeing the state of the schooner. He pointed out that the captain's duty lay in transferring to the gunboat with the others.

Lt. McClelland directed the rescue. It was conducted with the gunboat's whaleboat, which was a steadier platform in the high sea–a boon for the wounded. Orders passed on from the English commander expressly forbade taking anything from the *Montenegro*, including personal effects. Undoubtedly this was prompted by space limitations aboard the English vessel. The lightly wounded were removed first. Niox-Chateau went along on the second trip. On the third and final passage, Lemerle, Soulimant, and the seriously wounded Fournier were evacuated. Twenty-three hands in all (counting those in hiding on the minesweeper) were transferred without mishap. Rescue operations were completed about 5:00 p.m. The *Montenegro* was approximately 40 miles south of Cape Sicie in the south of France.[229]

When they left the schooner, she had sunk well below her freeboard marks. Captain Lemerle told the Board he expected that the *Montenegro* would founder during the night, but he hoped the schooner would last until daylight. He attributed her condition to serious damage received in combat, which he said contributed to her loss of navigability and resistance to bad weather and the sea.

Lemerle asked the English captain to stand by the schooner because he hoped they might be able to return on board the next day. The English captain complied for several hours. At 8:00 p.m. the French torpedo boat *Catapulte* came on the scene and exchanged signals with the *Petunia*. At 9:00 p.m. the *Catapulte* departed for Toulon and the *Petunia* proceeded to Marseille. She arrived at her berth there at 5:00 a.m. on the 16th. Niox-Chateau said the crew was well-treated aboard the *Petunia*.[230]

Three of the *Montenegro* survivors were taken ashore at 11:00 a.m. (presumably the more seriously injured) and the rest at 12:45 p.m.[231] The *Petunia* took on coal and depth charges and her decks were washed down. Next morning on the 17th she sailed out on convoy duty.[232]

The Board of Inquiry convened in Marseille to look into the loss of the *Montenegro*. Depositions were taken and witnesses interrogated from 18 to 21 February, 1918. The investigation covered a broad range of subjects, including measures taken by the gun crew to immobilize their weapons before abandoning the schooner. Niox-Chateau and Soulimant were questioned in detail about these matters. They explained that most of the loose materiel on deck had been swept away by the sea. But spare cases, machine guns, etc., were left in the paint locker. This equipment wasn't placed in a completely secure site because of the swift evacuation; the danger in trying to store materials in certain areas of the ship; and because of the proximity of land. If the ship was still afloat the following day, these items might be recovered.

Soulimant stated that what was transportable was lowered into the magazine. A diagram was prepared outlining where everything was stored. Much of the materiel was effectively immobilized because of damage, as with the cannons. Machine-gun breeches and spare parts were not jettisoned since the ship might be saved.

Niox-Chateau was asked about the destruction of documents, instructions and journals. He said he took care of the gun crew's documents and those from the Directorate of Shipping, such as orders for convoys, entrance to ports, etc. He placed them in a packet and dropped them in the sea before leaving the schooner. He did not get involved with books and journals.

The Board wanted to know what had been done to preserve the integrity of the other three masts after the foremast broke. Did those holding responsibility think to install a stay for the mainmast, which was supporting all the other masts? Answers were profuse to the effect that this would have required sending someone up the mast under the most adverse conditions of weather and sea. It was an absolutely perilous situation produced by: great movements of the vessel; oscillations of the mast, abruptly stopping and jerking back; and the topmast hanging down and beating against the mainmast. Anyone ordered up the mast would not be able to cling to it and would risk being thrown down at any moment. The men were inexperienced and it would have been life-threatening to send someone aloft under those conditions.

Captain Lemerle was asked why he hadn't attempted to preserve the rear masts by running before the wind immediately after the foremast broke instead of waiting all night. His answer was that he hadn't thought of this maneuver until daylight.

He also was questioned about his sea report. He stated that he had used information furnished by the second captain and he consulted the mate's logbook. He later talked to Niox-Chateau, who approved the report after some slight modifications concerning changes in tacks at the time of combat. Next the Board wanted to know why he had not advised that his command had been taken away from him during the greatest part of the voyage. As he replied:

> *If I have given incorrect information in my first deposition in responding to the title of captain, it is merely a question of self-respect and because I was ashamed to say that my command had been taken away. I knew well enough that the matter would become clear because Mr. Niox, as a military man, was obliged to render an account and I did not dare to confess myself.*

On 1 March, 1918, Captain Lemerle was furnished copies

of all depositions given to the Board so that he might prepare a defense in writing. He delivered this defense the next day in the form of a five-page letter. The letter follows except for one paragraph whose contents already have appeared:

To the President of the Board of Inquiry re the four-masted schooner *Montenegro*[233]

> *Commander:*
>
> *My testimony clearly shows that I was engaged by my company as second captain to deliver the vessel in tow from Algiers to Marseille. When authorities in Paris appointed me permanent captain on 2 January, nothing had changed. But if I had known I was being sent to sea with the crew I had, I would not have accepted the command in spite of the loyalty I had shown the shipowners.*
>
> *Being the only officer on board at Algiers and taking over a vessel that hardly was French, I had to contend with numerous problems. I had to take care of commercial matters and at the same time tend to matters concerning the ship. I was backed up only by a bos'n who always showed antipathy towards me, although I don't know why. This man was always insubordinate to my orders, capitalizing on me being the only Breton aboard while he and the rest of the men were Corsicans. I would have dealt severely with him and ordered him off the vessel; but where would a replacement be found in view of the dearth of available men and what would the company have said? It was better to suffer and wait for the captain who was to take command of the ship, and for whom I waited every day. Unfortunately, he never appeared.*
>
> *Thus, in spite of everything, I put the ship in order at Algiers and got it ready to go to sea. However, a few days before departure, a gunnery officer and his crew came aboard by order of the navy. The situation, therefore, was completely changed. With sailors (of the navy) accustomed to running the usual risks from submarines, we took to sea with a ship armed with 4 guns, 12 gunners (actually 10) and the gunnery officer. My men made me*

understand that they had not been employed for such a mission and that I should not leave under these conditions. Morally, however, I could not refuse to get underway but I would have left feeling better had my crew been volunteers.

Beginning then, I always had a feeling of remorse in leading a crew on a mission for which they had not signed up. I believed then, and I still believe, that I took too great a responsibility with respect to my crew. It is true that all went relatively well, as our only casualties in battle were one killed and one severely wounded. But what would have happened to my men in case of defeat or if they had been captured by the enemy?

That is why all these responsibilities came to mind like a flash of lightning at the time of the attack on the 7th. I looked upon myself as a sort of criminal. The shots, which I had never experienced before, affected me opposite from what I would have expected. I have always been considered to be fearless and unconcerned about danger but I lost my head.

Anything I might say about that day of the 7th would be useless as everything happened like a nightmare and I remember absolutely nothing. I have read and reread the testimony of Mr. Niox-Chateau with regret and I wonder at what point I would have been so deranged as to mouth such inconsistencies. It is all in such contrast to my normal character that I could not be more upset.

Putting that fateful day aside, I pride myself for always having gone out of my way for the gunnery ensign. I anticipated his every desire, giving him every possible comfort aboard the sailing vessel. I put my cabin at his complete disposal beginning with the departure from Algiers. For myself, I slept on a couch in the salon. I do not believe that Mr. Niox-Chateau could complain about my courtesy and hospitality.

In my defense, I can do no more than repeat that on the 7th I was in a state of unconsciousness and am unable to remember anything.

I want to point out one very inaccurate item in the bos'n's testimony when he says that two days after the battle I tacked at an inappropriate time. The truth is this. I was not in command anymore, and that afternoon when I was on the poop deck I saw the second captain vainly try to tack. The bos'n, during his watch from 4 to 6 p.m., also tried to tack but didn't succeed. At 6 p.m. both went below to eat. It is true that it was almost calm but as we were proceeding on a south-southeast heading, I asked the ensign's permission to try my turn. He granted permission and, assisted by some crewmen, I succeeded in tacking. As Mr. Niox-Chateau was present, he can certify the success of my ship handling. As the bos'n said, the maneuver wasn't possible. I find it painful that a petty officer whom I always considered unworthy of his duties permits himself to judge my ability as a sailor. I was schooled by eminent officers, my father among others, who always considered me to be an expert seaman. I do not believe that any man aboard could honestly say that I was unqualified or whatever in the handling and command of the ship. This simple fact shows the state of the bos'n's thoughts about me and the antipathy he showed me. Anyway, I never mistreated him nor any of the rest of the crew. I have absolutely nothing to criticize myself about in this respect.

As to the means taken to put the mast and rigging back together after the battle, I can say they were limited due to the lack of material aboard ship. Mr. Niox-Chateau told me on the 8th that he had relieved me of command. I asked him to reconsider but he told me he would only authorize me to take the watch from 4 to 8 a.m. under his orders. During the days that followed I begged him to give me back the handling and direction of the ship but he reiterated he would keep command as far as Marseille. He also told the second captain and bos'n that they did not have to obey my orders any more. Under these circumstances how could I act? Did I morally have the right to give counsel to an ensign? Wouldn't that have led him to believe that I seemed to belittle his ability as a sailor? Who knows if he would not have taken the advice as an insult? My role was difficult and I suffered for it since we had several days of good weather after the battle when we would have been able to do something.

I know the foremast was pierced right through about eight meters above the deck. It had lost much of its strength and with a strong gust of wind, it would be in danger. To lessen the stress on it, I would have lowered the topmast to where it joins the foremast at the front of the damaged part. Then with the cargo boom that was on deck, I would have been able to strengthen the rear part. And I would have used rope (in place of the mast), allowing me to bend (tie on) the foresail. It is true that the flying jib, standing jib and (normal use of) the foremast would have been done away with. But by taking two reefs in the spanker, it (the ship) would have been balanced again and we would have been able to navigate. It is true that the work would have been hard but with the help of the crew it would not have been impossible. If I had suggested such a thing, the bos'n would have said I was a fool. He was happy not to have to take orders from me anymore and he had already told the men not to listen to me. Afterward, I would have tightened the lower shrouds where there was some slack. And with the steel wire I had from Algiers, we would have been able to make four or five pairs of new stays to replace those that were damaged. We also had some new rope for the hawsers to strengthen the rigging. Those were the ideas that came to me but I understood Mr. Niox-Chateau's attitude. He knew what he had to do and he didn't want to have anything more to do with me. Therefore, I had nothing to do but keep quiet, remain in my enforced state of inaction and suffer again in silence.

I am surprised that during those days the second captain and the bos'n didn't take more initiative. I still can see a spanker lanyard on the starboard side completely separated by a shell. They passed by it more than ten times a day but the lanyard wasn't ever changed.

I am also surprised that during the night of the 13th-14th, when the wind began to blow quite briskly about 9:30 p.m., the watch officer didn't think about lowering the flying and standing jibs to help the foremast at that time. These are the things that absorbed me because I loved my ship and it will be the regret of my whole life to have been involved in the loss of such a beautiful schooner. Unfortunately I was powerless at the time and looked upon as a zero. . . .

In conclusion, even when I took command again, my crew did not help me. During the whole critical time that passed after we lost the masts, only the ensign's staff remained loyal to me and showed some respect.

At the time when there was no mast at all and believing the men's lives to be in danger, I ordered the abandonment of the ship and the preparation of the life rafts to receive everyone. The bos'n and two of my men were the first on the rafts. I know that it took two men to clear the length of the broadside so it would not be smashed. But I do not believe it was the place of a bos'n to remain in a lifeboat from 2 p.m. to 7 a.m. the next morning when his help would have been more valuable aboard ship.

This, Commandant, is what remains to bring to your attention. I would like to have a more auspicious way of redeeming my weakness of the 7th. But the war continues, and if the country has need of volunteers to arm ships like the Montenegro, I would be obliged if you would recommend me to the navy so that I can restore myself completely in an impressive way so that the name of an honorable family and the honor of oceangoing captains will not be tarnished.

Given at Marseille, 2 March, 1918

The Captain of the *Montenegro*
C. Lemerle

The Board came to several conclusions. It considered that

the *Montenegro* left Algiers in a defective condition. The crew did-n't know anything about handling a sailing vessel. The men sent by the Algiers Flotilla were, save for one, just as ignorant about this as the others.

The bos'n had not performed his duties in restoring the rigging after the attack nor in proposing repairs of the masts to his superiors.

Responsible authorities aboard ship did not effect dam-age-control measures to restore the vessel between the end of the battle and the advent of the storm. A bit of sea sense or more familiarity with the handling of a sailing vessel would probably have saved the ship.

Captain Lemerle, by his conduct during combat, rendered himself unworthy to be commander. The Board considered that his provisional title be lifted from him. However, due to his favor-able actions at the time of the wreck, the Board thought he should be permitted to continue as a captain in the merchant service.

Reprimands were requested for Seamen Luciani and Giafferi, Apprentice Cayla, and Engineman Pasqualini. It was noted that T.S.F. Petty Officer Pleven's stripes obliged him to behave with more dignity. A proposal was made to reward Second Captain Manya, who stayed at his post despite wounds and con-ducted himself well during the battle and the wreck. Also noted for staying at their posts despite being slightly wounded and for not attempting to save themselves by going aboard the gunboat were Seamen Crasto, Pappalardo and ship's boy Ferrero.

Niox-Chateau recommended citations for every man on his gun crew for their performance during the battle and evacua-tion. He recommended Soulimant for promotion to petty officer.

The rear admiral in command at Marseilles agreed with all of the above. He further recommended that Pleven be stripped of his rating. He commented that when Niox-Chateau assumed com-mand, the gun crew chief also assumed responsibility for execut-ing damage-control measures to preserve the ship. His nonperformance of these measures at the very least indicated a lack of fore-sight and perhaps of judgment.

The rear admiral also noted that while Captain Lemerle's actions were laudable during the last hours preceding evacuation, they didn't sufficiently attenuate the unworthiness of his conduct during the battle.

Under Secretary of the Navy Jules Cels administered a censure against Luciani, Giafferi and Cayla, which was to be placed on their record. If they came under any further censure, serious punishment would result.

Under Secretary Cels admonished Niox-Chateau: for exceeding his authority in taking command of the sailing vessel; for not exercising damage-control measures; and for not utilizing his military personnel in default of a shiphandling crew he had declared incompetent. Nevertheless, for his very positive military qualities shown in combat, he was cited with the Order of the Division.

As for Captain Lemerle, the under secretary suspended his captaincy for one year for causing disorder aboard his ship during combat with a submarine.

The under secretary pointed out to the Algiers naval commander that his command had completed the *Montenegro*'s staffing with personnel incapable of serving on a sailing vessel. This was done after previous notification that the schooner would not be towed. Attention was called to the necessity of assigning competent personnel for duty, particularly on small ships.

Regarding Engineman Jean Pasqualini's punishment, no further record was located in the file. He was not cited in the directive from the under secretary concerning Luciani, Giafferi and Cayla. Nor was he cited with Pleven by the rear admiral, although this officer agreed he should be reprimanded. But, as stated before, Pasqualini's hiding aboard the *Petunia* was particularly resented. It was Pasqualini who was most familiar with the steam machinery that ran the pumps, and if he had been working together with the

English engineroom artificer they might have been able to get the boiler operating and save the ship. It would seem that Pasqualini must have received some special punishment for abandoning the *Montenegro*.

But this is only the French and English story. What was happening on the other side?

The following action of the German U-boat, *U-64*, under command of Kapitaenleutnant Robert Wilhelm Moraht, was reported in German military records for 7 and 8 February, 1918:

7 February. At dawn during return trip southeast of the Balearic Islands, had 2-hour firefight with heavily armed sailing ship. The enemy guns were substantially superior to the U-boat's weapons, enemy fire control was excellent. Impact of projectiles was in very close proximity to the U-boat, which for its part achieved five hits on the sailing ship at distances up to 8 hm (sic). After having fired 218 grenades with just one 10.5 cm gun, the *U-64* commandant disengaged from the fight, which appeared to be futile. The U-boat's torpedos were fired (in a previous action). The ship was the armed French four-masted fore-and-aft schooner *Montenegro* "(U-boat trap?)" that, according to official reports from Italy, sank anyway as the weather turned bad.

8 February. South of Sardinia the Italian sailing vessels *Emma-Felice*, 128 tons, and *Agnese Madre*, 235 tons, were blown up.[234]

Kapitaenleutnant Moraht wrote a book about his U-boat experiences in the war. Although he didn't name the *Montenegro* per se, there is no question that she was his intended victim in the following battle he described in his book:

Since all torpedoes had been used up, we started on the return trip.

Southeast of the Balaeric Islands, just before daybreak the next morning, we intercepted a big four-masted gaff-rigged schooner which did not heave to after we fired a warning shot. Consequently, we commenced firing for effect with only a slight narrowing of range. This developed into a surface fire fight. At the start, our port side was facing northeast; then we moved southeast of the target so we eventually had the sun at our back.

The sailing vessel commenced firing from three guns at a distance of about 8,000 meters. From the splashes, it was clear that the caliber of the guns was about 15 centimeters. Now we were sure it was a U-boat trap. At 8,000 meters range, the schooner's shells were falling short while ours were hitting but without apparent effect. With the low rising and blinding sun behind us, I decided to turn towards port and slowly advance on the schooner. We soon observed a hit towards the front of the enemy ship. Apparently blinded, the schooner ceased fire but started again at a distance of 5,500 meters. Now his salvos, quickly following one after another, were blanketing the area. We had many impacts in very close proximity, some of them only ten meters away.

It was a situation which no U-boat should generally allow itself to be drawn into because any hit would, in all probability, sink the vessel. I immediately stopped firing, came about and set off on a high speed zigzag course in the direction of the sun to get out of range. The sailboat followed with a remarkable speed in spite of the prevailing low wind. In all probability it had a motor.

Fighting with the sun at our back was so advantageous that I decided on another sortie, trusting in our shooting accuracy but at a greater range. On a westward course that was almost parallel (to the enemy), we stopped both our diesels and were just about to start the electric motor (in order to move slowly) when the sailboat started firing again with a well-aimed rapid fire blanketing attack. So we came about again and I gave up all further attacks. We resumed our regular cruising speed on an eastern course while the sailboat continued on its original westward course. On his deck, we could make out a number of uniformed crew.

As far as this incident was concerned, the Admiralty later noted that since the commander realized his artillery was not

KAPITÄNLEUTNANT MORAHT.

equal to the enemy's, it was senseless to expose the U-boat to enemy fire for a long time. However, the commander's war diary was declared to be very readable and the commentary closed with the words "ship and crew have done an excellent job."

As noted in Moraht's report, *U-64* had good hunting the day after the encounter with the *Montenegro:* "South of Sardinia, we sank two small Italian sailboats, the *Emma-Felice* of 128 tons and the *Agnese Madre* of 235 tons."[235]

There is another story that needs telling, which could relate to the battle with the *Montenegro,* and may add to the already antic adventures of schooner and submarine. At some unspecified time Kapitaenleutnant Moraht made a promise to his ship's cook Miedtank. The crew had become dissatisfied with their steady diet of canned food, particularly peas and bacon, which were featured in many if not most of the meals aboard the submarine. The crew complained not only about the food, but about the cooking and the cook. Miedtank, a simple soul who was sensitive to criticism, complained to the captain and asked for a transfer. Moraht recognized the limited culinary talents of his chef, but he also took notice of the materials the cook had to work with–as well as the possibility that a new cook might be even worse. Moraht did his best to placate Miedtank by praising his cooking and telling him the men were merely teasing. Additionally, the captain was aware that Miedtank regarded his wife, Mrs. Moraht, as one of the great ladies of the world. Whenever she passed him on the street, Miedtank came to rigid attention. Moraht used the cook's awe of his wife to embellish his point. He told Miedtank that he had just written a letter to his wife describing Miedtank's pancakes as absolutely delicious and saying that nobody ever cooked better peas and bacon. Miedtank was beguiled by the captain's words. For him to be praised to the great lady was not merely consolation, it was glory. Moraht encouraged him to cook the best he could, and if he did he would be given a chance to fight and become a hero. In fact, Moraht promised him the Iron Cross.[236]

The opportunity arrived on the day of a long surface fight with an unnamed armed merchantman. (Whether this was the battle with the *Montenegro*, we don't really know.) Every man who could be spared was needed to carry shells on deck, so Captain Moraht assigned Miedtank to this duty. The cook responded with enthusiasm, carrying shells along with the other men during the battle and undoubtedly considering his performance heroic. Although Miedtank did nothing more gallant than work his arms sore, the U-boat captain cited Miedtank's labors under fire and the cook received the Iron Cross. This proved to be the balm that Miedtank needed. He swelled and strutted from then on, scornfully ignoring any new insults or complaints hurled at him or his cooking.[237]

In the engagement with the *U-64*, the *Montenegro* was not confronting the average U-boat commander. She was coming up against one of Germany's best. Kapitaenleutnant Moraht was born in 1884 on Alsen Island, now part of Denmark. He grew up in Hamburg and joined the Imperial German Navy in 1901. In 1916 he was first assigned to submarines. Within two years he had accounted for 44 merchant vessels sunk, totaling approximately 150,000 tons along with two warships. On 19 March, 1917, he sank the largest warship to be vanquished by a submarine during the war. It was the French battleship *Danton*, which carried 806 men, of whom 296 were lost, including the captain. Moraht was awarded Germany's highest military decoration, the *pour le mérite*, on 7 November, 1917.[238]

END NOTES

1. Parker, *Great Coal Schooners*, 41.
2. *NYMR*, 9, 16 September 1891, 4.
3. Ibid., 9 January 1895, 11, 16 January, 10.
4. Ibid., 18 October, 1899, 10; 14, 21, 28 January & 4 February, 1891, 4.
5. Ibid., 10; 8 January, 1896, 10.
6. Ibid., 21 December, 1910, 12.
7. Ibid., 13 February, 1889, 4; 17 November, 1897, 11.
8. *NYMR*, 4 November, 1914, 12; 6 March, 1901, 11, 34; 27 January, 1904, 10; 2 December, 1908, 11; 9 December, 1908, 35.
9. Ibid., 13 August, 1902, 10, 29; 14 December, 1904, 10.
10. Ibid., 9, 30 August & 18 October, 1905, 10.
11. *NYMR*, 14 March, 1888, 4; 21 March, 1888, 4-5.
12. Ibid., 26 October, 1898, 10. *Register*, 21 October, 1898, 1. *Journal*, 22 October, 1898, 2. *Tropical Cyclones of the North Atlantic Ocean, 1871-1977* (Washington, D.C: U.S. Government Printing Office, 1978), 60. Certificate of Enrollment, *Edward M. Reed*, 20 March, 1896.
13. *Register*, 21 October, 1890, 1. U.S. Customs Service Wreck Report, *Edward M. Reed*, 1 October, 1898.
14. *Register*, 21 October, 1898, 1.
15. Ibid., *NYMR*, 8 January, 1896, 10; 24, 31 March, 1897, 11; 9 March, 1898, 11. During the winter of 1896 the only listing of the *Reed* by the *NYMR* concerned her grounding on Romer Shoals. There was no mention of her in the compendium, or voyage section. This suggests that she might have made only that voyage during the 1896 winter, and perhaps the extensive repairs were made sometime after the grounding on Romer Shoals. At any rate, whatever was done, whenever it was done, was insufficient to withstand the ravages of the hurricane.
16. *Register*, 21 October, 1898, 1.
17. Ibid., U.S. Customs Service Wreck Report, *Edward M. Reed*, 1 October, 1898. Certificate of Enrollment, *Edward M. Reed*, 20 March, 1896. Security Insurance Co. records pertaining to this insurance contract have long since been destroyed, per 7 January, 1981, letter to author from Security Insurance Group.
18. *NYMR*, 26 December, 1906, 10.
19. Ibid., 13 October, 1909, 12, 32. *Register*, 11 October, 1909, 1. *Journal*, 12 October, 1909, 4. U.S. Life-Saving Service Wreck Report, *James Boyce*, 10 October, 1909.
20. Wreck Report, *Boyce*.
21. Ibid.
22. Ibid., Certificate of Enrollment, *James Boyce*, 21 March, 1877, 1 November

1906. *Register*, 11 October, 1909, 1.

23. *NYMR*, 3 April, 1889, 4, 5.
24. Ibid., 28 July, 1897, 11.
25. Ibid., 15, 22 June, 1898, 11.
26. *NYMR*, 12 December, 1906, and 9 January, 1907, 11. *Providence Journal*, 8 January, 1907, 16. *Baltimore American*, 9 January, 1907, 11. U.S. Life-Saving Service Annual Report, 1907, Table 64, 405. Certificate of Registry, *Henry Sutton*, 18 November, 1906.
27. *Morning Chronicle* (Halifax, Nova Scotia), 1 November, 1906, 2; 5 November, 1906, 1-2.
28. Ibid., 3 November, 1906, 1; 5 November, 1906, 1-2; 6, 7, 8, 9; 12 November, 1906, 1.
29. Ibid., 5 November, 1906, 1-2.
30. Ibid., *Providence Journal*, 8 January, 1907, 16.
31. *Providence Journal*, 8 January, 1907, 16.
32. Certificate of Registry, *Henry Sutton*, 18 October, 1906.
33. *NYMR*, 20 February, 1884, 7. U.S. Customs Service Wreck Report, *Orville Horwitz*, 8 February, 1884, RG 36, NA.
34. Wreck Report, *Horwitz*, 8 February, 1884. Certificate of Enrollment, *Orville Horwitz*, 3 October, 1883, RG 41, NA.
35. *NYMR*, 23 March, 1887, 5. *Register*, 17 March, 1887, 1. *Journal*, 18 March, 1887, 2. Both New Haven newspaper articles erroneously described the location of *Winter Quarter Lightship* as being off the New Jersey coast. Dr. Robert L. Scheina, U.S. Coast Guard historian, advised on 13 February, 1986, that the lightship was located off Virginia near the Maryland line. *Notice to Mariners from No. 1 to No. 52 for 1887*, (Washington, D.C.: U.S. Government Printing Office, 1888), 173.
36. *Register*, 17 March, 1887, 1. *Journal*, 18 March, 1887, 2.
37. *NYMR*, 22 February, 1887, 4. *Register*, 21 February, 1887, 1. *Journal*, 22 February, 1887, 4. Certificate of Enrollment, *Harry A. Barry*, 5 July, 1886. U.S. Life-Saving Service Annual Report, 1887, *Harry A. Barry*, 230-31, 300-01.
38. *NYMR*, 22 February, 1887, 4. U.S. Life-Saving Service Annual Report, *Barry*, 230.
39. U.S. Life-Saving Service Annual Report, *Barry*, 230.
40. *NYMR*, 22 February, 1887, 4. U.S. Life-Saving Service Annual Report, *Barry*, 230-31.
41. *Register*, 21 February, 1887, 1.
42. Ibid., U.S. Life-Saving Service Annual Report, *Barry*, 230-31.
43. *NYMR*, 5, 12 December, 1883, 7. 25 December, 1883, 6.
44. Ibid., 15 November, 1893, 10.

45. Ibid., 12 May, 1897, 11, 16 June, 1897, 10.

46. Ibid., 6 October, 1897, 11.

47. Ibid., 25 March, 1903, 11.

48. *Register*, 22 September, 1906, 1-2.

49. Ibid., *Tropical Cyclones of the North Atlantic Ocean, 1871-1977* (Washington, D.C.: U.S. Government Printing Office, 1978), 68. Letter to author from U.S. Coast Guard dated 19 March, 1981, fixing eye of hurricane #4 at 7:00 a.m. on 17 September, 1906.

50. *Journal*, 24 September, 1906, 3; 26 September, 1906, 9. *Register*, 22 September, 1906, 1; 9 October, 1906, 1. *NYMR*, 26 September, 1906, 10, 31; 10 October, 1906, 10. U.S. Life-Saving Service Annual Report 1906, Table 64, 402.

51. *Register*, 22 September, 1906, 2; 29 October, 1906, 1; 19 April, 1906, 1. Certificate of Enrollment, *James D. Dewell*, 18 February, 1903.

52. *NYMR*, 17 December, 1884, 6.

53. Ibid., 14 January, 1885, 7.

54. Ibid., 6 April, 1887, 6.

55. U.S. Life-Saving Service Wreck Report, *Nathan Easterbrook, Jr.*, 20 February, 1893. *Register*, 21 February, 1893, 1. *Journal*, 22 February, 1893, 4.

56. U.S. Life-Saving Service Wreck Report, *Easterbrook*. David Stick, *Graveyard of the Atlantic* (Chapel Hill: University of North Carolina Press, 1952), 131. U.S. *Life-Saving Service, Appleton's*, 763.

57. U.S. Life-Saving Service Wreck Report, *Easterbrook*. *Register*, 21 February, 1893, 1. *Journal*, 21 February, 1893, 4.

58. Certificate of Enrollment, *Easterbrook*,19 July, 1889.

59. *The Federal Reporter* (First Series) 300 vols. (St. Paul Publishing Co., 1880-94), 44, (1891): 445-48.

60. *NYMR*, 4 April, 1894, 11.

61. *Register*, 29 January, 1895, 1. Records of the U.S. Coast Guard, letters received by the Lighthouse Board, wreck of *James Ives*, 27 January, 1895, RG 26, NA.

62. *Journal*, 31 January, 1895, 1. USCG records, *James Ives*.

63. *NYMR*, 30 January, 1895, 11.

64. *Journal*, 31 January, 1895, 1. Certificate of Enrollment, *James Ives*, 19 March, 1891.

65. USCG records, *James Ives*.

66. *NYMR*, 18 August, 1886, 6.

67. U.S. Customs Service Wreck Report, *General S. E. Merwin*, 11 May, 1887. *Register*, 12 May, 1887, 1. *NYMR*, 18 May, 1887, 5.

68. Ibid., *Boston Daily Globe*, 12 May, 1887, 1. *Register*, 12 May, 1887, 1. *Lloyd's Register of British and Foreign Shipping* (London: William Clowes & Sons Ltd.,

1886), *Iowa* (Steamers).

69. *Boston Daily Globe*, 12 May, 1887, 1. *Register*, 12 May, 1887, 1.

70. Ibid., *Register*, 13 May, 1887, 1. *NYMR*, 18 May, 1887, 5. *Journal*, 18 May, 1887, 2.

71. *Boston Daily Globe*, 12 May, 1887, 1. *Register*, 12 May, 1887, 1.

72. *Journal*, 18 May, 1887, 2.

73. *NYMR*, 25 May, 1887, 5.

74. Ibid., 3 June, 1887, 5.

75. Ibid., U.S. Customs Service Wreck Report, *Merwin*. *Register*, 12, 13 May, 1887, 1. Presumably the crew recovered their personal property or its value if water damaged, although there was no mention of this.

76. Certificates of Enrollment, *General S.E. Merwin*, 3 December, 1884; 30 June, 1887.

77. *NYMR*, 12 September, 1894, 10.

78. Ibid., 8, 16 November, 1898, 10.

79. Ibid., 22 March, 1899, 10; 19 April, 1899, 10.

80. Ibid., 12 July, 1899, 10.

81. *Register*, 21 February, 1893, 1. *St. Thomae Tidende*, 13 February, 1889, 2, 3. *NYMR*, 13, 20, 27 February, 1889, 4; 20 March, 1889, 4.

82. *Register*, 7 March, 1889, 1. *St. Thomae Tidende*, 17 April, 1889, 2, 3. *NYMR*, 8, 29 May, 1889, 4.

83. *Register*, 4 March, 1901, 1. U.S. Life-Saving Service Wreck Reports, *General S.E. Merwin*, 4 March, 1901. (Gull Shoal and Little Kinnakeet Life-Saving Stations, District 7).

84. *Register*, 4 March, 1901, 1. *NYMR*, 13 March, 1901, 10.

85. Ibid., U.S. Life-Saving Service Wreck Reports, *Merwin*. *NYMR*, 6 March 1901, 11, 27.

86. U.S. Life-Saving Service Wreck Reports, *Merwin*. *Journal*, 8 March, 1901, 1. *NYMR*, 13 March, 1901, 10.

87. U.S. Life-Saving Service Wreck Reports, *Merwin*. *Register*, 4 March, 1901, 1. *NYMR*, 6 March, 1901, 11. Certificate of Enrollment, *General S.E. Merwin*, 21 June, 1900.

88. *NYMR*, 18 November, 1891, 3.

89. Ibid., 4 December, 1895, 10.

90. Ibid., 27 October, 1897, 11; 29 December, 1897, 10.

91. Ibid., 30 September, 1903, 10.

92. Ibid., 9 November, 1904, 10.

93. *Register*, 22 September, 1906, 1. *Journal*, 24 September, 1906, 3.

94. Ibid., *Tropical Cyclones*, 68.

95. *Register*, 22 September, 1906, 1. *Journal*, 24 September, 1906, 3. *NYMR*, 26

September, 1906, 10, 20. Letter to author from U.S. Coast Guard dated 19 March, 1981, fixing rescue coordinates at 140 miles east of Charleston.

96. *Register*, 22 September 1906, 1, 2. Certificate of Enrollment, *Tuttle*, 28 May, 1906.

97. *Register*, 13 April, 1888, 1; 5 January, 1900, 2. *Journal*, 13 April, 1888, 2. *NYMR*, 18 April, 1888, 4. U.S. Life-Saving Service Annual Report, 1888 *Henry H. Olds*, 262, 320-21. Certificate of Enrollment, *Henry H. Olds*, 26 August, 1887.

98. *Register*, 13 April, 1888, 1. *Journal*, 13 April, 1888, 2. *NYMR*, 18 April, 1888, 4.

99. Ibid., *NYMR*, 6 June and 19 December, 1888, 4. U.S. Life-Saving Service Annual Report, *Olds*.

100. *Register*, 3 July, 1889, 4.

101. *Register*, 13 April, 1888, 1. *Journal*, 13 April, 1888, 2. U.S. Life-Saving Service Annual Report, 1888, *Olds*. Certificate of Enrollment, *Henry H. Olds*, 26 August, 1887.

102. *NYMR*, 20 April, 1892, 10, 11.

103. *Norfolk Virginian*, 16 June, 1894, 2. U.S. Customs Service Wreck Report, W. *Wallace Ward*, 14 June, 1894. *Register*, 15 June, 1894, 1; 20 February, 1903, 1. *Journal*, 16 June, 1894, 2. *NYMR*, 20 June, 1894, 10. Coast Chart #131, Chesapeake Bay, U.S. Coast & Geodetic Survey, August, 1890.

104. *Norfolk Virginian*, 16 June, 1894, 2. *Register*, 15 June, 1894, 1; 20 February, 1903, 1. *Journal*, 16 June, 1894, 2. *NYMR*, 3 July, 1894, 10.

105. *Norfolk Virginian*, 16 June, 1894, 2. Certificate of Enrollment, *R.& T. Hargraves*, 21 December, 1891. *Camden Herald*, 11 December, 1891, 3. *NYMR*, 20 June, 1894, 10.

106. *Register*, 15 June, 1894, 1. *NYMR*, 20, 27 June, 1894, 10; 11, 25 July, 1894, 10.

107. *NYMR*, 3 July, 1894, 10.

108. Ibid., 8 August, 1894, 10.

109. Certificates of Enrollment, *R.&T. Hargraves*, 4 August, 1894; 21 December 1899.

110. *Register*, 5 January, 1900, 1. *Journal*, 5 January, 1900, 1. U.S. Customs Service Wreck Report, *W. Wallace Ward*, 5 January, 1900.

111. *Register*, 5 January, 1900, 1, 2. *Journal*, 5 January, 1900, 1. *NYMR*, 10 January, 1900, 11, 48. Norsk Sjofartsmuseum in Oslo advised by letter dated 2 July, 1981, that the author's prior letter to the Norwegian Government requesting further information about the dramatic rescue of the *Ward* mariners met with negative results both in the government and with the Norwegian shipping company, Wilh. Wilhelmsen, which is still in business in Oslo. The museum librarian, Else Marie Thorstvedt, concluded by writing: "In this case you are the one that have (sic) supplied us with information, and a copy of your letter will be kept in our archives together with material on the 'Themis.'" A copy of the

newspaper article in the *Register* concerning the *Themis* rescue was furnished to both the museum and the shipping company in 1994.

112. U.S. Customs Service Wreck Report, *Ward*. Certificate of Enrollment, *W. Wallace Ward*, 21 December, 1899.

113. New Haven Colony Historical Society Scrapbook Collection, 1906, reel 138, B27, box 13, fol. E. *NYMR*, 7, 14 March, 1906, 10.

114. *NYMR*, 30 November, 1904, 10, 27; 15 February, 1905, 10. *Tropical Cyclones of the North Atlantic Ocean, 1871-1977* (Washington, D.C.: U.S. Government Printing Office, 1978, 66.

115. U.S. Coast Guard Casualty Report, Fiscal Year 1917 #360, *George M. Grant*, 14 October, 1916.

116. Ibid., Certificate of Enrollment, *George M. Grant*, 14 September, 1916. Certificate of Registry, *George M. Grant*, 25 September, 1916. *Tropical Cyclones of the North Atlantic Ocean, 1871-1977* (Washington, D.C.: U.S. Government Printing Office, 1978), 78. Data regarding the position of the *Grant* furnished by U.S.C.G. in letters to author dated 19 March, 1981, and 7 April, 1981.

117. U.S.C.G. Report, *Grant*. *Journal of Commerce* (New York), 18 October, 1916, 20. The rescuer of the *Grant*'s crew, the *Seward*, ran aground on a Haitian coral reef later in the month but was pulled off undamaged. Six months after the *Grant*'s rescue, the *Seward* was reported torpedoed and her crew was landed at Vigo, Spain. *Journal of Commerce*, 23 October, 1916, 20; 10 April, 1917, 20.

118. U.S.C.G. Report, *Grant*.

119. *NYMR*, 5 December, 1900, 10, 11; 12 December, 1900, 10, 35.

120. Ibid., 8 May, 1907, 10, 34.

121. Ibid., 11 February, 1903, 10.

122. Ibid., 4 February, 1903, 10.

123. *The Federal Reporter* (First Series), 300 vols. (St. Paul: West Publishing Co., 1880-1924), 122 (1903): 816-28.

124. *The New International Year Book for the Year 1916, 1917* ed., s. v. "Shipping." *Journal*, 15 February, 1917, 1. *Bangor News*, 15 February, 1917, 1. *NYMR*, 19 August, 1916, 10.

125. The story of the *Law*'s destruction was previously published in 1987 in *The Connecticut Historical Society Bulletin*, vol. 50, Winter 1984, No. 1. *New York Times*, 16 February, 1917, 2.

126. Ibid., 15 February, 1917, 2. Unnamed, undated Jacksonville, Florida, newspaper clippings plus notes written by the late Walter McDonough about his father, Captain Stephen McDonough. These papers were furnished by Mrs. Walter McDonough, who also made available unnamed, undated Maine and Boston newspaper articles about Captain McDonough. *Encyclopedia Americana*, 1984

ed., s. v. "Macdonough, Thomas." *Bangor News*, 15 February, 1917, 1. *Bangor Daily Commercial,* 14 February, 1917. *Waldo County* (Maine) *Herald*, 8 March, 1917. *Journal*, 19 February, 1917, 1.

127. *Maine Sunday Telegram* (Portland), 4 January, 1959, 10 D.

128. *Bangor News*, 6 January, 1917, 1; 9 January, 1917, 2. *Maine Telegram*, 4 January, 1959, 10, D.

129. *New York Times*, 15 February, 1917, 2. *Bangor News*, 15 February, 1917, 1.

130. Translation of German Foreign Office note of 31 January, 1917, sent by U.S. Ambassador to Germany, James W. Gerard, to U.S. Secretary of State, U.S. Department of State, Decimal File 763.72/3437, RG 59, NA, Microfilm Publications M 367, roll 32. The note delineated a narrow 20-mile corridor through the Mediterranean to Greece that was excluded from this prohibited area (see 137 below). U.S. Department of State, *Papers Relating To The Foreign Relations of The United States, 1917, Supplement 1, The World War* (Washington, D.C.: U.S. Government Printing Office, 1931), 178.

131. *The Papers of Woodrow Wilson*, ed. Arthur S. Link (Princeton University Press, 1983), 41:111.

132. *Register*, 15 February, 1917, 3. U.S. Coast Guard Casualty Report #860, *Lyman M. Law*, 6 April, 1917. *Bangor News*, 15 February, 1917, 1. *Maine Telegram*, 4 January 1959, 10 D (source of paragraph quotation). Information reported from other sources shortly after the *Law*'s destruction was added to the *Maine Telegram* account where such information was compatible with that article and it appeared to be logical. *Journal*, 19 February, 1917, 1.

133. *Maine Telegram*, 4 January, 1959, 10 D. *Journal*, 19 February, 1917, 4.

134. *Maine Telegram*, 4 January, 1959, 10 D. *NYMR*, 21 February, 1917, 12, 35.

135. *Journal*, 17, 19 February, 1917, 4. Memorandum to President Wilson from U.S. Secretary of State Robert Lansing regarding *Housatonic* and *Lyman M. Law*, dated 21 February, 1917, RG 59, NA, M 743, roll 1, frames 305, 306. McDonough clippings and papers.

136. *New York Times*, 15 February, 1917, 1.

137. Letter from U.S. Ambassador to Italy, Thomas Nelson Page, to U.S. Secretary of State, dated 17 February, 1917, Decimal File 763.72/3346 for tel. #841 and 763.72/3550-1/2, RG 59, NA, M 367, roll 32. *The Times* of London, 15 February, 1917, 8. *Journal*, 15 February, 1917, 1. There was some question whether the *Law* might have been assaulted in the 20-mile corridor to Greece and later drifted out of the safety zone. The Italian Naval Ministry dispatch had reported the burning schooner's position just 12 miles from the corridor. *New York Times*, 15 February, 1917, 1, 2.

138. *Journal*, 15 February, 1917, 1. *New York Times*, 15 February, 1917, 2. After the start of the war, Germany listed wood as conditional contraband (considered

contraband if it could be understood to have some military use). But it generally proved impossible for either side to determine what might be useful in waging war. As a result, the distinction between absolute and conditional contraband was disregarded or abolished by most countries involved in the conflict. H. Reason Pyke, *The Law of Contraband of War* (Oxford: Clarendon Press, 1915), 182. Charles H. Stockton, *The Laws and Usages of War at Sea* (Washington, D.C.: U.S. Government Printing Office, 1900), 20-22. *Naval War College-International Law Situations, 1933* (Washington, D.C.: U.S. Government Printing Office, 1934), 10, 25-27. *Evening Star*, 16 February, 1917, 1. Freeman Snow, *International Law*, 2nd ed., C.H. Stockton (Washington, D.C.: U.S. Government Printing Office, 1898), 2.

139. Memo to Wilson from Lansing.
140. Ibid.
141. *New York Times*, 15 February, 1917, 2. James W. Ryan, *Freedom of the Seas and International Law* (New York: The Court Press, 1941), 18, 33-35.
142. *Evening Star*, 20 February, 1917, 1.
143. Robert Lansing, *War Memoirs of Robert Lansing. Secretary of State* (Indianapolis: Bobbs Merrill Co., 1935), 247. *Foreign Relations*, 40-41. *Papers of Wilson*, 185.
144. Lansing, *War Memoirs*, 246. *Foreign Relations*, 112, 178-79.
145. *New York Times*, 15 February, 1917, 2. *Republican Journal* (Belfast, Maine), 1 March, 1917, 7. *Portland* (Maine) *Evening Express*, 15 February, 1917, 1.
146. *Journal*, 16 February, 1917, 1.
147. Ibid., 15 February, 1917, 1. Law, *Allied Families*, 12.
148. *New York Times*, 18 February, 1917, 1.
149. Ibid., 3. Memo to Wilson from Lansing.
150. *Journal*, 19 February, 1917, 1. *New York Times*, 18 February, 1917, 3.
151. Telegram from Secretary of State Lansing to U.S. Embassy, Vienna, dated 14 February, 1917, Decimal File 763.72/3339a, RG 59, NA, M 367, roll 32, frames 171-73. *Foreign Relations*, 137. *Evening Star*, 20 February, 1917, 1. *Times* (London), 21 February, 1917, 6. Austria, Czernin to Hohenlohe, 21 February, 1917; Czernin to Tarnowski, 20 February 1917, Oesterreichisches Staatsarchiv, Haus-, Hof-, und Staatsarchiv, Krieg 61a, Amerika I, cited by Gerald H. Davis, *The Diplomatic Relations Between the United States and Austria-Hungary 1913-1917* (Ph. D. dissertation, Vanderbilt University, 1958), 248.
152. *Mobile* (Alabama) *Register*, 21 February, 1917, 1.
153. *Foreign Relations*, 152.
154. Ibid., 179, 191.
155. Austria, Tarnowski to Czernin, 20 March, 1917 (via Stockholm), Oesterreichisches Staatsarchiv, Haus-, Hof-, und Staatsarchiv, Politisches Archiv (PA. I) Karton 1047 (Krieg 61a Amerika) fol. 49 Cr. Information furnished

by Oesterreichisches Staatsarchiv in letter to author dated 13 September, 1983.

156. Lansing, *War Memoirs*, 251, 253, 259.

157. German military records were searched at Militaergeschichtliches Forschungsamt ({German} Armed Forces Office of Historical Research), Freiburg, Germany. Arno Spindler, *Der Krieg zur See*, 1914-1918, *Der Handelskrieg mit U-Booten* (Berlin: E. S. Mittler & Sohn, 1941) 4:162.

158. Bodo Herzog, Guenter Schomaekers, *Ritter Der Tiefe Graue Woelfe* (Munich: Welsermuehl, 1965), 57-58. Bodo Herzog, *60 Jahre Deutsche Uboote 1906-1966* (Munich: J.F. Lehmanns, 1968), 107, 146-51. Lowell Thomas, *Raiders of the Deep* (Garden City: Garden City Publishing Co., 1928) 127-28, 146-47, 150-51, 334-41. Von Arnauld also was credited with sinking two subchasers for an additional 2,500 tons, but they were accounted for differently. According to Thomas, von Arnauld attributed much of his success to giving warning to his victims. By this means, he could produce the names of ships and verify their sinkings, thus gaining full credit for his efforts. It also went a long way towards making his patrols free from torpedo dependence since he was in a position to sink most of his victims with bombs or gunfire. Therefore, he could remain at sea as long as shells and food lasted. In May of 1918 he was given command of the big new submarine, *U-139*, and ordered to raid the east coast of the U.S. The *U-139* was less than halfway across the Atlantic when armistice negotiations interrupted the mission. But before von Arnauld returned to base he had destroyed five more merchantmen, accounting for 7,008 additional tons of shipping.

159. Thomas, *Raiders*, 145-46, 151-59, 336-41. Lothar von Arnauld de la Periere, *U-35 auf Jagd* (Guetersloh: C. Bertelsmann, 1938), 3-32. Herzog, *Deutsche Uboote*, 149, 152. Von Arnauld died in 1941 in an airplane crash at Le Bourget airport in Paris while on a flight to assume command as Admiral of the Southeast. A new German submarine group, formed in the Mediterranean in 1941, was named after him.

160. Spindler, *Der Handelskrieg*, 2 (1933): 200-01. W. Aichelburg, *Die Unterseeboote Oesterreich-Ungarns*, 2 vols. (Graz: Akademischer, 1981), 1:126-128; 2:417. Aichelburg offers two reasons for continuing the false flag deception. First, strategic concepts dictated misleading the enemy as to the size of the Austrian submarine fleet. Second, a total discontinuance would have raised doubts about prize court decisions. (This, in turn, would have invited potential retroactive legal considerations which were not wanted.) Herzog, *Deutsche Uboote*, 101, 144.

161. Herzog, *Deutsche Uboote*, 146-50. Von Arnauld sank two more American ships in the *U-35* during the war. Both were sailing vessels and both were sunk in the Mediterranean in 1917. The 1,553-ton schooner *Marguerite*, built in Bath,

Maine, in 1889, and with Fall River as her home port, was sunk on 5 April. The 404-ton schooner *Fannie Prescott*, built in Stonington, Connecticut, in 1906 with her home port New York, was sunk on 25 October. *List of Merchant Vessels of the United States, 1917* (Washington, D.C.: U.S. Government Printing Office, 1918), 46, 24.

162. U.S. Coast Guard Casualty Report, *Lyman M. Law*, 6 April, 1917. *New York Times*, 15 February, 1917, 2. U.S. Department of State Document No. 300.115 L98 Sub No. 34, Purport List (1910-29), RG 59, NA. A claim against the German government such as the one considered by the *Law*'s owners would have come within the jurisdiction of a German prize court. In principle, prize courts were not international, but national; they operated under the laws of the nation that authorized them. In 1917 the German Supreme Prize Court openly rejected the principles of international law, claiming they were not binding on the court. But if no national law was applicable, the court said it could then look to international law. H. Reason Pyke, *The Law of Contraband of War* (Oxford: Clarendon Press, 1915), 216. James W. Garner, *Prize Law During The World War* (New York: Macmillan Co., 1927), 45. C. John Colombos, *A Treatise on the Law of Prize* (London: Sweet & Maxwell, Ltd., 1926), 17-18, 24.

163. *Bangor News*, 4 April, 1917, 12; 30 March, 1917, 14.

164. *Maine Telegram*, 4 January, 1959, 10 D. *Republican Journal* (Belfast, Maine), 9 May, 1963, 11. Interviews with Mrs. Frances Hewitt, Mrs. Grace Young, Mrs. Cora McLeod, all of Winterport, Maine, on 16 June, 1983; Mrs. Helen McInnis, Bangor, Maine, on 16 and 20* June, 1983 and 28* May, 1984; Mrs. Sara Fernald, Oceanside, L.I., New York, on 22* June, 1983; Mrs. Mildred Luosey, Warner Robins, Georgia, on 7* May, 1984; Mrs. Oleta (Walter) McDonough, Jacksonville, Florida, on 22* June, 1983 and 27* May, 1984. (Mrs. McInnis, Mrs. Fernald, and Mrs. Luosey are daughters of Captain Stephen W. McDonough and Mrs. McDonough is his daughter-in-law.) * Denotes telephone interview.

165. *Maine Telegram*, 4 January, 1959, 10 D. McDonough clippings and papers. *Bangor News*, 30 March, 1917, 14. Memo to Wilson from Lansing.

166. *New York Times*, 18 February, 1917, 3. Memo to Wilson from Lansing. *Journal*, 19 February, 1917, 4. *Bangor News*, 30 March, 1917, 14.

167. *New York Times*, 18 February, 1917, 1. Memo to Wilson from Lansing. *Bangor News*, 30 March, 1917, 14.

168. *New York Times*, 18 February, 1917, 1. *Journal*, 19 February, 1917, 1, 4. *Maine Telegram*, 4 January, 1959, 10 D.

169. Herzog, *Ritter Der Tiefe*, 57. Thomas, *Raiders*, 120, 159-61. Great Britain, Imperial War Museum, shot sheet from movie film taken aboard the *U-35*, No. 560 Part 1, Sec. 4 and Part 2, Sec. 6, captioned *U-35*. This movie was

forwarded to German Army headquarters on the western front and was captured by the British. *New York Times*, 18 February, 1917, 1. *Journal*, 19 February, 1917, 1. On at least one occasion McDonough tired of telling the tale about the *Law*. Upon returning to the U.S. after her destruction, he informed an inquiring newspaper reporter that it was the same old story which he had told and retold, then he changed the subject. *Bangor Daily Commercial*, 31 March, 1917, 5. McDonough clippings and papers.

170. Interview with Mrs. Oleta (Walter) McDonough on 27 May, 1984.

171. Aichelburg, *Unterseeboote*, 1:101. *Foreign Relations*, 135-36. The former French submarine *Curie*, sunk at Cattaro in December, 1914, was salvaged by the Austrians and recommissioned the *U-14* in June of 1915. She was dispatched on offensive operations in the Ionian Sea in April, 1917, and in the central Mediterranean in May, 1917, thereby contradicting the Austrian military attaché's statement. Aichelburg, *Unterseeboote*, 2:335-44.

172. *Papers of Wilson*, 284. Lansing, *War Memoirs*, 225.

173. Amy Lowell, "Before War Is Declared," *Pan American Magazine*, April, 1918, 328. This publication incorrectly used the middle initial "W" instead of "M" in citing the *Lyman M. Law*.

174. *Bangor Daily Commercial*, 7 August, 1917, 10. *Regulus* dossier (SS G 71) and (SS YA 86), Service Historique de la Marine, Vincennes, France. Letters to author dated 30 July, 1991, and 28 January, 1992, from Militaergeschichtliches Forschungsamt.

175. *Dictionary of American Naval Fighting Ships* (Washington, D.C.: U.S. Government Printing Office, 1968) Vol. III, 294-95. Logs of U.S. ships *Helvetia, E-2, L-5* and *N-6*, RG 24, NA. Carroll Storrs Alden, "American Submarine Operations in the War," *U.S. Naval Institute Proceedings*, 46 (June, 1920): 827-37. Letters to author dated 31, October, 1991, 25 February and 9 November, 1992, from National Personnel Records Center, RG 24 NA.

176. Records Group 125, Office of the JAG, NA. Navy Court Martials of Lt. (j.g.) Robert W. Dempsey and Lt. Martin A. Hansen. Roosevelt signed Office of the Secretary, Department of the Navy attachment #26251-18758 K-SM on October 3, 1991.

177. McDonough clippings and papers.Carroll Storrs Alden, "American Submarine Operations in the War," *U.S. Naval Institute Proceedings*, 46 (June, 1920), 827-37. Letters to author dated 31, October, 1991, 25 February and 9 November, 1992, from National Personnel Records Center. Logs of U.S. Ships, *Helvetia, E-2, L-5,* and *N-6*. Arno

178. *Maine Telegram,* 4 January, 1959, 10 D.

179. *NYMR*, 13 December, 1898, 11; 12 April, 1899, 11, 28.

180. Ibid., 10 January & 7 February, 1912, 12.

181. Ibid., 8 January & 12 March, 1913, 12; 19 March, 1913, 35; November, 1914, 12.

182. Ibid., 15 September, 1915, 11, 35.

183. Ibid., 15 March, 1916, 11; 21 June, 1916, 10; 3 January, 1917, 10. U.S. Coast Guard Casualty Report, Fiscal year 1917, #1425, *Lucinda Sutton*, 23 May, 1917. Federal Reserve System, *Banking and Monetary Statistics (1914-1941)*, 4 vols. (Washington, D. C.: Board of Governors of Federal Reserve System, 1976), 1:681.

184. USCG Report, *Lucinda Sutton*, 1917.

185. Ibid.

186. Correspondence with author in 1987 from *La Nueva Provincia* and from Jose Guardiola Plubins, author of both articles. *La Nueva Provincia*, 31 March, 1987, 16. *Gaceta Marinera*, 31 May, 1987, 10, 11.

187. Background material and maps sent by *La Nueva Provincia*.

188. Ibid. *NYMR*, 12 May, 1909, 10.

189. Background material from *La Nueva Provincia*.

190. Ibid.

191. Ibid.

192. Ibid.

193. Ibid.

194. Ibid.

195. *La Nueva Provincia*, 31 March, 1987, 16. *Gaceta Marinera*, 31 May, 1987, 10, 11.

196. *NYMR*, 6 June, 1917, 11. USCG Report, *Lucinda Sutton*, 1917.

197. Ibid., 13 June, 1917, 11.

198. Letter to author dated 7 December, 1988, from Assistant Naval Attache, Argentine Embassy, Washington, D.C., summarizing the investigation conducted by the Chief of the Naval Historical Department Studies in Argentina and enclosing typed copies of the cited articles in *La Prensa*, 3 & 4 April, 1917.

199. Ibid.

200. Ibid.

201. Telephone conversation on 14 September, 1993, with R. Thomas Crew, Jr., Archivist, The Mariners' Museum.

202. *NYMR*, 25 February, 1903, 10. *Register*, 20 February, 1903, 1. *Journal*, 20 February, 1903, 1. *Fall River* (Massachusetts) *Evening News*, 20, 21 February, 1903, 1. *The Federal Reporter* (First Series) 300 Vols. (St. Paul: West Publishing Co., 1880-1924), 135 (1905): 827.

203. Ibid.

204. *Register*, 20 February, 1903, 1. *Journal*, 20 February, 1903, 1. *Fall River News*, 20 February, 1903, 1.

205. Ibid. *NYMR*, 25 February, 1903, 10.

206. *Register*, 20 February, 1903, 1. *Fall River News*, 21 February, 1903, 1. *NYMR*,

25 February, 1903, 10. Certificate of Enrollment, *R.& T. Hargraves*, 5 November, 1902. Apparently the *Hargraves* began breaking up some time after sinking. The steamer *El Norte*, enroute from Galveston to New York, reported that on 4 March she passed two masts with rigging attached, some broken rails and other wreckage, about 18 miles off Absecon. Supposedly the wreckage was that of the *Hargraves*. *NYMR*, 11 March, 1903, 11.

207. *NYMR*, 25 February, 1903, 10. *Federal Reporter*, 827.

208. *NYMR*, 4 March, 1903, 10. *Federal Reporter*, 827.

209. *Federal Reporter*, 828.

210. Ibid.

211. Ibid., 829.

212. Ibid., 829-30.

213. *Federal Reporter*, 830-31.

214. Ibid., 831.

215. Ibid.

216. Ibid., 831-32.

217. Ibid., 162 (1908): 882-83. *U.S. Supreme Court Reports*, Lawyer's Edition, 100 Books, (Rochester, New York: The Lawyers Cooperative Publishing Co., 1882-1956), 53 (vol. 212), (1909): 659. Ironically, on 27 January, 1911, the *Eagle Wing* collided with the Danish steamship *Nordamerika*. Amidst conflicting evidence, both claimed the other ship's change of course was responsible for the collision. In this case, the court found the *Eagle Wing* to be without fault. *Federal Reporter*, 191 (1912): 997-99.

218. *NYMR*, 21 December, 1910, 11, 28.

219. Certificate of Registry, *General E.S. Greeley*, 13 July, 1917, surrendered at Algiers, Algeria 19 January, 1918. *Lloyd's Register of Shipping* (London: *Lloyd's Register of Shipping*, 1918) unpaged: Sailing Vessels. *NYMR*, 13 March, 1918, 13.

220. *Montenegro* Dossier, Guerre Sans-Marine [ss G 71], Service Historique de la Marine Archives Centrales de la Marine, Vincennes, France.

221. The overall length of the submarine was 224.4 feet, which was five and one-third feet longer than the *Montenegro*. Bodo Herzog, *60 Jahre Deutsche Uboote 1906-1966* (Munich: Lehmanns, 1968), 49.

222. Ibid. In fact, the submarine was armed with one 8.8 cm deck gun and one 10.5 cm deck gun.

223. *Lloyd's Register of Shipping* (1917) unpaged: Steamers.

224. Great Britain, KEW, Public Record Office, Admiralty 53, Log of HMS *Petunia*, 15 February, 1918.

225. Ibid.

226. Ibid.

227. Ibid.

228. Ibid.

229. bid.

230. Ibid., 15-16 February, 1918.

231. Ibid., 16 February, 1918.

232. Ibid., 16-17 February, 1918.

233. Captain Lemerle's five-page letter was replete with run-on sentences, and direct quotations were not used.

234. Lowell Thomas, *Raiders of the Deep* (Garden City: Garden City Publishing Co., 1928), 254. German military records were searched at Militaergeschichtliches Forschungsamt ({German} Armed Forces Office of Historical Research), Freiburg, Germany. Arno Spindler, *Der Krieg zur See 1914-1918*, *Der Handelskrieg mit U-Booten* (Frankfurt: Mittler & Sohn, 1966), 5:160.

235. Robert Moraht, *Werwolf der Meere* (Berlin: Schlegel, 1933), 123-25.

236. Thomas, *Raiders*, 263-64.

237. Ibid., 264. Militaergeschichtliches Forschungsamt advised author by letter dated 3 June, 1986, that records of Iron Cross awards were maintained by Zentrales Staatsarchiv in Merseburg, East Germany. Zentrales Staatsarchiv advised author by letter dated 4 August, 1986, that their World War I records were destroyed during a bombing attack in April of 1945.

238. Thomas, *Raiders,* 254, 272-74. Herzog, *Deutsche Uboote*, 144. On 17 June, 1918, in the *U-64*, Moraht attacked a British convoy in heavy weather in the Mediterranean between Sicily and Sardinia. He torpedoed the transport *Kandy.* Immediately after, the sloop *Lychnis* damaged the submerged U-boat with a depth charge, then rammed the submarine when it emerged from the sea. Ultimately forced to remain on the surface, the *U-64* engaged in a firefight with the ships of the convoy. The *Lychnis*, and *Kandy*, transport *Manitou*, and the armed boarding steamer *Partridge II* all were shooting at her. She took several hits and sank. *Partridge II* was credited by Moraht with the *coup de grace*. Thirty-eight men on the *U-64* were killed, including the cook, Miedtank. Moraht, who was manning one of the U-boat's deck guns, was one of five survivors rescued from the sea. He was imprisoned in England until October, 1919, when he was allowed to return to Germany. Thomas, *Raiders*, 279-283. Herzog, *Deutsche Uboote*, 90. Letter to author from British Naval Historical Branch, Ministry of Defense, dated 19 January, 1983. Moraht, *Werwolf*, 153.

C H A P T E R   8

THE EPONYMS

The eponyms are those individuals for whom the schooners were named. Their thumbnail sketches follow. Where local biographical histories were obtained, little or no additional background investigation was conducted—with a few exceptions. An effort was also made to try to locate any family record that might have been kept of the Sutton schooners, specifically by the managers of the fleet—i.e., through the Sutton and/or Dewell families. Henry Sutton's only direct descendant living as of 1990 was his great-grandson, Alvah D. Jones, of Brattleboro, Vermont. He advised that there are no family records of the schooners and he had no knowledge that Henry Sutton ever formed any company to build or manage his ships.[1]

With regard to James D. Dewell, his granddaughter, Miss Jane K. Dewell of New Haven, is the only direct-line descendant of the former lieutenant governor who was then living (23 February, 1988). She confirmed that there are no family records in existence pertaining to the Sutton or Dewell ships.[2]

EDWARD MORDECAI REED

Edward Mordecai Reed was born 17 November, 1821, in Lancaster County, Pennsylvania, where he attended common schools. At age 16 he was apprenticed to a machinist, and by the time he was 21 he was general foreman of a machine shop in Lancaster City, Pennsylvania. One year later he began his career in railroading as a locomotive engineer on the Baltimore and Ohio Railway. His job responsibilities rose as he worked successively for the Philadelphia and Reading Railroad Co., the Havana and

Engines Railway in Cuba, and the Hartford and New Haven Railway Company. In 1873, when the New York, New Haven and Hartford Railroad Company was consolidated, he was made its general superintendent. Two years later he became vice-president of the road.[3]

Edward M. Reed was both a civil and a mechanical engineer. He designed and/or built locomotives, stationary engines, bridges, and buildings. He also was responsible for advances in the field of communications. In 1885 Yale College recognized his scientific achievements and public service with an honorary master of arts degree.[4]

JAMES BOYCE

James Boyce was born in Chester, New York, on 8 January, 1823, the son of parents from Dublin, Ireland. He received a common-school education, then obtained employment as a grocery clerk in New York City. At age 16 he became a clerk in a coal office. At 19 he went into the coal business on his own. Five years later he invested his money in bituminous coal fields in Maryland and Virginia, operating mostly under his own name and as agent for a mining company in which he was a principal stockholder. During the Civil War he contracted for and delivered millions of tons of Pennsylvania anthracite coal to the U.S. Government. He was elected president of the Franklin Coal Company of Maryland, of which he became the sole owner in 1865. He became the largest stockholder in the Maryland Union Coal Company; half-owner of the Gaston gas and coal mine; and the largest owner of another gas and coal company in West Virginia. With these and other holdings, he was considered to be one of the largest producers and shippers of bituminous coal in Maryland and West Virginia and was sometimes called the autocrat of the trade. Anticipating the need for coal-shipping facilities in the port of Baltimore, he purchased waterfront property and built coal piers with direct railroad access. With this, he greatly enhanced the value of the property and facil-

itated the movement of coal from his own mines. Thousands of tons of coal were shipped out annually.[5]

Boyce invested in the first five schooners built by Sutton. He was married twice, in 1844 and 1850. His first wife died in 1845, leaving one daughter. With his second wife he had six more children.[6]

HENRY SUTTON

Henry Sutton was born 3 May, 1843, in Oxford, Connecticut, where he grew up on a farm. His father was a carpenter, builder and contractor. Henry was educated in a common school and became a carriage trimmer in Naugatuck while quite young. Early on, he moved to Canada, likely following many other young American males in avoiding the Civil War draft. He continued his carriage trimmer trade in Canada and New Haven, to which city he moved in 1865 at the war's end. In 1870 he started a grocery store. Two years later he became involved with activity in the port when he added a ship chandlery to the business, in partnership with George H. Story. Two years after that, the partnership was dissolved and Sutton continued the business alone. The ship chandlery and grocery prospered together in the provisioning of ships.[7]

Henry Sutton seemed to have a "feel" for shipbuilding, stemming no doubt from his experience as a ship chandler and carriage trimmer, and perhaps from whatever he might have learned about carpentry and construction through his father. He invested in all of his vessels except for the *Boyce*. For his shipbuilding, investment and management activities, see Chapter Three.

Sutton and James D. Dewell were two members of a five-man syndicate that was organized by Dewell to relocate the Connecticut State building in West Haven, moving it from the 1893 Chicago World's Fair after the fair closed. It was relocated on 500 square feet of beautiful ocean frontage on Ocean Avenue in West Haven. An electric railway, the West Shore Road, connecting New Haven with Woodmont, ran by the rear boundary of the building's grounds. Thus the building was easily accessible from New Haven, only four miles distant by the railway. Sutton managed the building and also became a stockholder, secretary and director in the West Shore Road in 1895. The building reportedly burned down sometime between 1916 and 1918.[8]

He married Lucinda Doney of Napanee, Canada, see "Eponyms—Lucinda Sutton." On 8 November, 1896, at age 53 he was killed in a runaway horse accident, leaving his wife and son, Harry D. Sutton.[9]

ORVILLE HORWITZ
Orville Horwitz was born in Baltimore in 1820, the son of a distinguished physician, Dr. Jonathan Horwitz. Dr. Horwitz was

a friend and student of Dr. Benjamin Rush, one of the signers of the Declaration of Independence.[10]

At age 16, Orville Horwitz graduated with high honors from St. Mary's College. He taught in Maryland and Virginia and became principal of Winchester Academy. In the next few years, he prepared a comprehensive history of the Anglo-Saxon language and literature, was admitted to the Maryland bar, studied and traveled in Europe, and became fluent in German, French and Italian. In 1841 he commenced his legal practice in Baltimore at age 21. Gifted with a remarkable memory and an acute and penetrating mind, he acquired a thorough knowledge of the law. As a speaker, he was effective, well-reasoned, and much sought after to argue cases in appellate court. He often contributed articles to journals and magazines. As one of the foremost attorneys in the area, he amassed a fortune of two million dollars. Two of his three brothers were attorneys and the third became medical director of the U.S. Navy.[11]

Orville Horwitz married Maria Gross of Philadelphia in 1861. His younger brother, Benjamin Franklin Horwitz, married Maria's sister, Louisa E. Gross, in 1862. Orville Horwitz died on 30 July, 1887, leaving his wife and four daughters.[12]

HARRY AUGUSTUS BARRY

With regard to the investigation of eponyms, the most troublesome of them proved to be Harry Augustus Barry. He was born 19 September, 1840, in Reading, Pennsylvania, and was called both Henry and Harry throughout his life. After completing his Civil War military service, he moved to Baltimore and entered the wholesale coal business.[13]

In 1865 he married Mary Alice Patterson of Baltimore. Before Barry died, he endured ill health for several years. On 30 May, 1919, he returned to his home in Catonsville, Maryland, from Decoration Day ceremonies and committed suicide by shooting himself through the mouth. He was 78 years old and left his wife and one daughter. Another daughter had predeceased him.[14]

Harry A. Barry's obituary in the *Baltimore Sun*, 31 May, 1919, stated that Colonel Barry served with the 127th Pennsylvania Volunteer Regiment and was one of the organizers and the first commander of the 4th Maryland Regiment. He also was listed as a member of the Loyal Legion, and a past commander of Beauseant Commandery, Knights Templar. The *Sun* reported that Colonel Barry was the general manager of the Susquehanna Coal Company for 35 years and that he retired 20 years before. Trying to verify these assertions in the obituary brought the trouble into focus.[15]

Barry's military record disclosed that on 13 August, 1862, he was mustered into military service as a musician in the 127th Pennsylvania Infantry, which was assigned to the defense of

Washington, D.C. At his own request, he became a private on 29 September, 1862. He contracted typhoid fever in December, was hospitalized, then sent to a convalescent camp. By February of 1863 he was back on active duty. His regiment participated in the Chancellorsville campaign for ten days during April-May 1863, after which his nine-month enlistment terminated. He was mustered out of service on 29 May, 1863.[16]

The 4th Maryland Infantry Regiment was organized at Baltimore during July and August 1862, which was when Barry enlisted in the 127th Pennsylvania Infantry–at age 21. Barry wasn't mentioned in *The Historical Register of the U.S. Army* (1789-1889) or in *The List of Officers of the U.S. Army 1779-1900*. Furthermore, Barry applied for a U.S. Government pension on 29 July, 1889, due to a rheumatic disability caused by typhoid fever during his duty with the 127th. He certified on the form that he had not been in the U.S. military service since 29 May, 1863. He recertified this information on 13 May, 1912.[17]

Records of the Military Order of the Loyal Legion of the U.S. disclosed that Harry Augustus Barry was elected a member in 1896 through inheritance of his father who had been a surgeon in the Pennsylvania infantry. On Harry A. Barry's application for membership, dated 17 December, 1895, in addition to his Civil War service, he listed further military duty as Lt. Col., commanding Baltimore Light Infantry, April 1885 to August 1889, Maryland National Guard.[18]

The State of Maryland Military Department reported finding no record that Barry, either as Henry or Harry, had ever served in the Maryland National Guard.[19]

The Grand Commandery of Knights Templar of the State of Maryland advised that Harry A. Barry was knighted in the Baltimore Commandery Knights Templar No. 2 and withdrew in 1887. However, he never was a past commander in the history of the Beauseant Commandery.[20]

Barry actually moved to Baltimore in 1864. A review of

Baltimore City Directories from 1864-1903 failed to disclose that he ever was listed as general superintendent of the Susquehanna Coal Co. The only years when the Susquehanna Coal Co. was named in connection with Barry was from 1874-78, when he was listed as a sales agent and coal dealer for the company. In 1870 and 1871 his office address was the same as that of fellow eponym James Boyce. And from 1884-91 he was located in the same building as Boyce but in an adjacent office. In 1884 he was listed as a sales agent for the Maryland Pavement Co., and in 1885-86 as a salesman for J. Hilles and Co., a coal company. However, most of his listings between 1865 and 1897 didn't mention any company at all. He simply was carried as a clerk, sales agent, salesman, coal dealer or merchant. Finally, from 1897-1903, he was listed as a clerk and sales agent for an apartment house in Baltimore, after which he moved to his retirement home in Catonsville.[21]

One can conclude that Harry A. Barry exaggerated his stations in life, and that Henry Sutton may have been taken in by these misrepresentations to the extent of naming his fifth schooner after him.

JAMES DUDLEY DEWELL

James Dudley Dewell was born 3 September, 1837, in Norfolk, Connecticut, where he had a limited common-school education. He clerked in a country store until 1858 when he moved to New Haven and became a salesman in a wholesale grocery store. Two years later he was made a member of the firm, and in 1879 the firm name was changed to J.D. Dewell & Co.[22]

Mr. Dewell helped organize the State Board of Trade and became its first president in 1890. He was retained in this position for many years, at least through 1902. In addition, he served as president of the New Haven Chamber of Commerce for a number of years. At the close of the 1893 Chicago World's Fair, a five-man syndicate, organized by Dewell and including Henry Sutton, relocated the Connecticut State building to West Haven, where Sutton became its manager. Dewell also served as a director or officer in banking institutions as well as other mercantile and civic enterprises. As a Republican, he was elected lieutenant governor of Connecticut in 1896. After Henry Sutton's death, he became manager of most of the remainder of the Sutton fleet. He also invested in at least eight of the Sutton schooners.[23]

In 1860 he married Mary Elizabeth Keyes of Norfolk, Connecticut, and they had six children, one of whom died in infancy. Mr. Dewell died on 19 April, 1906.[24]

NATHAN EASTERBROOK, JR.

Nathan Easterbrook, Jr. was born 30 March, 1836, in Herkimer, New York. He organized a company of volunteers at the outbreak of the Civil War, and these were enrolled in the army on 15 June, 1861, at Albany, New York. Easterbrook was commissioned a lieutenant and was made regimental quartermaster for the 34th Regiment, New York Volunteer Infantry. On 15 October, 1861, he was promoted to captain and became quartermaster, First Brigade, Second Corps, Army of the Potomac. He participated in all the military actions of the brigade, some of which included the siege of Yorktown; battle of Seven Pines; covering Pope's retreat from Bull Run; battles of Antietam and Fredericksburg; and the Chancellorsville campaign. He was mustered out at Albany on 30 June, 1863, upon completion of his enlistment.[25]

In 1865 he moved to New Haven, where some nine years later he became president of the Easterbrook Co., an oleomargarine manufacturing firm that employed from 60 to 75 people. Still later he was president of the Humiston Preservative Co., another food manufacturing company.[26]

For a number of years he was Special Deputy Collector of U.S. Customs for the Port of New Haven, as well as an owner of vessels in coastwise shipping. He also was president of the New Haven Chamber of Commerce and was active in humane, patriotic and civic organizations.[27]

On 4 October, 1864, he married Mary Catherine Feeter of Little Falls, New Jersey. He lived until 18 July, 1922, and was survived by his wife and three sons. His only daughter had died earlier.[28]

JAMES IVES

James Ives was born 8 December, 1815, the 13th and last child of Elam Ives, a Mt. Carmel, Connecticut, farmer. At age 17 James apprenticed under a master mechanic who manufactured brass surgical instruments. He was paid eight dollars a month, out of which he paid for his board. At age 20 he established his own business, the Mt. Carmel Brass Works, which specialized in carriage and harness hardware. He obtained higher prices than his competition because of the excellence of his products. In making brass, he used old copper from the West Indies. He contracted to purchase all the copper that the vessels of New Haven shipper N.H. Gaston might bring back from Barbados in excess of their regular cargo of molasses. Many years later, Ives and his partner at the time, Joseph Granniss, doing business as "Ives & Granniss," attributed part of their financial success to certain principles. These

were: never give a business note; employ no traveling salesmen; and, except on rare occasions, use no newspaper advertising.[29]

James Ives helped found other companies such as a bank, a bolt company, a screw works, and a water company. He owned a general store in Ivesville, Connecticut, which he leased out with the provision that no drinks were to be sold except "small beer, soda, ginger pop or lemonade." No lights were to be used that would "endanger the insurance on the store." The lessee could use the hay scales and half the icehouse but only if he did half the work in filling it.[30]

After approximately 50 years in business, Ives retired in 1883, the same year that his namesake schooner was launched in West Haven. Hobart Ives was her captain but no information was developed in this investigation as to whether he and James Ives were related.[31]

James Ives was married to Lucy Ann Candee of Oxford, Connecticut, in 1838. They had five daughters. He died on 21 September, 1889.[32]

SAMUEL E. MERWIN

Samuel E. Merwin was born 23 August, 1830, in Brookfield, Connecticut. He received a district-school education plus an additional year in a neighboring village school and some brief private instruction before starting a business career. He clerked for two years and then joined his father in the pork packing business in New Haven in 1850. Six years later the firm name was changed to S.E. Merwin & Son, which continued until 1889 when Swift and Co. bought out the 50-employee business. General Merwin was an officer or director of many civic organizations and corporations and was president of the New Haven Savings Bank at the time of his death.[33]

Merwin had a full career in the Connecticut state militia, serving as captain of the New Haven Grays, colonel of the Second Regiment, and for three years adjutant-general of the state. During

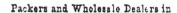

S. E. MERWIN & SON,

Packers and Wholesale Dealers in

PROVISIONS,

And Curers of the Elm City Brand Hams,

354 and 356 STATE STREET, NEW HAVEN, CONN.

the Civil War, he commanded the Grays, whose duties consisted mainly of conducting ceremonial rites and guarding conscript camps. On one occasion, he and his company were kept under arms for 30 days during an alert caused by draft riots in New York.[34]

While serving as adjutant-general, the governor ordered him to assist the New Haven county sheriff in preventing a prize fight from taking place near Milford, Connecticut. This fight was being promoted by roughnecks from New York City. Through coordination effected by General Merwin, the fight party was arrested and incarcerated in the New Haven jail. As an added dividend, according to the general's biographical history, . . . "our state has from that time been saved from any attempt of a like disgraceful nature."[35]

Samuel Merwin ran unsuccessfully as a Republican candidate for mayor, congressman, and twice for governor, but in 1876 was elected state senator in a heavily Democratic district. He also was elected lieutenant governor of the state, to serve from 1889-91. After completing his term of office, he ran again. The new election involved four political parties and it proved to be both a very close election and an absolute fiasco. The sitting governor and lieutenant governor (Merwin) were Republicans; the senate was controlled by Democrats; Republicans controlled the assembly. Under the state constitution, if no majority prevailed, the assembly was empowered to elect a governor from the two candidates with the highest totals. Democrats claimed a majority of all the votes cast but Republicans denied there was an absolute majority, stating that 126 votes from Bridgeport had been improperly voided. The senate then swore in the whole Democratic ticket, which the governor disallowed. The matter was finally resolved unanimously by the state supreme court, which found that in the absence of a constitutionally chosen successor to the state's highest office, the sitting governor was the de jure as well as de facto governor (which also applied to the lieutenant governor). So Samuel E. Merwin was held over in office for another two years.[36]

General Merwin never lost his interest in the Grays. In the summer preceding his death, when failing health prevented him from attending the Grays' annual outing, they paid tribute to him by marching past his home on Orange Street and saluting as he stood on his front porch and bowed.[37]

He died on 5 March, 1907, and was survived by his wife. The Grays attended his funeral.[38]

CHARLES F. TUTTLE

Charles F. Tuttle was born 25 April, 1831, in New Haven but nearly didn't achieve his proper niche in the family history. As an infant, Charles was in a cradle at home when a fire burned down the house. In the "fright and hurry" of the occasion, Charles "was forgotten." Before the house—and Charles—were fully consumed, several Yale students came to the rescue. They entered the burning building, rescued the child and "cared for him until he was returned to his distracted family." Having survived this catastrophe, Charles attended the John E. Lovell school and finished at the "Gunnery" in Washington, Connecticut.[39]

His career began in a grocery store, but when his family established a liquor business in New Haven in 1848 he joined the firm. Eight years later he assumed control of the business and

operated it for another 43 years. He also owned a large farm in Hamden, Connecticut.[40]

In 1856 he accompanied two balloonists in the first flight of its kind over New Haven. They lifted off from the New Haven green, drifted over Long Island Sound and landed on one of the Thimble Islands, Governor's Island, which he later bought.[41]

Tuttle would invest in at least six of the Sutton schooners. He married Mary C. Sperry in 1857 and they had one son, Charles Allen, who became one of the founders of the *New Haven Morning News*. Charles Allen later joined his father in the family business.[42]

Charles F. Tuttle died of paralysis on 30 September, 1899. His holdings included 23 pieces of real estate as well as stock in four vessels. The value of his estate was estimated between $150,000 and $200,000.[43]

HENRY HOMER OLDS

Henry Homer Olds was born 6 July, 1824, in New Haven, Connecticut. His employment began at age 14 as a farmer's boy. He followed this as an errand boy in a livery office. Then, he worked successively at blacksmithing, boilermaking, running stationary engines, molding, and finally, of all things, pie-making. He worked for eight years in a pie bakery before he and his wife started their own pie-baking business in Providence, Rhode Island, in 1859. Later that year they moved the business to New Haven. At the end of the first year they were making from 200 to 300 pies a day. By 1887 their business was the second largest pie bakery in the country, the only larger one being in New York. Investments in the Olds' bakery totaled $100,000. Approximately 75 employees worked there, and they turned out 8,000 to 10,000 pies each day.[44]

On his 31st birthday in 1855 Henry married Elizabeth

Campbell, who was born near Belfast, Northern Ireland. She had worked in some of the best pie bakeries in the business. He attributed much of his financial success to his wife's knowledge of the business and her personal supervision of the bakery.[45]

Mr. Olds was characterized as a retiring man who enjoyed his home and kept strict business habits. He had no interest in public affairs or politics. He was interested in sailing ships and invested in four of Henry Sutton's schooners. He also displayed an interest in things nautical in his trade mark—anchors and waves of the sea superimposed upon a pie crust.[46]

Henry H. Olds died on 16 June, 1888. More than a year later, Mrs. Olds invested in another of Henry Sutton's vessels, the *George M. Grant.*[47]

W. WALLACE WARD

William Wallace Ward was born in West Haven in June 1830, and received his education in the common schools. His father, three uncles and two of his three brothers were seafarers during part of their lives. Two of the uncles later engaged in shipping goods from the New Haven area to the West Indies. One brother, Minott Ward, a sea captain, was lost at sea off Cape Hatteras in 1865.[48]

W. Wallace Ward's early working years were spent in various businesses. In 1867 he was made superintendent of the New Haven Horse Railroad Co., and after some years of business success he was induced by his Republican friends to become a candidate for state representative. He won the election and served one term. Although he maintained an interest in public affairs, was approved by his party, his constituents and the general public, he declined to be renominated. Instead, he returned to his former position on the 4-1/2-mile-long horsecar railroad that served New Haven. He was described as a man of stalwart build, with a hearty handshake and ready sympathy. Four years before he died he began to be in failing health, and despite intervals of convalescence death took him on 18 May, 1896.[49]

During his lifetime, he maintained his family's interest in ships and the sea. He invested in at least seven of the Sutton schooners.[50]

GEORGE MILES GRANT

George Miles Grant was born in New Haven on 18 January, 1834, the son of one of the first regular policemen in the city. He was educated in the public schools and the Lancasterian School. His career was that of a stone mason, first as a journeyman, then as a contractor. In 1871 he joined a firm that became Chatfield and Grant four years later. After 1886 the business was conducted under Mr. Grant's name.[51]

Mr. Grant was one of New Haven's leading builders, and his firm constructed many of the principal buildings in the city. He was active in a number of New Haven's clubs and civic organizations, and was described as a kindly man who gave freely of his time. Once he was publicly praised as being "radically honest." In politics he was a Democrat, but when proposed as a candidate for mayor he declined to be a candidate.[52]

His first marriage was to Julia M. Freeman of New Haven, who died about 1877. Two years later he married Mrs. Jane P. Judson, a widow. On 3 February, 1901, George M. Grant died of apoplexy, survived by his wife and an adopted daughter.[53]

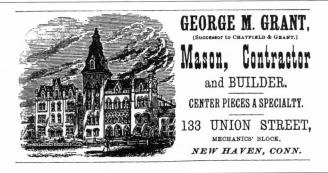

GEORGE M. GRANT,
(Successor to CHATFIELD & GRANT.)

Mason, Contractor

and BUILDER.

CENTER PIECES A SPECIALTY.

133 UNION STREET,

MECHANICS' BLOCK,

NEW HAVEN, CONN.

LYMAN MARCUS LAW

Lyman Marcus Law was born 9 June, 1825, in Orange, Connecticut. He attended school in New Haven, and began his business career in the city as a clerk. He worked for Dr. Nathaniel Booth, learning the druggist's trade from him. Later he was associated with Dr. Booth in manufacturing varnish and coach lacquers. The firm also dealt in paints, oils, glass, and brushes, doing much of this business with New Haven's carriage-building trade. In 1857 he married Dr. Booth's daughter, Anna, and the next year the firm's name was changed to "Booth and Law." After some years, Lyman M. Law became senior partner and manager, continuing in the business until he retired about 1897.[54]

As a member of the New Haven Chamber of Commerce, Mr. Law actively promoted better business. He also invested in sailing ships, not only in all of Henry Sutton's vessels but in the Benedict-Manson fleet as well. He was elected president of the latter fleet in 1909 when he was 84 years old.[55]

The Laws had three daughters, one of whom died in infancy. Mrs. Law passed away in 1886. Lyman M. Law died on 23 January, 1921, leaving his two daughters.[56]

LUCINDA SUTTON

Lucinda Sutton, nee Doney, was born in Napanee, Ontario, Canada, in 1845 and raised there. Her grandfather had served as an officer in the American Revolution. During the

American Civil War, Lucinda was employed in Napanee making fringe for surreys. Henry Sutton, who had followed his trade in Canada as a carriage trimmer, met Lucinda, wooed and married her. A son, Harry D., was born in 1864. In 1865 the family left Canada and moved to New Haven where Henry's business success enabled them to establish a beautiful home in West Haven in 1887. By August of 1887 Henry Sutton's fleet of schooners numbered 11 vessels. Henry's son, Harry D. Sutton, also was involved in ship investment and management for awhile but it didn't last. After Henry's death in 1896, Mrs. Sutton repeatedly attempted to establish Harry D. in several businesses, but her efforts all failed. Harry D's interests were in other areas. He was, according to his great-grandson, quite handsome and a ladies man. Another member of the family also was involved with the Sutton fleet. One of Mrs. Sutton's sisters, Lisle, married Captain H.A. O'Brien of Thomaston, Maine. He sailed for Henry Sutton and was the first master and later managing owner of the *Lucinda Sutton*.[57]

Lucinda Sutton died in her 68th year on 10 December, 1913, at West Haven.[58]

R.& T. HARGRAVES

R.& T. Hargraves stood for the brothers Reuben and Thomas Hargraves. Reuben was born in Belmont, England, on 22 September, 1834. Thomas was also born in England (presumably Belmont) on 8 October, 1836. At an early age, the two boys and their sister were brought to the U.S. by their parents. They settled in Fall River, Massachusetts. Their father, Cornelius, founded the Hargraves Soap Works in Bristol County, Massachusetts, in 1841. Twenty years later, father and sons organized the Hargraves Manufacturing Co. in Fall River, for the production of soap and glue substitutes. About 1867 Reuben and Thomas took over the entire business after buying out a third party to whom their father had sold his interest. In 1888 the Hargraves Mill was incorporated to produce textiles. It was built on land purchased from Reuben and Thomas, with Reuben becoming president of the mill. The brothers also became directors of another textile mill, Cornell Mills, when it was first established. Reuben's son, John W., was the first treasurer of Cornell Mills.[59]

Reuben and Thomas were both investors in sailing vessels, the best known of which were the *Cornelius Hargraves* and the *R. & T. Hargraves.*[60]

Reuben was married twice. With his first wife, Sarah A. Alty, he had two sons and a daughter. Reuben's second wife was Mrs. Lucy E. Streeter. Thomas married and had two daughters.[61]

Both men died in Fall River, Thomas of pneumonia on 10 April, 1904, and Reuben of Bright's disease on 7 December, 1905.[62]

EDWIN SENECA GREELEY

Edwin Seneca Greeley was born 20 May, 1832, in Nashua, New Hampshire. At age 12, he began to work in a Nashua cotton factory for three years. During this time he also trained in an artillery battalion for boys under age 16. Then he worked in locomotive shops in New York and New Jersey as a machinist. In 1854 he came to New Haven, where he was employed by the New York and New Haven Railroad. At the outbreak of the Civil War, he began drilling a squad at the railroad. One hundred men volunteered with him to serve in the state's military forces. On 22 October, 1861, Lt. Greeley and the company he commanded were mustered into the Union Army as part of the Tenth Connecticut Volunteers.[63]

They were ordered south almost immediately, seeing action in battles in North Carolina at Roanoke Island, New Bern, Kinston, Whitehall, and Goldsboro. After New Bern, Greeley was made Captain. At Kinston, 106 officers and men of his regiment were casualties in less than 30 minutes. Greeley was promoted to Major in 1863 and commanded the Tenth in the siege of Charleston, South Carolina, where the fighting was without respite for almost four months. The regiment mounted an assault on Fort Sumter itself during this campaign. By this time the Tenth was reduced by heavy casualties to only 175 men and seven officers. The regiment was ordered to St. Augustine, Florida, to recruit.[64]

During June of 1864 Major Greeley was praised for a successful exploit at Bermuda Hundred, Virginia, when he correctly deduced that rebel troops were withdrawing from the line. In spite of disbelief by his superiors, he moved into the breach with only his picket line. He captured 30 stands of small arms, a 15-gun battery, and a tactical advantage.[65]

Also in 1864 the Tenth fought bloody engagements at Petersburg and Richmond. The regiment maintained a picket line at Cemetery Hill in Petersburg, where the men were under continuous fire for one month, and Greeley became a Lieutenant Colonel. The remnants of the Tenth then participated in a withering attack against a heavily defended position at Richmond. Nearly half the men in that charge fell. Due to the loss of senior officers, Greeley became a full Colonel. At this point the regiment was down to just 150 men and two front-line officers.[66]

Col. Greeley was assigned 500 additional men, many of whom were professional bounty jumpers. He promoted his veterans and put all his men through a regimen of schooling, drills, and rigid discipline, so that by early 1865 the Tenth was once again a first-class unit. It was soon to prove itself and the Colonel's training regimen even though Col. Greeley was up north on a short furlough at the time. He was chagrined to learn that the spring campaign had started in his absence. The regiment was assigned Fort Gregg, the key to the Petersburg front, as its target. In a desperate charge, the regiment swept up the rebel position.[67]

In March of 1865 Col. Greeley was breveted Brigadier General for gallant and meritorious services. His military record was exemplary with but one blemish. This occurred when the Tenth was detached for duty at New York City during the presidential election of 1864. On 9 November, Lt. Col. Greeley left a military transport ship in New York harbor, went ashore and spent part of the night in a hotel with his wife. Since specific instructions had been given to military personnel not to go ashore, Greeley was arrested and could have been dismissed from service. Instead, due to his outstanding military record, he received a reprimand.[68]

Greeley's physical appearance belied his military experience. General Ord once referred to him as "that boy colonel of the Tenth Connecticut Volunteers."[69]

On 25 August, 1865, Gen. Greeley was mustered out of military service. He returned to New Haven and formed a business partnership with a retired telegrapher. They manufactured and imported railway and telegraphic supplies. Upon his partner's death in 1885, Gen. Greeley bought out his interest and continued the business as E.S. Greeley & Co. At one time the firm carried the most diverse inventory of railway and telegraphic supplies in the U.S., and its trade was worldwide. Although the business was successful, it went into receivership in 1896. This was caused by nonexistent profits over a three-year period due to an economic depression in the U.S. However, the company's assets outweighed its debts. Gen. Greeley and the company secretary were appointed as receivers. In 1893 the company strung wires for the opening of the Chicago World's Fair. President Cleveland inaugurated the fair by pressing a gold telegraph key that was given to Greeley. President McKinley used this same key to begin the Exposition of 1898. It was used to transmit Chauncey M. Depew's famous 68-word message around the world in what was then the astounding time of 21-$^1/_2$ minutes.[70]

Gen. Greeley helped organize other businesses that were successful, including the New Haven Electric Light Company, and he served as an officer or director of manufacturing enterprises and banking institutions. Through his business ventures, he became wealthy and was a public benefactor. He was an alderman for one term in New Haven's city government.[71]

In 1856 he married Elizabeth Corey of Taunton,

Massachusetts. They lost one child in 1860 but reared Mrs. Greeley's daughter, Jennie. In 1906 they celebrated their golden wedding anniversary, although Mrs. Greeley was then in feeble health. On 23 February, 1916, Gen. Greeley was severely injured in a railroad wreck in Milford, Connecticut, from which he never fully recovered. Indeed, it was thought he wouldn't survive the accident. He died in January of 1920 at age 87.[72]

END NOTES:

1. Interview with Alvah D. Jones 25 July, 1990.
2. Letter to author from Miss Jane K. Dewell, dated 23 February, 1988.
3. *History of New Haven*, 371.
4. Ibid.
5. *History of Baltimore*, 1:391-392.
6. Ibid.
7. *New Haven Record*, 1224-25. *Leading Businessman of New Haven County* (Boston: Mercantile Publishing Co., 1887), 197.
8. *New Haven Record*, 1225. *Connecticut at the World's Fair* (Hartford: Press of the Case, Lockwood and Brainard Co., 1898), 52-55.
9. *Register*, 9 November, 1896, 2. Certificate of Enrollment, *Lucinda Sutton*, 26 October, 1905.
10. *The Sun* (Baltimore) *Supplement*, 1 August, 1887, 1. *The Biographical Cyclopedia of Representative Men of Maryland and District of Columbia* (Baltimore: National Biographical Publishing Co., 1879), 647.
11. *Biographical Cyclopedia*, 227, 362, 647-48. *History of Baltimore*, 2:701-702. *Baltimore American*, 31 July, 1887, 8. *Baltimore Sun*, 30 April, 1905.
12. *Baltimore American*, 31 July, 1887, 8. *Biographical Cyclopedia*, 227, 648.
13. Pension certificate, #l,101, 574, Henry A. Barry, (U.S. Pension Office), records of Veterans Administration, RG 15, NA.
14. Ibid. *Baltimore News*, 31 May, 1919, 8. *Baltimore Sun*, 30 May, 1919.
15. *Baltimore Sun*, 30 May, 1919.
16. Compiled military service record, Co. E, 127th Pennsylvania Infantry, Henry A. Barry, records of Office of Adjutant General, RG 94, NA. Frederick H. Dyer, *A Compendium of the War of the Rebellion* (Dayton: Press of Morningside Bookshop, 1978), 1614.
17. Frederick H. Dyer, *War of the Rebellion*, 1234. Compiled military service record, Henry A. Barry. No references to Barry in *The Historical Register of the U.S.*

Army (1789-1889) by Heitman or in *The List of Officers of the U.S. Army 1779-1900* by Pavell, per letter to author dated 1 July, 1981, from the State of Maryland General Services. Pension certificate, Henry A. Barry.

18. Letters to author from the Military Order of the Loyal Legion of the U.S. dated 2 November, 1982, and 28 January, 1983.

19. Letters to author from the National Guard of Maryland dated 10 November, 1982, and 11 January, 1983.

20. Letters to author from the Grand Recorder of the Grand Commandery of Maryland dated 31 February, 1981, and 9 July, 1986.

21. Pension certificate Henry A. Barry. *Woods's Baltimore City Directory*, 1864-1883; 1885-1886. *Sheriff & Taylor's Baltimore City Directory*, 1884. *R.L. Polk & Co. Baltimore City Directory*, 1887-1903.

22. *History of New Haven*, 521. *New Haven Record*, 30. *Leading Businessmen of New Haven County*, 95.

23. *New Haven Record*, 30, 1225. Connecticut at the World's Fair, 52-55.

24. Ibid., *History of New Haven*, 521. *Register*, 19 April, 1906, 1.

25. Pension certificate #1,088,648, Nathan Easterbrook, Jr., records of Veterans Administration. Compiled military service record, 34th Regiment, New York Volunteer Infantry, Nathan Easterbrook, Jr, records of the Office of Adjutant General. Frederick H. Dyer, *A Compendium of the War of the Rebellion* (Des Moines: The Dyer Publishing Co., 1908), 1416-17. New Haven Colony Historical Society MSS B51 (2), Nathan Easterbrook, Jr.

26. *New Haven City Directory*, 1883, 1889, 1893. *History of New Haven*, 612. *Register*, 18 July, 1922, 4. New Haven Colony Historical Society, Arnold G. Dana collection, *New Haven and Yale Old and New*, vol. 125, 67.

27. *Register*, 18 July, 1922, 4.

28. Pension certificate, Nathan Easterbrook, Jr. New Haven Colony Historical Society, MSS B51 (2), Nathan Easterbrook, Jr.

29. William P. Blake, *History of the Town of Hamden, Connecticut* (New Haven: Price, Lee & Co., 1888), 257-58, 148, 151, 153. Rachel M. Hartley, *The History of Hamden Connecticut 1786-1959* (Hamden: The Shoe String Press, Inc., 1959), 209-10, 290-92.

30. Blake, *History of the Town of Hamden*, 104-05, 157-58. Hartley, *History of Hamden*, 291-92.

31. Hartley, *History of Hamden*, 339-40. *Register*, 28 November, 1883, 1.

32. Blake, *History of the Town of Hamden*, 258. Hartley, *History of Hamden*, 357. *Register*, 26 September, 1889, 3.

33. *History of New Haven*, 607. *Leading Businessmen of New Haven County*, 96. *Register*, 5 March, 1907, 2.

34. *History of New Haven*, 608.

35. Ibid.
36. *Register*, 5 March, 1907, 1. *History of New Haven*, 608. Albert E. Van Dusen, *Connecticut* (New York: Random House, 1961), 256-58.
37. *Register*, 5 March, 1907, 2.
38. Ibid., 1-2.
39. *New Haven Record*, 780-81.
40. Ibid., 781. *Leading Businessmen of New Haven County*, 204.
41. *New Haven Record*, 781.
42. Ibid., 781-82. *Register*, 30 September, 1899, 1.
43. *New Haven Record*, 781. *Register*, 30 September, 1899, 1.
44. *History of New Haven*, 541. New Haven Colony Historical Society, Arnold G. Dana collection, *New Haven and Yale Old and New*, vol. 125, 69.
45. *History of New Haven*, 541.
46. Ibid. Certificates of Enrollment, *James D. Dewell*, 3 October, 1882, *Nathan Easterbrook, Jr.*, 12 September, 1883, *James Ives*, 30 November, 1883, *Henry H. Olds*, 26 August, 1887. *New Haven City Directory*, 1888.
47. *New Haven Record*, 536. Certificate of Enrollment, *George M. Grant,* 13 September, 1889.
48. *History of New Haven*, 371, 372. *Register*, 18 May, 1896, 10.
49. Ibid. *Register*, 21 May, 1896, 5. *New Haven City Directory*, 1888.
50. Review of Certificates of Enrollment, NA.
51. *New Haven Record*, 563.
52. Ibid., 563, 564. *Register*, 4 February, 1901, 5.
53. *Register*, 4 February, 1901, 5.
54. *Leading Businessmen of New Haven County,* 106. *Journal,* 15 February, 1917, 1. *New Haven City Directory,* 1897. *History of New Haven*, 600. *Law-Booth and Allied Families* (Hartford, Connecticut: States Historical Society, Inc., 1929), unpaginated.
55. *Law-Booth and Allied Families*. Original Certificates of Enrollment of all vessels built or managed by Henry Sutton. Holcomb, *Magnus Manson and the Benedict-Manson Marine Company,* 9.
56. *Law-Booth and Allied Families*.
57. *New Haven Record*, 1225. *Register*, 10 July, 1891, 1; 9 November, 1896, 2. Certificates of Enrollment, *Lucinda Sutton*, 29 July, 1891; 24 December, 1901; 11 September, 1903; *Henry H. Olds*, 26 August, 1887. New Haven Colony Historical Society, Scrapbook collection, box XI, fol. B, reel 138. Interviews with the great-grandson of Henry Sutton, Alvah D. Jones of Brattleboro, Vermont, on 26 February, 6 June, and 7 and 25 July, 1990.
58. *Register*, 11 December, 1913, 2.
59. Frank Walcott Hutt, *History of Bristol County*, 3 vols. (New York: Lewis Historical

Publishing Co., 1924), 3:175. Letter to author from A.F.& A.M. Grand Lodge of Massachusetts (Boston), dated 11 March, 1981. *Fall River Daily Herald,* 11 April, 1904, 5. *Fall River Evening Herald,* 8 December, 1905, 2.

60. *Fall River Daily Herald,* 11 April, 1904, 5. *Fall River Evening Herald*, 8 December, 1905, 2.

61. Ibid.

62. Ibid.

63. *History of New Haven*, 572-73. *New Haven Record*, 52. Frederick H. Dyer, A *Compendium of the War of the Rebellion* (Dayton: Press of Morningside Bookshop, 1978), 1011.

64. *History of New Haven*, 573. *War of the Rebellion*, 1011.

65. *History of New Haven*, 573.

66. Ibid., 574.

67. Ibid.

68. Ibid. Compiled military service record, Co. A,C,F & S, Tenth Connecticut Infantry, Edwin S. Greeley, records of Office of Adjutant General.

69. *History of New Haven*, 575.

70. Ibid., 574. Military service record, Edwin S. Greeley. *Register*, 8 October, 1896, 2. *Journal*, 12 January, 1920, 4.

71. *History of New Haven*, 575. *Journal*, 12 January, 1920, 4.

72. *New Haven Record*, 55. Letter to author from A.F.& A.M. Grand Lodge of Connecticut (Wallingford), dated 4 March, 1981. New Haven Colony Historical Society, Scrapbook collection, 1906, B27, box 13, fol. E, reel 138. *Journal,* 12 January, 1920, 1, 4.

EPITAPH

Some of Henry Sutton's schooners were among the largest ever
built in Connecticut. They were said to be among the finest
afloat. In a sense they were works of art—beautiful to the eye of
many a beholder. They also were workhorses of their day.
Their transport capabilities were significant and needed.
Their performance was impressive. They helped the nation grow.
In all, they sailed from 1875 to 1918, more than 42 years.
They sail no longer—they are no more.
They are but memories in the waters of time.

ILLUSTRATION CREDITS

Page 1 . . . . .Robert W. Feuer

Page 3 . . . . .Robert W. Feuer

Page 8 . . . . .The Mariners' Museum

Page 14 . . . . .Courtesy of Alvah D. Jones

Page 15 . . . . .Courtesy of Captain W.J. Lewis Parker

Page 16 . . . .*Commemorative Biographical Record,*

vol. II, 44.

Page 33 . . . . .Mystic Seaport

Page 39 . . . . .New Haven Colony Historical Society

Page 41 . . . . .New Haven Colony Historical Society

Page 49 . . . . .Courtesy of Captain W. J. Lewis Parker

Page 57 . . . . .Courtesy of Captain W. J. Lewis Parker

Page 59 . . . . .Courtesy of Captain W. J. Lewis Parker

Page 74 . . . . .Author's collection

Page 77 . . . . .New Haven Colony Historical Society

Page 84 . . . . .Courtesy of Captain W. J. Lewis Parker

Page 87 . . . . .Courtesy of Captain W. J. Lewis Parker

Page 103 . . . . .Mystic Seaport

(Claire White-Peterson photo)

Page 112 . . . . .The Mariners' Museum

Page 117 . . . . .Courtesy of Mrs. Helen McInnis

Page 120 - 121 . . . . .Courtesy of Engineer R. Greger

Page 128 . . . . .Courtesy of Militargeschictisches

Forschungsamt

Page 141 . . . . .New Haven Colony Historical Society

Page 150 . . . . .Courtesy of Captain W. J. Lewis Parker

Page 156 . . . . .The Connecticut Historical Society

Page 158 . . . . .Robert W. Feuer

Page 162 . . . . .Deutsches Museum, Munich

Page 188 . . . . .Archiv Bibliothek für Zeitgeschicte,

Stuttgart

INDEX

Page references in italics indicate pages with illustrations. Those followed by n indicate endnotes.

Easterbrook, Nathan, Jr., 91, 212-213
Easterbrook Co., 212
Edward M. Reed, 54, 73-75, *74,* 190n15
  captains, 58, 75
  cargo, 26-27
  collision with *Gaskill,* 73
  construction, 13
  decks, 36
  design and construction details, 17, 36
  destruction, 73-75
  groundings, 71
  measurements, 13
  namesake, 27
  ownership shares, 20, 75
  value, 75
Edwin A. Gaskill, 73
El Norte, 202n205
El Recreo (Recreation Place), 144
Ellis, Alfred, 79
Elmer E. Randall, 77
Elsie, 95
Emery, Ralph C., 23
Emma-Felice, 186, 188
Emma J. Kennedy, 75-76
engineers, 62
eponyms, 5, 38, 204-230
E.S. Greeley & Co., 226

F
Fairbrothers, Godfrey, 92-93
family members onboard, 58-60
Fannie Prescott, 199n161
Farnham, Arthur N., 1, 5
Farnham, Letty, 5
Farnham, Mrs.Hortense G., 5
Farnham, Myrlon A., 1
Farnham, Ne, 1, 5
Feeter, Mary Catherine, 213
Ferrero, 166-167, 169, 184
financial procedures, 20
fires, 73
first mate, 62
Five Fathom Shoal, 92-93
five-masters, 8-9. *See also specific schooners*
flags, 38, *39*
Flamboro, 88
foreign trade, 53-54

Fort de Vincennes, 157, *158*
four-masters, 7-8. *See also specific schooners*
Fournier, Auguste, 164, 176
France, 54-55
Francis Shubert, 111-112
Freeman, Julia M., 220
Freeman House, 4
freight, 8-9
French Foreign Legion, 157-158
French Naval Archives, 157-159

G
Gaceta Marinera, 143, 149
Gallia, 128
Gasperini, Joseph, 165
Gaston, N.H., 213
General E.S. Greeley, 8, 49, 155. *See also Montenegro*
  captain, 57
  certificate of enrollment, 53
  certificate of registry, 53
  collision, 155
  colors, 38
  construction costs, 36
  design and construction details, 19
  intercontinental travel, 55
  launching, 16, 42-43, 45-47
  maiden voyage, 49
  masts, 37
  measurements, 14
  namesake, 38
  performance, 50
  repair costs, 73
  sale to out-of-state interests, 24, 55, 156
  size, 35
General Maritime Law (Virginia), 105
General S.E. Merwin, 70, 93-98
  building time, 33
  captain, 58-59
  collisions, 59, 93-97
  construction costs, 35
  design and construction details, 17-18
  destruction, 97-98
  dismasting, 72, 97
  foreign trade, 54
  grounding, 70-71